TRADITION AND CHURCH REFORM

Tradition and Church Reform

Perspectives on Catholic Moral Teaching

Charles E. Curran

ORBIS BOOKS
www.orbisbooks.com

Copyright © 2016 by Charles E. Curran
Published by Orbis Books, Maryknoll, New York 10545-0302.

Manufactured in the United States of America.

Library of Congress Cataloging-in-Publication Data

Curran, Charles E.
    [Essays. Selections]
        Tradition and church reform : perspectives on Catholic moral teaching /
            Charles E. Curran.
        pages cm
        Includes index.
        ISBN 978-1-62698-171-3 (pbk.)
        1. Christian sociology—Catholic Church.   2. Church renewal—Catholic Church.
    I. Title.
    BX1753.C87 2016
    241'.042—dc23

2015027823

CONTENTS

PREFACE

This book brings together essays and articles originally published elsewhere. The individual chapters, however, fit into three specific areas: Social Perspectives, Bioethical and Sexual Perspectives, and Reform at Vatican II and Afterward. The original essays have been somewhat modified to fit into this structure. Each of the three parts begins with a short introduction. A final chapter, written specifically for this volume, brings a greater unity to the whole by exploring the reform that Pope Francis has brought to the church, especially with regard to the Catholic moral tradition as discussed in the preceding chapters.

I am grateful to all those who have assisted me in the research and writing of this volume. For the last twenty-five years I have been privileged to hold the Elizabeth Scurlock University Professorship in Human Values at Southern Methodist University. My students and colleagues, the librarians at the Bridwell Library, and the university administration have made my years at SMU enjoyable and challenging. I remain ever grateful to the late Jack and Laura Lee Blanton, who established the professorship that I hold. Special thanks goes to Robert Ellsberg, the publisher and editor-in-chief of Orbis Books, for his strong encouragement and support for this volume. The book would never have seen the light of day without the dedicated help of my assistant, Leslie Fuller, in preparing the manuscript for publication. I also appreciate the permission to use in this volume material originally published elsewhere.

Part I

SOCIAL PERSPECTIVES

INTRODUCTION

The chapters in part I were originally individual essays written for particular occasions, but they share a common focus on contributing to the understanding of the social tradition of the church.

Chapter 1, "Overview of the Development of the Catholic Social and Political Tradition," provides a logical starting point. This overview presents the basic aspects of the Catholic social tradition, touching on its sources, its theory of politics, the methodology employed, the message and content of the teaching, and its relevance for nonbelievers. In addition, as the title clearly indicates, the chapter recognizes the growth and development that has occurred. The Catholic social tradition, like the best of all traditions, is a living tradition. Subsequent chapters underscore this reality of a living tradition, which is characterized by continuities as well as discontinuities. The danger of any tradition, including the Catholic tradition, is to be closed in on itself, failing to recognize the need to be a living tradition. A living tradition, however, must be willing to recognize growth and change but also the fact that the tradition itself has at times been in error. The Catholic Church in general has found it difficult to admit that the tradition itself has been in error. Some of the subsequent chapters treat the discontinuities and even the errors in the Catholic social tradition.

Chapter 2, "The Reception of Catholic Social and Economic Teaching in the United States," deals with what Pope John Paul II and others have called "Catholic social teaching." This teaching consists of the papal and hierarchical documents on social issues, beginning with the 1891 encyclical of Pope Leo XIII, *Rerum Novarum,* and continuing with a string of official documents to the present time. These documents propose authoritative teaching for the whole church, but chapter 2 focuses on the reception of this teaching in the United States. Here, too, significant changes have occurred. As the twentieth century developed, the church in the United States, including the bishops, the theologians, and laypeople involved in social action, gave more importance and significance to this teaching. In the immediate post–Vatican II times, Catholic theoreticians recognized that in the reception of this teaching they had failed to appreciate its own cultural and historical limits. One sees here the growing acceptance of the importance of historical consciousness in Catholic understanding as a result of Vatican II. As a result, this Catholic social teaching was received in a somewhat different manner after Vatican II.

Throughout the twentieth century and even into the twenty-first, the lament has often been heard that the average Catholic in the pew was totally unaware of this social teaching. Attempts have been made on all levels in the church to make the teaching better known. In the 1980s, the US bishops issued two significant pastoral letters on peace and the economy, which plowed new ground in both areas. First, the bishops wrote their letters after a very broad consultation, even making public the various drafts of the documents and asking for feedback on the drafts. Second, the letters purposely decided to go beyond the principles given in Catholic social teaching to propose particular programs and actions, while recognizing that on these particular issues they were proposing solutions that Catholics should seriously consider but could legitimately disagree with. Catholic social teaching, precisely because it sees itself as authoritative teaching, has restricted itself to principles and has not proposed particular programs or strategies.

Chapter 3, "George G. Higgins: Catholic Social Teaching and Social Action in the United States," develops the general topic even more by looking at the teaching and actions of Msgr. George G. Higgins, who was universally recognized as the most important figure in this area in the Catholic Church in the United States. Higgins's prominence was due to his role with the United States Bishops' Conference and his involvement in many different areas of social action. In keeping with his official capacity, Higgins tried to make Catholics throughout the country more aware of Catholic social teaching, but he also engaged in many discussions and activities with regard to Catholic social action. He strongly supported workers and labor unions. Higgins played a leadership role in getting the United States Catholic bishops to support the farm workers and César Chávez while using his union connections to garner union support for the farm workers. Higgins recognized the problem of racial discrimination and supported attempts to overcome it. He strongly criticized Catholic neoconservatives because they failed to appreciate the legitimate role of government. He also chided the Catholic right-to-life movement for making alliances with the New Right and for its failure to recognize and promote the other aspects of Catholic social teaching. Higgins also criticized some of the "new breed" of Catholic social activists for failing to give enough importance to the role of the laity and insisting on the primacy of prophetic statements and demonstrations.

Chapter 4, "Human Rights in the Christian Tradition," points out how dramatically the Catholic tradition changed on this issue. The Catholic Church went from open hostility to enthusiastic support for human rights. This history of the Catholic view of human rights serves as an excellent example of discontinuity and even error in the Catholic tradition. World history helps explain how this substantial change occurred. Catholic approaches to the Enlightenment in the eighteenth and nineteenth centuries formed the basis for the rejection of human rights, but the Catholic opposition to totalitarianism in the twentieth century paved the way for the reversal. The changed teaching on religious liberty at Vatican II well illustrates this dramatic change. To its credit, the Declaration on Religious Freedom of Vatican II recognizes that this teaching was true even before the council made its declaration. Thus the church had been in error in holding on to the earlier teaching. Ironically, contemporary Catholic scholarship shows that the concept of subjective rights did not originate with the Enlightenment but rather with thirteenth-century canon lawyers.

Chapter 5, "The Catholic Tradition in Dialogue with the Black Theological Ethics of J. Deotis Roberts," well illustrates how dialogue keeps the tradition alive. To its credit, the Catholic theological tradition has always been open in theory to dialogue. Recall, for example, that the most important figure in the tradition, Thomas Aquinas, learned much from the approach of Aristotle. The theological grounding for the importance of dialogue comes from the Catholic recognition that on the basis of creation, the Catholic tradition shares much with all others. The Catholic understanding has recognized not only the role of faith but also the role of human reason in coming to moral wisdom and knowledge. Unfortunately, at times a certain defensiveness has prevented or downplayed the role of dialogue. The contemporary theological scene, for example, shows how the Catholic tradition has learned much from feminism. In the specific dialogue considered in this chapter, communalities in method exist between the Catholic approach and the black theology of J. Deotis Roberts. However, the Catholic tradition should learn from Roberts's critique about the racism that has existed and still continues to exist in the Catholic tradition. In this dialogue, the Catholic tradition also learns the need to recognize the particular and not just the universal and the important role of power in social ethics.

Chapter 6, "White Privilege," discusses this reality from a more personal perspective, but there is no doubt that the Catholic tradition in the United States and in Europe has failed to recognize and deal with the white privilege of the tradition itself and its leading figures. The perennial danger in any tradition is to fail to recognize its own failures and problems. The Catholic Church has always had a difficult time in admitting its failures. History and contemporary realities, however, remind us that we are a pilgrim church and a sinful church. The particular issue of white privilege makes clear the need for the Catholic tradition to be resolutely self-critical.

Chapter 1

OVERVIEW OF THE DEVELOPMENT
OF THE CATHOLIC SOCIAL AND
POLITICAL TRADITION*

While emphasizing the gift and goal of eternal life, Roman Catholicism has consistently had a concern for this world and how life is lived in this world. Catholic faith touches all aspects of human existence. The ultimate basis for such a concern for life in this world comes from the doctrine of creation according to which God made all that exists and saw that it was very good. Some Christians emphasize the doctrine of sin as radically affecting the temporal world and making it evil; but the Catholic tradition has insisted that, although sin does affect the goodness of creation, sin clearly does not destroy the basic goodness of the human and all that God has made. Contemporary Catholic thought also sees the redemptive love of Jesus and God's grace affecting and transforming the temporal realm while recognizing that the fullness of justice and peace will never be present in this world. Critics both inside and outside Catholicism have pointed out the danger that Catholicism might be too optimistic about the temporal realm and the political order and not give enough importance to the negative effects of sin. Catholicism today in continuity with its past insists that Catholic Christians are called to work together with all people of good will for a better or more just temporal order in general and political order in particular.

In this chapter's consideration of the Catholic understanding of the political order, I first discuss the classical sources, texts, method, and audience of Catholic social and political teaching and in a second section develop the substance of this understanding of the political order and the role of Catholics and others in the political realm.

* Originally published as Charles E. Curran, "Roman Catholic Christianity," in *God's Rule: The Politics of World Religions,* ed. Jacob Neusner (Washington, DC: Georgetown University Press, 2003), 61–84. Used with permission. www.press.georgetown.edu.

Classical Sources of
Roman Catholicism on Politics

What are the generic sources that the Catholic approach uses to develop its understanding of the political order? Where does the Catholic approach find wisdom and knowledge for its understanding of how the political order should function?

Sources in General

Catholicism, in keeping with the Judeo-Christian tradition, believes that God reveals God's self to us and this revelation provides wisdom and knowledge. Revelation includes both scripture and tradition, but these are not understood today in a dualistic way as two distinctly different realities. Scripture or the word of God includes the Hebrew Bible (often called the Old Testament) and the New Testament. The scriptures are the inspired word of God, although diverse interpretations of inspiration exist. Tradition refers to both the process and the content of what has been handed over in the church from generation to generation. Catholicism believes that the Holy Spirit is given to the church so that down through the centuries the church will be able to understand, live, and appropriate the word and work of Jesus in light of changing historical circumstances. The scriptures themselves are historically and culturally conditioned, so tradition helps us understand the call of faith in light of the different historical and cultural circumstances in which we now live. Perhaps the best example of tradition in early Catholicism concerns the creeds of the early church, which spelled out Catholic Christian belief even in basic areas such as the Trinitarian nature of God and the divine and human natures in Jesus. The Trinitarian doctrine of three divine persons in one God is not found explicitly as such in the scripture, but the church proposed this teaching in its early councils and creeds.

Most Christian churches recognize scripture and tradition as sources of moral wisdom for believers, but Catholicism also acknowledges a distinctive source of moral wisdom and knowledge—the gift of the Holy Spirit has been given to the pope and the bishops in the church to assist them in teaching authoritatively about faith and morals for the members of the church. This teaching office, exercised especially by the bishop of Rome, or the pope, has in recent times proposed authoritative teaching in many moral areas including the political order. In addition, Catholicism accepts human sources of moral wisdom—reason and experience. Since Catholicism recognizes the goodness of all that God has made, human reason and human experience can be sources of moral wisdom and knowledge. Catholicism relies heavily on human reason for its understanding of the political order. Again, the danger in Catholicism is to forget that limitation and sinfulness also affect but do not totally distort human reason and human experience.

Texts

In relation to these sources various authoritative texts exist in Catholicism. The Bible itself with all its parts is the most significant text, but for the area of politics the Bible does not provide that much guidance and direction. Subsequent Christians often refer to the saying in Matthew 22:15–22 to give to God what is God's and to Caesar what is Caesar's. They also recognize the teaching in the letter of Paul to the Romans 13:1–7 about the obedience that is due to civil rulers. However, there are also passages in the New Testament that cause problems for many Christians today such as the apparent acceptance of slavery. Christians have tried to explain in different ways how this came about. The primary purpose of revelation in general and the Bible in particular is not to give details about the political order, although it does provide guidelines and even commandments for life in this world. However, the dramatic difference between political life then and political life today means that any specific biblical teachings might not be applicable to our very different situation.

Early church councils and creeds usually did not address issues of politics, but the writings of the leaders of the early church (often called the Patristic Age, embracing the first six or even more centuries) frequently did discuss aspects of life in the temporal and political spheres. For example, the question of Christian participation in the army was frequently discussed. Many other issues of daily life as well as the broader question of what today we call the relationship of church and state were discussed by these church leaders and thinkers. Augustine of Hippo (d. 430) was the most famous of these "fathers of the church," and he wrote on many subjects dealing with life in the temporal and political realms. The writings of this period from these leaders tended to be ad hoc and dealt with particular issues primarily from a pastoral perspective.

A more systematic study came to the fore in the second millennium with the rise of universities under church auspices. Here again notice the Catholic acceptance of the goodness and power of human reason to arrive at truth. Systematic theology began at this time as an attempt to explain the

Catholic faith and morals in a systematic way, putting all the parts together into one whole. In the thirteenth century religious orders came into existence, such as the Dominicans and the Franciscans, who engaged in the systematic study of theology.

The most important figure in the thirteenth-century context was Thomas Aquinas (d. 1274), an Italian Dominican friar whose *Summa theologiae* became the most significant book (three volumes) in Catholic theological tradition. By definition Aquinas's *Summa* is a synthesis of all theology, but the second of the three parts deals with the moral life, which Aquinas explains on the basis of the three theological virtues (faith, hope, and charity) and the four cardinal virtues (prudence, justice, fortitude, and temperance), with justice, dealing with life in the world, receiving the most coverage.[1] Aquinas uses all the five sources mentioned above, but in a distinctive manner he employs Aristotelian thought in trying to explain Christian faith and morals. Aquinas's discussion of justice relies heavily on Aristotle.

At the same time, the Franciscan School, represented by Alexander of Hales (d. 1245), John Duns Scotus (d. 1308), and St. Bonaventure (d. 1274) made significant contributions to systematic theology. Thomism competed with both Scotism and nominalism, an approach associated with William of Ockham (d. 1347), during the next few centuries. However, in the sixteenth century a revival of Thomism throughout Europe, beginning in Germany and moving to Italy and especially Spain, made Thomism the primary approach to Catholic theology and understanding. At this time the *Summa* became the textbook of theology in all universities. Spain became the principal center of the Thomistic renewal with such leading figures as Francis de Vitoria (d. 1546), who has been called the father of international law, and Dominic Soto (d. 1560), who like many others wrote long commentaries on the *Summa*, especially the section on justice.

In the eighteenth century, however, Thomism lacked vitality and began to wane. In the nineteenth century Italian Jesuits started a successful campaign to renew Thomism or scholasticism, as it was sometimes called. One of their students later became Pope Leo XIII, who in 1879 issued an encyclical (an authoritative letter to the bishops of the world) titled *Aeterni Patris*, which called for the renewal and teaching of Aquinas in Catholic

---

[1] For a Latin and English version of the *Summa*, see *Summa theologiae: Latin Text and English Translation, Introductions, Notes, Appendixes and Glossaries*, ed. Dominicans from English-speaking Provinces of the Order (New York: McGraw-Hill, 1964–), 61 vols. The treatise on justice is found in the second part of the second part of the *Summa* and is generally referred to as II–II, q. 57–122.

universities and seminaries "for the defense and beauty of the Catholic faith, for the good of society, and for the advantages of all the sciences" (no. 31).[2] Later church documents maintained that philosophy and theology in Catholic institutions should be taught according to the method, outline, and approach of Thomas Aquinas. Note here the importance of Aquinas not only for teaching the faith but also for the Catholic understanding of society as a whole. Thomism or neoscholasticism from the nineteenth century reigned as *the* Catholic theology and philosophy with some different emphases under the one Thomistic umbrella until the Second Vatican Council (or Vatican [Council] II), when Catholicism opened itself to other possible approaches. Many have viewed Pope Leo's imposition of Thomism in the late nineteenth century, which was continued by his successors, as a very forceful way for the church to speak in a convincing way to the modern world and its problems, but others criticized this as imposing an older approach and showing an unwillingness to dialogue with contemporary thought.

Leo XIII played an even more significant role in terms of the Catholic approach to the social and political orders. In 1891 he issued the encyclical *Rerum Novarum* dealing with problems for workers brought about by the Industrial Revolution. The encyclical recognizes the right of workers to a living wage, the need for them to organize into unions, and the proper role of government to intervene to protect the rights of workers and others who are in need. This encyclical inspired other encyclicals and letters by subsequent popes dealing with social, economic, and political questions. These documents were often issued on anniversaries of *Rerum Novarum* and together they constitute what Pope John Paul II has called the social teaching of the church. These documents, including documents from Vatican Council II (1962–65), have addressed the broad range of issues for national and international society in the social, political, and economic realms. In the US context, two pastoral letters of the US bishops on peace (1983) and on the economy (1986) are generally included in the group of documents pertaining to Catholic social teaching.[3] Thus, these documents

---

[2] For an English translation of Pope Leo XIII's encyclicals, see Claudia Carlen, ed., *The Papal Encyclicals, 1878–1903* (Wilmington, NC: McGrath, 1981). Encyclicals and other church documents take their official title from the first two or three Latin words of the document.

[3] There is no official canon or list of these documents. For a readily available collection of these documents in English, see David J. O'Brien and Thomas A. Shannon, eds., *Catholic Social Thought: The Documentary Heritage*, exp. ed. (Maryknoll, NY: Orbis

form an authoritative source of official teaching on the social and political order. The documents themselves employ all the sources mentioned earlier but tend to highlight official church teachings. These documents of Catholic social teaching have spawned many commentaries throughout the world. Before Vatican II most of these commentaries were quite uncritical, but later commentaries employ more sophisticated hermeneutical principles.

Catholic social teaching, since it authoritatively proposes teaching for all Catholics, tends to be somewhat broad and general, involving principles of reflection, criteria of judgment, and basic directives for action. On the US scene the two pastoral letters by the bishops have proposed more specific guidelines (e.g., no first use of counterforce nuclear weapons) but the bishops recognize that on these more specific issues there is room for disagreement among Catholics. The somewhat general nature of the papal documents means that different commentators can and will interpret them differently. The basic thrust of Catholic social teaching, as will be illustrated later, tends to the more progressive side in emphasizing the needs of the poor and workers. However, a group of Catholic neoconservative scholars in the United States have disagreed with the approach taken by the US bishops, characterizing it as being too negative on US policy and capitalism and have interpreted the papal documents from their perspective.[4]

Roman Catholicism's Theory of Politics

Thomism, Catholic social ethics (the academic discipline), and Catholic social teaching are obviously interrelated and employ in general a natural law methodology based on that found in Aquinas. Natural law, from a theological perspective, is the participation of the eternal law in the rational creature. From a theological vantage point, natural law is the understanding that divine eternal law exists independent of human opinion or construction, but rational beings participate in it. The eternal law is the plan that God has for the world. How do we discover God's plan? Do we go directly and immediately to God to find out what to do? The Catholic answer is No. One of the distinctive characteristics of Catholic theology is the idea of mediation. God has created the world and has given

---

Books, 2010). The text will give the paragraph numbers from the documents cited which then can be found in this volume or any other source.

   [4] Michael Novak, "Neoconservatives," in *The New Dictionary of Catholic Social Thought*, ed. Judith A. Dwyer (Collegeville, MN: Liturgical Press, 1994), 678–82.

us the faculty of reason, that mediates God's own reason. Human reason, reflecting on the creation that God has made, including of course human beings, can discover how God wants us to act and use what God created. Thus the natural law is the participation of the eternal law in the rational creature. Such a natural law approach means that Catholics and all others are called to do the same thing in working for a better or more just temporal and political realm. The later encyclicals explicitly address not only Catholics but all people of good will.

From an ethical and philosophical perspective, natural law is human reason directing us to our end in accord with our human nature. Of course, there are disputed questions about what is meant by human reason and human nature. By examining human beings, human reason comes to the conclusion we are not isolated monads but are social by nature and meant to live in many different communities from the family on up to the broader political community. To fulfill ourselves as human beings we need to exist in these many different relationships. Another example: reason discovers that through work human beings earn what is necessary to provide for themselves so that they might have at least a minimally decent human existence. The just wage, therefore, is not simply what the employer and the employee agree on but rather what is necessary to provide the worker with a minimally decent human existence.

Commentators have raised various questions and criticisms about natural law both from within and from outside the Catholic tradition. More recent documents of Catholic social teaching and commentaries on these have responded to these criticisms and thus modified to some extent the neoscholastic natural law approach as found in Leo XIII.

A first criticism concerns the fact that the natural law approach does not give enough importance to the central faith aspects of Jesus Christ, revelation, and redeeming grace. Vatican Council II (1962–65), which renewed Roman Catholicism, in *Gaudium et Spes*, the Pastoral Constitution on the Church in the Modern World (no. 41), lamented that the split between faith and daily life is a major error of our times. Neoscholasticism, perhaps not totally faithful to Aquinas, had seen the temporal as the realm of the natural distinguished from the supernatural aspects of grace, redemption, and Jesus Christ. Subsequent to Vatican II the documents of Catholic social teaching have tried to understand life in the world also in the light of Catholic faith and all that it entails.

One advantage of the newer Christological or faith approach is the centrality of working for a better human society or, as it is called, the social mission of the church. Previously the church's mission was seen as twofold—divinization and humanization, with the latter carried out by laypeople in their daily life in the temporal, social, and political orders. Divinization occurred on the supernatural level in the life of the church, and humanization occurred on the natural level in the life of the world. *Justitia in Mundo* (1971), the document of Catholic social teaching coming from the International Synod of Bishops, maintained: "Action on behalf of justice and participation in the transformation of the world fully appear to us as a constitutive dimension of the preaching of the gospel, or in other words, of the church's mission for the redemption of the human race and its liberation from every oppressive situation." Working for a better human society in this world was always a consequence of Catholic faith, but before Vatican II it tended to be secondary to the spiritual and supernatural elements. Now it is a constitutive part of the preaching of the gospel, which means that without a social mission there is no true preaching of the gospel or redemptive mission of the church.

A second criticism of natural law concerns its failure to give enough importance to history, change, and development. The natural law is a participation of the eternal law, which is understood as absolute, universal, and unchanging. The nature of things is something already given and does not recognize much change and development.

There have been some rejoinders to this criticism within the documents of contemporary Catholic social teaching. First, the teaching itself has developed over time, as this chapter will explain below. For example, Catholic social teaching in the twentieth century came to a greater appreciation of freedom, equality, and participation in public life and even changed its teaching on religious freedom. In other areas (e.g., sexuality and medical ethics) contemporary Catholic teaching has not been that open to change or development.

Second, many more recent documents have employed a more inductive methodology. Thomism, at least as it was interpreted in the neoscholasticism of the nineteenth and early twentieth centuries, was deductive in its method. Conclusions were deduced from their premises. Pope Paul VI clearly employed a much more inductive method. Induction by definition begins, as *Gaudium et Spes*, the Pastoral Constitution of the Church in the Modern World of the Second Vatican Council, does with "the signs of the times" or the contemporary realities.

Third, Paul VI in *Octogesima Adveniens* (1971) explicitly moves away from the backward glance of the natural law to the eternal law and appeals rather to forward-looking utopias as "criticism of existing society [which] often provokes the forward-looking imagination both to perceive in the present the disregarded possibility hidden within it and to direct itself toward a fresh future" (no. 37). John Paul II, the successor of Paul VI, moved away from the historical consciousness and more inductive approach found in *Octogesima Adveniens.*

A third criticism refers to natural law's penchant for insisting on universality, absolute principles, and unity at the expense of particularity, flexibility, and greater diversity. Here again some effort has been made to meet this criticism, but the documents still propose principles of reflection, criteria of judgment, and directives for action for the whole world with all its cultural diversity. At the very minimum any approach that tries to speak for the whole world must be conscious of the existing diversity and be self-critical enough to recognize that no perspective is without its limitations and prejudices. In the global reality of the modern world, however, some universal ethical concerns touching all human beings seem to be most necessary.

A fourth criticism points to the tension involved in a teaching claiming to be authoritative for Catholics but also claiming to be based on human reason. The criticism has been phrased as seeing the teaching more as law and less as rational. This is obviously a tension within the Catholic community itself in terms of the legitimacy of disagreement within the church about hierarchical church teaching on social and political matters. Within Roman Catholicism there has been considerably less discussion about disagreement and dissent in the realm of Catholic social teaching than in the areas of hierarchical sexual teaching such as contraception and divorce. Perhaps the very general nature of the social teaching, which by definition allows for different interpretations, makes the issue of dissent or disagreement less likely.

The Message of Roman Catholicism's Politics

In the Catholic understanding the temporal realm embraces all that occurs in human existence in this world. The temporal realm includes the broad area of the social as well as the cultural and the political. Thus for our purposes the political order is narrower than the temporal order and is differentiated from the cultural realm. The political realm refers to the ordered political life of the community.

Anthropology constitutes the grounding for the Catholic understanding of the political order. The Catholic tradition usually addresses the political order in terms of the state. State is the word that is usually used to refer to all aspects of government be it local, state (in our US understanding), or federal. Catholic anthropology insists that the human person ("person" is much more recent; the older term was "human being") has an inherent, God-given dignity and sacredness but is also social and political by nature. Genesis, the first book of the Bible, tells us that God created human beings in God's own image and likeness. The human person has an inherent, God-given sacredness and dignity and is thus different from all other creation. However, the human being is not an isolated monad but is called by the nature God has given us to live together in various structures such as the natural structure of the family as well as the natural institution of the state or the political order. This twofold aspect of anthropology grounds the Catholic understanding of the state as natural, necessary, and good but also limited.

The State as Natural, Necessary, and Good

Aquinas, in harmony with the biblical emphasis, accepted the Aristotelian understanding of the human being as social and political by nature. Human beings by their very nature (notice the natural law approach) are made by God and called to live together in political society. Only in and through political society can human beings achieve some of their fulfillment. No human being is an island or an isolated monad.

Such an understanding of the state differs from two other common approaches. Some Christian traditions (especially the Lutheran) see the state as fulfilling the promise made to Noah that God will never again destroy the world. Sin by its very nature leads to death and sinful human beings cannot live peacefully together. God thus uses the state as an order of preservation which through the power of coercion tries to keep sinful human beings in check and from killing one another or creating chaos. The state thus has the somewhat minimal and negative function of restraining evil and maintaining order.

In the thirteenth century Aquinas raised what seems today to be a totally irrelevant question: Would the state or political order exist if Adam and Eve had not sinned? (I, q. 96, a. 4). But the question is very relevant. Is the nature and existence of the state due primarily to human sinfulness or to human nature as created by God? Aquinas responded that the state would have existed without sin because wherever a multitude of human beings exist, they need someone to direct them to the common good. The different orders of angels remind us that even angels need a political authority. In this conception the state has a very positive role to play in bringing about the common good of society. In the Catholic understanding the state is primarily directive and not coercive. If citizens feel that government is primarily coercive, such a government will be very insecure. Note again that the perennial danger in Catholic understanding involves a too optimistic view of human nature and the state primarily because not enough importance is given to the role of sin.

From a philosophical perspective, the Catholic approach differs from the more individualistic approach that prevails among many people in the United States today. Individualism sees different individuals concerned about themselves wanting to protect their own interests in the light of the existence of other people and their interests. These individuals then come together to work out a contract for a society that can best protect their individual interests with the realization that some compromises will be necessary in order to accommodate others. This is often called the contract theory of the state where individuals enter into a contract with each other as the best way of trying to protect their own individual interests. The Catholic approach does not begin with isolated individuals but with a person who is social and political by nature and thus destined to live in political community.

Role of Government

Anthropology also governs the role of the state. An anthropology that recognizes both the inherent dignity or sacredness of the human person and the social and political nature of the person avoids the opposite dangers of individualism and collectivism. Individualism sees only individuals and downplays the role of the community itself, whereas collectivism so emphasizes the collectivity that it fails to give enough importance to the individual.

This complex anthropology governs two important roles of the state— its purpose and its relationship to individual persons and other groupings in society. In the Catholic tradition the purpose of the state has been to work for the common good, which differs in theory from both individual goods and the collective good. An individualistic approach acknowledges only individual goods that each one tries to protect and promote as much as possible. The collective good so emphasizes the collectivity that it denies individual goods and is even willing to sacrifice the individual for the good of the collectivity.

The Catholic tradition insists that the purpose of the state is to work for the common good. In theory the common good by definition flows back to the good of individuals and does not contradict or limit the proper good of

individuals. The state, for example, pursues the good of clean air that benefits all. The encyclical of Leo XIII, *Rerum Novarum* (1891), made explicit,
however, that the common good requires the good of all parts of society. The
state can and should intervene to help a particular group such as workers,
but this too ultimately contributes to the common good and the good of
other members of society (nos. 28–29).

The description of the concrete common good tends to be somewhat general. Pope John XXIII in *Mater et Magistra* (1961) describes the
common good as "the sum total of these conditions of social living whereby
human beings are enabled more fully and readily to achieve their own
perfection" (no. 65). The criterion of the common good as the purpose of
society thus clearly differentiates the Catholic approach from both individualism and collectivism.

In keeping with that same basic anthropology, the state in the Catholic
understanding is natural, necessary, and good, but its role is limited. The
proper role of the state is governed by two principles—subsidiarity and
socialization. Pope Pius XI in *Quadragesimo Anno* (1931) developed the
principle of subsidiarity (no. 79), but the basis of this principle is clearly
found in Aquinas. The primary limit on the role of the state comes from the
dignity and sacredness of the human individual who is prior to the state.
Likewise, the Catholic tradition sees the family as a natural society that is
prior to the state. In addition to the individual person and the family, public
society includes structures and institutions such as extended families and
neighborhoods. Then there exist voluntary groups or institutions of all
types that are necessary for the total good of society—educational, cultural,
social, and professional groups. Think of the media, colleges and universities, labor unions, management groups, and also religious groups such as
churches, synagogues, mosques, and temples—all of which exist in society
and contribute to the good of the public society as a whole. Only then do we
come to the levels of government beginning with the local, then the state,
and finally the federal as these are understood in the United States.

Subsidiarity comes from the Latin word *subsidium*, which means "help."
The description of society in the preceding paragraph begins with the most
fundamental level of the human person moving upward to given institutions
and structures, then to voluntary associations, and finally to government
with its different levels. According to the principle of subsidiarity, the higher
level should do everything possible to help the lower level achieve its own
purposes and should intervene only when the lower and more basic level
cannot do something on its own.

The way higher education is funded in the United States well illustrates the principle of subsidiarity at work. Individuals and families bear primary responsibility for providing for higher education. Originally many colleges and universities were religious in origin; private institutions also came into existence. However, these alone could not meet the demand, so the state government founded universities, land-grant institutions, teachers' colleges, and community colleges. The federal government helps all types of higher education through grants and low-interest loans. The state government had to start its own institutions in order to provide higher education for all, but individuals and families must still pay something. Likewise state governments do not demand the extinction of private institutions. In fact many if not most private colleges could not survive if it were not for various forms of government help. Thus the government does not usurp the role of the family or more basic groups but helps them achieve their purposes while providing for others who otherwise would not have access to higher education. Contemporary political scientists often speak of the need for mediating structures and institutions between the individual and government.

The principle of socialization exists in some tension with the principle of subsidiarity. Pope John XXIII developed this principle in *Mater et Magistra* (1961): "One of the principal characteristics of our time is the multiplication of social relationships, that is a daily more complex interdependence of citizens" (no. 59). In this light, to a greater extent than heretofore, public authorities have to intervene in a more organized and extensive way to adapt institutions, tasks, and means to the common good. However, this does not do away with the principle of subsidiarity. Thus the complexity of the modern world with its many interrelationships, including the level of globalization, calls for greater government intervention since the government alone can direct these complex forces to the common good.

Development in the Values of the Common Good

As mentioned, the common good in Catholic social teaching is described in broad and somewhat vague terms. The values constituting the common good have changed over time, and the authoritative documents of Catholic social teaching show a very significant development, even though the documents themselves do not explicitly call attention to this change.

One must also see the values composing the common good in the light of the Catholic self-understanding of the state as a middle position between the two extremes of individualism and collectivism. In the eighteenth and nineteenth centuries the Catholic Church saw the individualism of liberalism as its primary foe. According to Catholic understanding, liberalism extolled reason and the freedom of the individual cut off from any relationship to God and God's law. The Catholic Church was the implacable enemy of all forms of liberalism. The term is used here as it is used in philosophical thought, not in contemporary political thought. Religious liberalism, according to a generally understood Catholic approach, started with Luther, who exalted the conscience of the individual believer over the church. Philosophical liberalism emphasized human reason cut off from God and God's law.

Political liberalism supported democracy and the rights of the majority over the rights of truth. Economic liberalism in the form of capitalism affirmed the freedom of owners and entrepreneurs to make as much money as possible and forgot about the rights of workers and the poor. Leo XIII's *Rerum Novarum* (1891) emphasized the role of government to intervene and protect the workers and the poor. In a very triumphalistic way, Pope Pius XI in *Quadragesimo Anno* (1931) maintained that, "*Rerum Novarum* completely overthrew those tattering tenets of liberalism which had long hampered effective intervention by the government" (no. 27).

Pope Leo XIII's authoritative writings clearly illustrate the opposition to liberalism with its emphasis on human freedom. Leo strongly attacked the modern freedoms including freedom of religion, which violates the "highest duty" of worshipping the one true God in the one true faith; freedom of speech and the press means that truth will not remain sacred. In addition Leo did not see human equality as a value because in his concept of the organic society each individual has a different role to play for the good of the whole. Civil society is based on an analogy with the human body which has many distinct and unequal parts that have to work together for the good of the whole. If all the parts were the same and equal, there would be no unified human body. Equality erodes the glue that keeps society together. Also, Leo did not advocate the participation of people in government. His favorite word for the leaders of society was "rulers" (*principes*), and the people were the illiterate multitude that had to be led.

As the twentieth century developed, however, the Catholic Church began to see totalitarianism, especially in the form of communism, as the biggest problem. Pius XI, in the 1930s, issued encyclicals condemning totalitarianism on the right (Nazism and fascism) and especially totalitarianism on the left in the form of communism. Communism trampled on the dignity, freedom, and rights of the individual. In this context, Pius XI was happy and proud to wage the good fight for the liberty of consciences, which he was quick to point out does not mean the absolute independence of conscience from God's law.

A fascinating development took place in the two encyclicals issued by John XXIII in the early 1960s. *Mater et Magistra* (1961) develops the vision that the values of truth, justice, and love constitute the good society (nos. 212–65). But *Pacem in Terris* (1963) adds a fourth value to this triumvirate—freedom (nos. 86–129). The documents themselves do not call attention to this very significant change, but the growing importance of freedom comes to the fore here.

Vatican II (1962–65) moves even further in its promotion of human freedom in general and freedom in political life as illustrated in its changed teaching on religious freedom (which will be analyzed shortly). Pope Paul VI in *Octogesima Adveniens* (1971) develops two aspirations that have come to the fore in the light of recent developments: "the aspiration to equality and the aspiration to participation, two forms of human dignity and freedom" (no. 22). At the end of the nineteenth century the Catholic Church strongly opposed freedom, equality, and participation, but in the twentieth century the same Catholic Church became a strong proponent of human dignity and freedom. Pope John Paul II made human freedom and dignity an essential part of his many teachings on the political order.

The shift to a greater emphasis on freedom, equality, and participation in political society helps explain the Catholic move to the acceptance of and support for democratic forms of government. The Catholic Church strongly opposed the French Revolution and even supported the monarchy and the *ancien régime*. Liberal democracy seemed to involve all the negative aspects of liberalism in general. Catholic teaching did not give that much emphasis to the form of government but simply insisted that whatever form existed should strive for the common good of society. But as the twentieth century progressed, the developments mentioned above called for an acceptance of democracy. In his 1944 Christmas message, Pope Pius XII stated that a democratic form of government appears to many people as a natural postulate imposed by reason itself. Catholic thinkers such as Jacques Maritain and Catholic democratic parties in Europe after World War II espoused the cause of democracy. Vatican II firmly accepted the democratic form of government. John Paul II was a strong advocate of democracy both in the countries behind the former Iron Curtain and in the developing countries of the world.[5]

Church and State

Historically Roman Catholicism has been associated with the union of church and state. In fact it was only at Vatican II (1962–65) that the Catholic Church accepted religious freedom and the so-called separation of church and state.

The Gospel of Matthew 22:21–22 recognizes the duality between church and state with the warning to give to God what is God's and to Caesar what is Caesar's. Catholic tradition has recognized two different orders—the spiritual and the temporal with different authorities ruling these two orders. In the course of history, however, the Catholic Church has accepted significantly different ways of relating the church and the state.

In the time of the Roman Empire, the conversion of the Emperor Constantine brought about a very close relationship between church and state. Constantine and his successors saw themselves as defenders of the faith who could and did intervene directly in the spiritual affairs of the church as illustrated by their calling ecumenical councils. The Middle Ages witnessed an attempt by popes in the Catholic Church to establish a Christian commonwealth with all people and princes bound together under obedience to the pope. The confessional state arose after the Reformation in accord with the famous principle—*cuius regio eius religio*—the religion of the place (and the people) follows the religion of the prince. The Peace of Augsburg (1555) established the confessional state, which was based on the understanding that religious unity was necessary in order to achieve civic unity. Thus there came into existence Protestant and Catholic states. Note how the founding of the United States in the eighteenth century introduced a new reality—the possibility of political unity in the midst of religious diversity and pluralism.

Catholic theology in general fought against control of the church by the state and developed various theories for understanding the relationship. In the Middle Ages, many Catholic theologians espoused the direct power of the papacy and the church over the state and thus supported the Christian

---

[5] Paul E. Sigmund, "Catholicism and Liberal Democracy," in *Catholicism and Liberalism: Contributions to American Public Philosophy*, ed. R. Bruce Douglass and David Hollenbach (Cambridge: Cambridge University Press, 1994), 217–41.

commonwealth of the Middle Ages. This hierocratic theory, however, still recognized the existence of two different powers or societies but maintained that Christ who was both priest and king delegated to Peter and his successors, the popes, a direct jurisdiction over temporal affairs as well as spiritual ones. According to the metaphor, the pope has the two swords but delegates the temporal sword to the princes. If the prince is delinquent, the pope can take the temporal sword away. Such was the justification of Christendom. During the Reformation, Robert Bellarmine (d. 1621) supported a theory of indirect power of the pope over the temporal realm. For spiritual reasons the pope can depose the ruler.

By the nineteenth century official Catholic teaching still held that the state ought to publicly support the Catholic religion. Individuals could privately practice different faiths, but the state should prohibit the public expression of all faiths except the Catholic faith. A distinction, however, was made between thesis and hypothesis. The thesis, which was meant to prevail, called for the legal establishment of the Catholic Church and legal intolerance for all others. In certain circumstances in which a greater good could be achieved or a greater evil avoided, however, the "hypothesis," which involved the legal toleration of all religions, could be accepted. What happened in practice was that where Catholics were a vast majority, the thesis existed; where Catholics were a minority, as in the United States, the hypothesis could be tolerated. This remained the official teaching until Vatican II.

It is helpful, especially in our own age, which is so different, to give the reasons behind the denial of religious freedom. First, the primacy of the spiritual order called for the temporal to be in service of the spiritual. They were two different realities, but they had to work together.

Second, the most important reality involved was objective truth. The truth, according to the Catholic understanding, meant that the Catholic Church was the one "true religion." But what about the consciences of people who disagreed? The response was that error has no rights. Just as one is not free to sell poison, which can cause death to our physical life, so one cannot permit religious error, which can cause spiritual death. Objective truth is the primary consideration.

Third, the understanding of the state bolstered this denial of religious liberty. The state is a creature of God, and like all creatures of God it too must acknowledge the one true God and the one true religion. The state has an ethical and even religious function of directing the illiterate multitude to their spiritual and ethical good. Such a state is authoritarian or paternalistic at best.

Fourth, the Catholic Church strongly opposed the European arguments in favor of religious freedom as proposed in the name of continental liberalism. According to this theory, there was no dyarchy (no two societies—the temporal and the spiritual) but only a thoroughgoing political and juridical monism—one sovereign, one society, one law, one secular faith. This was a thoroughgoing secularism that removed the church entirely from the public realm and left it existing only in the private sphere. The church could have no influence whatsoever on what happened in public life.

Roman Catholicism at Vatican II in 1965, however, accepted the principle of religious liberty, meaning that no one is to be forced to act against one's conscience in religious matters or prohibited from acting in accord with religious conscience. What brought about this significant change?

The primary reality in this change was the greater appreciation and acceptance of the dignity, rights, and freedom of the human person, as mentioned earlier. Its implications for religious liberty are decisive.

First, the emphasis moved from the primacy of the objective reality of truth to the primacy of the subjective reality of the human person and her or his conscience. The freedom of the human person calls for a free response, and no secular authority can take away the basic freedom of the individual person in one's response to God.

Second, the growing emphasis on the freedom and dignity of the human person dramatically changed the understanding of government and its role. For Leo XIII the state was authoritarian, or at best paternalistic, in directing the illiterate multitude to their own good. Now the freedom of the individual limits the role of the state. The Declaration on Religious Freedom of Vatican II insists that "the usages of society are to be the usages of freedom in their full range. These require that the freedom of human beings be respected as far as possible and curtailed only when and insofar as necessary" (no. 7). Here the Catholic Church accepts the principle of the free society and of limited constitutional government.

Third, the contemporary understanding of religious freedom as enshrined in limited constitutional government does not call for the removal of the church from the public order and its relegation only to the private sphere. The church is free to carry on its own mission in the world, including the mission of working for a more just human society. The church has a right to influence the temporal society in and through the conscience and works of church members who are both members of the church and citizens of the nation. The government thus recognizes the freedom of the church to carry out its mission and in this way the primacy of the spiritual is safeguarded.

The recognition of religious freedom also means the acceptance of a limited constitutional government and the rejection of the authoritarian, paternalistic, and ethical state that Leo XIII had proposed in the late nineteenth century.

On the basis of the teaching found in the Declaration on Religious Freedom, Catholic teaching insists on the important distinction between the broader public society and the narrower concept of the public order where the coercive power of government is employed. The broader public society includes all the individuals, natural groups, and voluntary associations that influence and affect public society. The end of public society and all those who participate in it is the common good. The political order or the state with its power of coercion has the limited purpose of protecting and promoting the public order. The basic principle of the free society is as much freedom as possible with government intervening for the sake of public order. The question then naturally arises: What is public order? According to the declaration, public order involves the three goods of justice, public morality, and public peace (no. 7). Government can and should intervene and promote these three values. In keeping with the anthropology and understanding of the state developed previously, I add social justice to the generic concept of justice because people often do not give enough importance to social justice in our society.

Public order with its threefold goods or values also puts legitimate limits on religious freedom. In the United States, despite our rhetoric, we recognize restrictions on religious freedom that are basically governed by the threefold values of public order. If a religion calls for child sacrifice, public authorities can and should stop this because of justice—the need to protect the right to life of all citizens. If your religion calls for you to march through a residential neighborhood at 3 a.m. with a hundred-piece band, peace justifies the government in preventing such a march.

In the nineteenth century (in a disputed move) the US Supreme Court ruled that polygamy for Mormons was illegal despite the directives of their religion to practice polygamy. Note that the criterion of public morality by definition differs from private morality, but there exists much discussion about what constitutes public morality.

The Declaration on Religious Freedom thus sets forth the contemporary Catholic acceptance of limited constitutional government. But in a surprising move subsequent papal documents of Catholic social teaching issued by Paul VI and John Paul II fail to mention public order as the end of the state but still regularly invoke the common good. The possible reasons for this somewhat astonishing silence lie beyond the scope of this essay. Since Catholic social teaching deals primarily with justice issues, however, both the criterion of public order and the criterion on the common good would come to the same conclusions about the role of the state with regard to justice. The following section deals with justice in Catholic social teaching.

Justice

In this section I discuss material goods, private property and the poor, the different types of justice, human rights, and the economic systems of capitalism and Marxism.

The Catholic tradition based on the scripture and influenced by Thomistic Aristotelianism has maintained that material goods are not the most important human goods but are always subordinate to spiritual goods. Human dignity, however, requires a sufficiency of the material goods of this world. In any society or government the primary issue concerns the just distribution of material goods in society.

Catholic social teaching emphasizes the universal destiny of the goods of creation to serve the needs of all. Pope John Paul II in *Sollicitudo Rei Socialis* (1987) succinctly summarizes the teaching: "It is necessary to state once more the characteristic principle of Christian social doctrine: the goods of this world are *originally meant for all.* The right to private property is *valid and necessary*, but it does not nullify the nature of this principle. Private property, in fact, is under a 'social mortgage,' which means that it has an intrinsically social function, based upon and justified precisely by the principle of the universal destiny of goods" (no. 42).

Since the beginning of the church Catholic teaching has recognized both a social and an individual dimension to material goods in keeping with its basic anthropology, but there has been some development over time about the exact relationship between the two aspects. The social aspect of the goods of creation rests on the intention of the creator that the goods of creation exist to serve the needs of all. On this basis, the criterion of distributive justice that will be developed later insists that all human beings have a right to the material goods necessary to live a minimally decent human existence.

The social dimension also limits the understanding of private property as something that one owns as one's own. Thomas Aquinas accepts the general teaching of the early church that private property is justified not on the basis of natural law but on the basis of human sinfulness. He acknowledges there would be no need for private property if it were not for sin. However, granted the need for possessing things as one's own in this imperfect and sinful world, the use of private property insists on its function to serve the needs of all (Ia, q. 98, a. 1, ad 3).

In the question of the distribution of material goods, the Catholic tradition has insisted on a special care and concern for the poor. According to the Hebrew Bible, God is the special protector of the poor, and God will hear their cry and take care of them. The New Testament also shows this special concern of God and Jesus for the poor as illustrated in the so-called last judgment scene in Matthew 25 where eternal reward is based on what one does for the poor and the least of our brothers and sisters. In the very beginning of *Rerum Novarum* (no. 2), Leo XIII insists "some remedy must be found and quickly found, for the misery and wretchedness which press so heavily at this moment on the large majority of the very poor." John Paul II insisted on the preferential option for the poor. The economic pastoral of the US bishops spells out the priorities involved in the preferential option for the poor (nos. 87–95). A preferential option is not an exclusive option. God loves all people but has a special concern for the poor. On the basis of the preferential option for the poor, three priorities emerge: (1) the fulfillment of the basic needs of the poor is the highest priority; (2) increasing active participation in economic life by those presently excluded or vulnerable is a high social priority; (3) the investment of wealth, energy, and human talent should be specifically directed to benefit the poor.

Keeping with an anthropology that emphasizes both the dignity and social nature of the human person, the Catholic tradition insists on three types of justice: commutative justice (coming from the Latin *commutare* meaning "exchange") governs one-on-one relationships such as contracts; distributive justice governs how society distributes its goods and burdens among the members; legal, social, or contributive justice governs the obligation of individuals to society and the state. Scholastic theologians, especially Thomas Aquinas and commentators on Aquinas, developed a similar understanding of justice and applied it to the problems of their own day. The economic pastoral of the US bishops (1987) describes these three types of justice and indicates their application to contemporary problems (nos. 68–76).

Commutative justice involves arithmetic equality, is blind, and is no respecter of persons. If I borrow ten dollars from you and ten dollars from the wealthiest person in the world, I owe each of you ten dollars. The characteristics of the individual person do not enter into the consideration. Those who propose a more individualistic anthropology see commutative justice as the primary or the only aspect of justice.

Distributive justice governs the relationship between society or the state and the individual. As pointed out above, society is broader than the state. In the light of space constraints, this section will discuss how the state should distribute its goods and burdens. A just distribution rests on recognizing that the political community involves members who have an equal human dignity.

Take first the distribution of material goods. What is a fair and just distribution of material goods in society? An individualistic approach asserts the right of individuals to acquire as much as possible for one's self, provided that equal opportunity is afforded to all. Often the metaphor of the race is invoked. Extreme collectivism argues for a total equality in the distribution of material goods. The Catholic tradition, once again, finds a middle way between these two approaches.

A basic or fundamental criterion for just distribution of material goods is human need. As mentioned earlier, in the Catholic understanding all human beings have a right to a minimally decent human existence. Above and beyond this criterion of need, other criteria such as creativity, hard work, risk, and reward all come into play. Not everyone should have the same amount of goods, but all should have that basic minimum necessary for a minimally decent human existence. In addition, the equality of members of society is jeopardized if there exists a huge gap between the highest and lowest in the possession of material goods.

Take now the distribution of burdens. The primary societal burden involves taxation. What is a just tax system according to the principles of distributive justice? Those who earn or have more money should contribute more. Distributive justice maintains that those who have more should pay not only arithmetically more but also should pay a higher percentage. A progressive tax system is called for.

Legal justice, or what is today sometimes called contributive justice, involves the relationship of the individual person or citizen to the society and state. In an older understanding the primary obligation was to obey the just laws of the state, hence the name legal. Now, however, the emphasis falls on the responsibility of individuals to participate actively in the total life of the state and the community and the corresponding obligation of society to recognize and encourage such participation. Especially today when many people feel they have no say or control over our political and economic institutions, we desperately need institutions that are open to participation by all.

As might be expected, the Catholic social tradition with its basic anthropology has historically criticized both capitalism and communism. Since this chapter deals primarily with the political order and its responsibilities, it will not include a detailed discussion of these two economic systems. The next chapter, however, will discuss economic issues.

Roman Catholicism and Nonbelievers: Politics and People Outside the Tradition

Is the message or teaching of Roman Catholicism about politics intended just for Catholics and Christians or for all humankind? The documents coming from the hierarchical teaching office in the Catholic Church insist that the teaching is for all humankind. From a methodological perspective the teaching has traditionally been based on the natural law approach, which by definition is open to all human beings and has no religious presuppositions with regard to its content. From a content perspective Catholic social teaching insists on one common good for political societies to which all members of the society, whether they are believers or not, must contribute. Since the 1960s the papal documents themselves have explicitly been addressed to all people of good will. Nowhere do these official teachings propose something different that Catholics are asked to do in the political order. From a practical perspective the Catholic approach recognizes that its teaching for a more just social order will be effective only if many people work together to try to put this teaching into practice.

In theory, Catholic social teaching is addressed not only to Catholics but to all people of good will. In practice, however, two problems arise. First, as mentioned above, ever since Vatican Council II, official church teaching documents have made more explicit references to scripture, Jesus Christ, revelation, and grace. But, as noted above, these documents still address all people of good will. At the very least, this new approach creates some tension because it addresses two different audiences. The US bishops in their pastoral letters have recognized this tension and claim they appeal to unique Catholic and Christian sources in addressing fellow Catholics and appeal to others on the basis of common human reason and experience. However, it is impossible to make this clear differentiation all the time.

Second, recall the tension mentioned above between the natural law as based on human reason and experience and the natural law as authoritatively proposed by the Catholic Church. With regard to non-Catholics the fact that the teaching is proposed as being in accord with reason and experience means that all people can enter into the discussion. Such an approach facilitates a civil dialogue among all people in a society. However, since the teaching is also proposed as authoritative church teaching, the Catholic Church and Catholic individuals at times have used their political muscle or power to make these authoritative teachings into law. Thus at times the paradigm of culture wars seems more fitting than the paradigm of deliberative rational discourse and civil discussion about what is good for society.

This chapter has discussed the Roman Catholic approach to politics in the light of its sources, its theory of politics, the medium or methodology used, its message and content, and finally its relationship to nonbelievers. The very nature of Catholicism, with its authoritative teaching office, means the official documents have developed in some depth the Catholic understanding of the political order. More than half of this chapter thus has dealt with the message or content of this teaching as found in the official documents of the Catholic Church. The Catholic approach, however, is also intended for all people of good will and thus is truly catholic or universal.

Chapter 2

THE RECEPTION OF CATHOLIC SOCIAL AND ECONOMIC TEACHING IN THE UNITED STATES*

The term "Catholic social teaching," according to Pope John Paul II, refers to papal encyclicals and other documents issued since the 1891 encyclical of Pope Leo XIII, *Rerum Novarum,* which deal with labor, social, and economic issues (*CA* 2).[1] Although there is no official canon or list of the documents of Catholic social teaching, general agreement exists on the major documents belonging to this tradition. Catholic social teaching is a much narrower concept than Catholic social thought or Catholic social ethics.

This chapter examines the reception and influence of Catholic social teaching in the United States. Both developments in Catholic self-understanding and the evolving changes in US society and culture have affected the way in which these documents have been received in the United States. Significant changes both in Catholic ecclesiology, especially at Vatican II (1962–65), and in the cultural and social issues facing the United States in the 1960s, ushered in a distinctively new context. This long chapter will consider two different time periods—from the beginning of Catholic social teaching in the late nineteenth century to the 1960s and the period from the 1960s to the present.

---

* Originally published as Charles E. Curran, "The Reception of Catholic Social and Economic Teaching in the United States," in *Modern Catholic Social Teaching: Commentaries and Interpretations,* ed. Kenneth R. Himes (Washington, DC: Georgetown University Press, 2005), 469–92. Used with permission. www.press.georgetown.edu.

[1] These documents can be found in a number of different sources. The best known collection is David J. O'Brien and Thomas A. Shannon, eds., *Catholic Social Thought: The Documentary Heritage* (Maryknoll, NY: Orbis Books, 1992). References to individual documents will give the paragraph number of the document and the page number from O'Brien and Shannon. The specific reference here is to Pope John Paul II, *Centesimus Annus* (abbreviated in the text as *CA*), no. 2.

Before the 1960s

The influence and reception of Catholic social teaching in the United States involves three different factors or sources—the teaching and documents of the bishops of the United States, the theological and theoretical writings on Catholic social ethics in general, and the practical and pastoral involvements of Catholics.

Teaching of the US Bishops

In the twentieth century before 1919 there were no letters or teaching documents from the bishops as a whole because the US bishops did not have any perduring national organization. The US bishops first formed a national organization in 1917 to coordinate the Catholic support for the war effort. This organization became the National Catholic Welfare Conference (NCWC) in 1923 and has gone through subsequent changes, especially at the time of Vatican II.[2]

The most famous document coming from NCWC was "Bishops' Program of Social Reconstruction" issued by the Administrative Board of the NCWC in February 1919. This document dealt with reconstruction plans for justice and peace after World War I, proposed eleven recommendations, ten of which were ultimately put into practice in the United States, but also pointed out three long-term defects in the present system that need continuing attention—inefficiency and waste in production and distribution, insufficient incomes for the majority of workers, and unnecessarily large incomes for a small minority of privileged capitalists.[3] This sixteen-page document in contemporary format contains only one reference to papal teaching—the encyclical *Rerum Novarum* of Leo XIII.[4]

What explains the lack of extensive citations from papal documents in the earliest and perhaps most significant document coming from the US bishops dealing with social justice in the first half of the twentieth century? Many influences are at work here. With regard to papal teaching in general,

---

[2] For the origins of the National Catholic Welfare Conference (NCWC), see Elizabeth McKeown, *War and Welfare: American Catholics and World War I* (New York: Garland, 1988).

[3] Administrative Committee of the National Catholic War Council, "Bishops' Program of Social Reconstruction," in *Our Bishops Speak, 1919–51*, ed. Raphael A. Huber (Milwaukee: Bruce, 1952), 243–62.

[4] Ibid., 259.

its role or importance was somewhat less in the early twentieth century than it became in subsequent years. In the case of social teaching in particular, there existed only one document (*Rerum Novarum*) and not a body of Catholic social teaching. Likewise, the 1917 program addressed the broad US audience as well as Catholics and perhaps purposely did not appeal that much to authoritative church teaching. The first draft of the document came from the typewriter of John A. Ryan, the foremost theoretician of Catholic social ethics at the time, and was not originally intended as a document to be issued by the bishops.[5]

The first pastoral letter of the US bishops in the twentieth century in 1919, however, differs markedly from the "Bishops' Program of Social Reconstruction" with regard to the use of papal teaching. The six-page section on "Industrial Relations," in this sixty-three-page document, starts by citing *Rerum Novarum* and begins each of its separate sections with a citation from Leo XIII, thus making the encyclical the primary source for the teaching in this area.[6] The different audience and subject matter of this document help explain the different emphasis on papal teaching. As a pastoral letter, the document is addressed to all members of the Catholic Church in the United States and not directed to non-Catholics. This long document also deals with the whole life of the Catholic Church in the United States, including its internal and devotional life as well as its relationship to the broader US society and the problems facing that society.

One should look at the statements of the US bishops on industrial relations in the period between 1919 and 1950 in the light of the bishops' statements and documents on other issues. In his 1952 book, Raphael Huber collected the various letters, resolutions, and statements of the US bishops in the period of 1919 to 1951 and included only eighty-two documents. Fewer than ten of the statements deal with issues of industrial relations. Here too there is a tendency in addressing the broader American society to downplay the teaching of the popes and to appeal to sources that all the people in the United States readily accept. See, for example, the 1947 statement, "Secularism" and the 1951 statement, "God's Law: The Measure of Man's Conduct."[7]

---

[5] Francis L. Broderick, *Right Reverend New Dealer: John A. Ryan* (New York: Macmillan, 1963), 104–8.

[6] The Hierarchy of the United States, "Pastoral Letter of 1919," in Huber, *Our Bishops Speak*, 46–51.

[7] The Hierarchy of the United States, "Secularism," in Huber, *Our Bishops Speak*, 137–45; Administrative Board of the National Catholic Welfare Conference, "God's Law: The Measure of Man's Conduct," in Huber, *Our Bishops Speak*, 368–75.

The Depression in the 1930s focused much attention in the United States on industrial relations. From the Catholic perspective, the issuance of the new encyclical *Quadragesima Anno* by Pope Pius XI in 1931 added another authoritative voice to the solution for industrial problems. Now the church had two encyclicals dealing with this issue. Thus, in the decade of the 1930s, the US bishops frequently addressed the problems of the Depression and gave priority to the solutions proposed by the papal encyclicals. These various statements include "Statement on Unemployment" (1930), "Statement on the Economic Crisis" (1931), "Statement on the Present Crisis" (1933), "Statement in Defense of the Rights of Workers to Organize" (1934), "Statement on the Christian Attitude on Social Problems" (1937), "Statement on Industrial and Social Peace" (1938), and "Statement on the Church and Social Order" (1940).[8] In the eyes of the US bishops the encyclicals of Leo XIII and Pius XI proposed solutions for the industrial problems that existed in the United States in the 1930s. In the 1940 statement of the administrative board, "Church and Social Order," the bishops insist on the role of the church "as the teacher of the entire moral law and more particularly as it applies to man's economic and social conduct in business, industry, and trade. To make our pronouncements authentic and to interpret truly the mind of the church, we follow closely the teachings of our late lamented pontiff, Pope Pius XI."[9]

In this document the US bishops strongly urge the United States to put into practice the principles found in this papal teaching.[10] Here the bishops emphasize the right of workers to organize, the right of workers to receive a living wage as a minimum requirement of justice, the need for federal and state appropriations and intervention to bring about justice and relief from the present crisis, and a more equitable sharing of the goods of creation. In proposing a just social order, the bishops insist that the papal principles and understanding are a *via media* between individualism on the one hand and collectivism or communism on the other. Economic liberalism wants no interference whatsoever on the part of government and insists on no restrictions on individual initiative and personal enterprise. The government is limited to the function of a policeman or umpire in enforcing private contracts with no responsibility for promoting justice and the common good. On the other extreme, collectivists and communists desire

---

[8] All these letters are found in Huber, *Our Bishops Speak.*

[9] Administrative Board of the National Catholic Welfare Conference, "Church and Social Order," in Huber, *Our Bishops Speak,* 326.

[10] Ibid., 324–43.

to centralize all power in the state and to socialize all resources, including private property.

The bishops in accord with the teaching *Quadragesima Anno* want to overcome the opposition between capital and labor and build a more organic society. Human society must be seen as an organic entity based on an analogy with the human body in which all the parts work for the good of the whole. We all belong to the same social organism, but unfortunately that social organism has been dismembered and broken up with different groups such as capital and labor seeking their own good and not the common good of all. The encyclical calls for new functional structures called occupational groups or vocational groups. These occupational groups well illustrate economic democracy at work and avoid the opposite extremes of laissez-faire capitalism and government dictating all economic policy. Labor and capital, together with the blessing and limited help of government, will thus form these public groups that determine production, prices, and wages in a particular industry, while an overall council coordinates and directs the individual industries to make sure they work for the common good. Thus, labor, capital, consumers, and government work together for the common good and replace the primary role of the free market. Chapter 3 will discuss George Higgins's understanding of these industry councils.

In the 1930s, the bishops were also worried that communist leaders in the United States might take advantage of the chaos to introduce their approach, which masquerades as the champion of the downtrodden, the archenemy of capitalistic abuses, and the redeemer of the poor and the working classes. Such atheistic communism fails to recognize the basic God-given dignity of the individual person. The bishops said that the United States needed to respond to the problems of the Depression in accord with the principles of papal teaching to avoid a radical takeover by communists.[11] This theme of the danger of communism on both the national scene and especially the international scene would become quite prominent in the rhetoric of the US Catholic bishops in the 1950s.[12] However, this topic extends well beyond the limited question of industrial relations being treated here.

New issues came to the fore in the 1940s and 1950s with World War II and its aftermath. In this period the US bishops at their annual plenary

---

[11] Administrative Board of the National Catholic Welfare Conference, "Christian Attitude on Social Problems," in Huber, *Our Bishops Speak*, 314–18.

[12] John F. Cronin, *Social Principles and Economic Life*, rev. ed. (Milwaukee: Bruce, 1964), 106–22.

meetings issued no statements or pastoral letters on industrial relations as such. As one might expect, they addressed the issues of the day, including war, peace, communism, the Cold War, and the family, and in 1958 they condemned "enforced segregation" of Negroes.[13] However, the bishops had already forcefully made the point that in the area of industrial relations the papal encyclicals, especially *Rerum Novarum* and *Quadragesima Anno*, provide the principles to bring about justice in this area and even a plan for a just social order based on the industry councils.

Theologians and Popular Writings

The writings of Catholic theologians and commentators on socioeconomic issues in the United States in the first sixty years of the twentieth century show a trajectory that gave an increasingly important role to papal teaching and encyclicals, culminating in these sources becoming the primary and principal sources for Catholic social thought. Likewise by the 1960s, the mainstream of Catholic writing on socioeconomic issues in the United States basically followed the same approach as the papal documents—a heavy natural law basis, a moderate reforming stance, a working together with all others for the common good, and an emphasis on change of structures rather than change of heart.

John A. Ryan (1869–1945), a diocesan priest of St. Paul, Minnesota, was the foremost exponent of Catholic social thought in his role as professor at the Catholic University of America from 1915 to 1939 and the most visible spokesperson for Catholic social thought in his role as director of the Social Action Department (SAD) of NCWC, one of the four original departments of NCWC founded in 1919. Ryan was a prolific author throughout his life, but he did his academic and scholarly publishing early, especially *The Living Wage* (1906) and *Distributive Justice* (1916).[14] In these two monographs Ryan gives practically no attention to papal documents. *Distributive Justice*, in its almost 450 pages, mentions Leo XIII's *Rerum Novarum* in only three places![15] However, by the 1930s papal encyclicals constitute the primary source for Ryan's ethical analysis of socioeconomic issues.[16] Four factors influence this change. First, in his role as director of

---

[13] See Hugh. J. Nolan, ed., *Pastoral Letters of the United States Catholic Bishops, vol. 2: 1941–1961* (Washington, DC: United States Catholic Conference, 1984).

[14] For the biography of Ryan, see Broderick, *The Right Reverend New Dealer*.

[15] John A. Ryan, *Distributive Justice* (New York: Macmillan, 1916), 64–66, 306–9, 377.

[16] John A. Ryan, *A Better Economic Order* (New York: Harper & Brothers, 1935).

the SAD, Ryan's charge called for him to make official church teaching known and applied. Second, papal teaching became more important in the life of the Catholic Church in general as the century progressed. Third, by 1931, there were now two papal encyclicals dealing with industrial relations. Fourth, Ryan himself had often been attacked by others within the Roman Catholic Church as being too advanced and liberal in his social positions, but many saw the new 1931 encyclical as a papal vindication of Ryan's positions. Ryan defended himself by calling on the teaching of the popes.

Throughout his over four decades of publishing, Ryan remained basically consistent in his approach to Catholic social ethics. He employed a natural law methodology, proposed a constantly reforming position while rejecting radical reconstruction, called for some government intervention to promote justice, worked with many groups and associations outside the church for social change, and emphasized the change of structures while neglecting the change of heart.[17]

Three somewhat different Catholic approaches to the social problem emerged in the period before 1940 in popular Catholic writings. These approaches addressed a Catholic audience from the perspective of a triumphalistic Catholic ecclesiology. The German American Catholics under the leadership of Frederick P. Kenkel, in their journal *Central Blatt and Social Justice*, which reached a peak circulation of 8,000 in 1913, were more negative than Ryan in their view of the US economic scene and called for more radical change in the social order, based on the corporatist theory proposed by German Catholics, especially Heinrich Pesch, a Jesuit. Corporatism called for a system analogous to the guild system of the Middle Ages and similar to the vocational groups proposed later by Pius XI as a middle road between the extremes of socialism and capitalism. As conservative Catholics, they referred to papal teaching, but their primary sources were Pesch and the German writers associated with him.[18]

Paul Hanly Furfey (1896–1992), a priest and a professor of sociology at the Catholic University of America, wrote significant popular works in the 1930s, especially *Fire on Earth* (1936), calling for a radical Christian personalism in opposition to the existing mores and institutions of US society and life. *Fire on Earth* explains the theoretical basis of the Catholic Worker Movement founded by Dorothy Day. Furfey advocated a supernatural

---

[17] For my analysis and criticism of Ryan's social ethics, see Charles E. Curran, *American Catholic Social Ethics* (Notre Dame, IN: University of Notre Dame Press, 1982), 26–91.

[18] Ibid., 133–71.

sociology (in opposition to the natural law approach of others), a literal and radical interpretation of the New Testament, and strategies of separation, nonparticipation, and bearing witness in relation to the existing ethos and culture in the United States. However, in the very first paragraph of *Fire on Earth* Furfey appeals to *Quadragesima Anno*'s call for a return to genuine Christian life as a justification for his very different approach.[19]

Virgil Michel (1890–1938), a Benedictine monk of Collegeville, Minnesota, with broad philosophical and theological interests, wrote often on social issues, including a commentary on *Quadragesima Anno*, in which he explains the problems of capitalism and the need for a reconstruction of the social order based on the encyclical's call for occupational groups. Addressing primarily a Catholic audience, he insists this more substantive change calls for a basic change of heart that could only take place in and through a living participation in the liturgy. He cites Pope Pius XI to justify his emphasis on bringing together social change, change of heart, and active participation in the liturgy.[20]

Joseph Casper Husslein, SJ (1873–1952), a Jesuit priest, associate editor of *America*, and professor and founder of the School of Social Service at St. Louis University, was a prolific popular writer on social justice beginning with his 1912 *The Church and Social Problems*. He even wrote a 1924 book for the Social Action Department of NCWC titled *The Bible and Labor*. His writings well illustrate the trajectory described in this section of gradually making the papal encyclicals the primary source for his teaching. In 1931 he published *The Christian Social Manifesto*, which was a commentary on *Rerum Novarum* and *Quadragesima Anno*. In 1940 and 1942 he first published under the general title of *Social Wellsprings* two different books bringing together the important encyclicals of Leo XIII and Pius XI.[21] For the later Husslein the papal encyclicals constituted the primary and governing source for Catholic social thought.

---

[19] Paul Hanly Furfey, *Fire on the Earth* (New York: Macmillan, 1936).

[20] Virgil Michel, *Christian Social Reconstruction* (Milwaukee: Bruce, 1937); *The Social Question: Essays on Capitalism and Christianity* (Collegeville, MN: St. John's University Press, 1987). See also R. W. Franklin and Robert L. Spaeth, *Virgil Michel: American Catholic* (Collegeville, MN: Liturgical Press, 1988).

[21] For different perspectives on Husslein, see Peter McDonough, *Men Astutely Trained: A History of the Jesuits in the American Century* (New York: Free Press, 1992), 50–64; Stephen A. Werner, *Prophet of the Christian Social Manifesto: Joseph Husslein, S.J., His Life, Work, and Social Thought* (Milwaukee: Marquette University Press, 2001).

John F. Cronin (1908–1994), a Sulpician priest, who taught in seminaries and served as the assistant or associate director of the SAD of NCWC from 1948 to 1967, wrote often on Catholic social thought.[22] His *Social Principles and Economic Life* (1959), based on an earlier work and later revised to include the encyclicals of John XXIII, served as a textbook in many Catholic colleges and universities. All seventeen chapters begin with extended citations from appropriate papal (and occasionally episcopal) documents, especially *Rerum Novarum* an *Quadragesima Anno*. Thus Catholic social thought involves a commentary on, and an application of, papal documents. In this book Cronin follows the natural law approach, adopts a reforming and not a radical approach to the social order, and insists on institutional and structural change while downplaying to a great extent the role of change of heart.[23] Writing in 1971, Cronin criticized his own naïve hermeneutic of the papal documents for failing to recognize their historical and cultural conditioning and also pointed out the limited and fundamentalist ecclesiology of the times.[24]

Thus by 1960 the Cronin book illustrates that Catholic social thought in the United States had become almost identified with the teaching of the papal social encyclicals as giving the principles for guiding and overcoming the problems still existing in the socioeconomic order.

Practical Influence of the Social Encyclicals

The SAD, despite a small staff, tried to disseminate the ideas of the social encyclicals and to show how these principles should affect pastoral life. This department strongly supported labor and union organizing with occasional criticisms about corruption and the failure to organize industrial workers in earlier times. The SAD in the 1920s, for example, started the "Catholic Conference on Industrial Problems" that sponsored conferences dealing with the industrial issues in the light of Catholic teaching. The department also ran conferences, short courses, and lectures to train priests to work in the labor apostolate, and help in the work of labor schools in many areas of the country. Later the department issued a monthly bulletin, *Social Action*

---

[22] For a biography of Cronin, see John Timothy Donovan, "Crusader in the Cold War: A Biography of Father John F. Cronin, S.S. (1908–1994)" (PhD diss., Marquette University, 2000).

[23] John F. Cronin, *Social Principles and Economic Life* (Milwaukee: Bruce, 1959).

[24] John F. Cronin, "Forty Years Later: Reflections and Reminiscences," in *Readings in Moral Theology No. 5: Official Catholic Social Teaching*, ed. Charles E. Curran and Richard A. McCormick (New York: Paulist Press, 1986), 69–76.

Notes for Priests. In many ways the department was the center for Catholic social action; some areas, such as family life, rural life, and international relations, eventually became separate entities within NCWC.[25]

Beginning in the 1940s George G. Higgins, a Chicago priest, worked in SAD and continued the work of Ryan and his hard-working associate, Raymond A. McGowan. In keeping with the history of the department, Higgins concentrated primarily on industrial relations, but he became the most influential figure in broader Catholic social action in the United States during this period. Higgins, like his associate John F. Cronin, championed the cause of Pius XI's occupational or vocational groups and was even able to influence some labor leaders to support this plan. However, by the 1960s Higgins and Cronin realized that there was no possibility for such institutions coming into existence in the United States.[26] The next chapter will discuss Higgins in great detail.

In addition to the SAD, the NCWC since 1922 housed the National Council of Catholic Women, which was organized to provide a voice for Catholic women and also addressed problems of unemployment and unjust industrial practices. The women's council sought a living wage for men and women, particularly working mothers.[27]

The social encyclicals inspired four significant pastoral involvements within the church. First, many dioceses and Catholic colleges and universities established labor schools with the practical goal of acquainting Catholic workers with the social teaching of the church about labor and industrial problems with a special effort to overcome the possible inroads of communist influence in labor unions. The labor schools aimed at both training leaders for the movement and a broader dissemination of Catholic social principles to all involved. Some were basic schools existing on a parish level, and some offered specialized technical courses on a diocesan level or at a college or university. In 1948, more than forty dioceses had such labor schools or related projects.[28]

---

[25] H. W. Flannery, "Social Movements, Catholic," *New Catholic Encyclopedia* 13:331–32.

[26] For Higgins's own story, see Msgr. George Higgins with William Bole, *Organized Labor and the Church: Reflections of a Labor Priest* (New York: Paulist Press, 1993); see also *Social Catholicism: Essays in Honor of George Higgins, US Catholic Historian* 19, no. 4 (Fall 2001).

[27] Patricia Ann Lamoureux, "Justice for Wage Earners," *Horizons* 28 (2001): 222–25.

[28] John F. Cronin, *Catholic Social Action* (Milwaukee: Bruce, 1948), 75–88;

Second, individual priests, basing their approach on the encyclicals, were collectively known as "labor priests" because of their strong support for workers and labor unions even though they often approached things in different ways. As early as the second decade of the century, Peter Dietz worked tirelessly in support of the AFL and other labor unions, but his attempt to found a national organization of Catholic workers was unsuccessful.[29] Later figures include Charles O. Rice of Pittsburgh, John P. Boland of Buffalo, and Francis J. Haas, later the bishop of Grand Rapids, Michigan.[30] From the 1953 movie *On the Waterfront* many Americans became familiar with the antiracketeering crusade of the Jesuit Father John Corridan on the waterfront in New York.[31]

Third, the Association of Catholic Trade Unionists (ACTU) came into existence in New York City in 1937 to help Catholics influence their unions to act in accord with Catholic principles and especially to overcome the danger of communist influence in unions. The group published *Labor Leader* and had about eleven chapters throughout the United States in its prime before its demise in the 1960s.[32]

Fourth, the Jesuit general told US Jesuits to start something similar to the existing Jesuit centers of social research and action in Europe so as to inspire their educational apostolate with a commitment to papal social teaching. The "Institute of Social Order," headquartered in St. Louis for most of its life, came into existence as such a center; it published the *Journal of Social Order*, which existed from 1951 until 1963.[33]

Two significant intellectual associations began under the impulse of papal social teaching. The American Catholic Sociological Society began in 1938. Its journal, the *American Catholic Sociological Review* was first

McDonough, *Men Astutely Trained*, 98–108.

[29] Mary Harrita Fox, *Peter E. Dietz, Labor Priest* (Notre Dame, IN: University of Notre Dame Press, 1953).

[30] Patrick J. Sullivan, "Monsignor George G. Higgins: The Labor Priests' Priest," *US Catholic Historian* 19, no. 4 (Fall 2001): 103–18.

[31] James T. Fisher, "The Priest and the Movie: *On the Waterfront* as Historical Theology," in *Theology and the New Histories*, 1999 Annual Publication of the College Theology Society, 44, ed. Gary Macy (Maryknoll, NY: Orbis Books, 1990), 167–85.

[32] For different views of ACTU, see Neil Betten, *Catholic Activism and the Industrial Worker* (Gainesville: University Presses of Florida, 1976), 124–45, and Douglas P. Seaton, *Catholics and Radicals: The Association of Catholic Trade Unionists and the American Labor Movement from Depression to Cold War* (Lewisburg, PA: Bucknell University Press, 1981).

[33] McDonough, *Men Astutely Trained*, 295–318.

published in 1940; its primary goal was to apply the principles of Catholic social teaching as found in the encyclicals to the US scene. The association did not want to cut itself off from the academic study of sociology in the United States but definitely wanted to bring Catholic principles to bear on the understanding of society. At its height the society had nearly five hundred members. A few years later some Catholic scholars founded the Catholic Economic Association, which published *Review of Social Economy*, with the same basic purpose as the American Catholic Sociological Society. Both groups ceased to exist as such in the 1960s.[34]

The apostolate of Catholics in the labor and intellectual realms sprang from the understanding of "Catholic action." Catholic action according to the popes was "the participation of the laity in the apostolate of the hierarchy." The pope and the hierarchy proposed the social teaching with its principles, and then laypeople carried out these principles in practice in their own respective areas. The role of the laity was to Christianize the social order through their efforts in their own fields in the light of the social teaching of the church.[35]

Thus by 1960 the papal social encyclicals had become identified with Catholic social thought and significantly influenced the role of elite lay Catholic leaders, who tried to implement this papal teaching especially in the labor movement and in the intellectual movements dealing with sociology and economics. The average Catholic, however, knew little or nothing about the social teaching of the encyclicals.

From the 1960s to the Present

By the end of the 1960s none of the associations, structures, and institutions associated with the social encyclical tradition in the United States survived. The encyclicals were no longer taught in Catholic colleges. The ACTU, the American Catholic Sociological Society, and the American Catholic Economic Association no longer existed as such. No new generation of labor priests came to the fore; labor schools and colleges ceased to exist. The social encyclicals with their emphasis on industrial relations no longer played a significant role in the life of the Catholic Church in the United States. John

---

[34] E. J. Ross, "American Catholic Sociological Society," *New Catholic Encyclopedia* 1:399; Thomas F. Devine, "The Origins of the Catholic Economic Association," *Review of Social Economy* 2 (1944): 102–3.

[35] Cronin, *Catholic Social Action*, 42–44.

Cronin pointed out "that the golden era of Catholic social thought, begin-ning in 1891, has ended by 1971."[36]

Cronin's statement needs to be nuanced. Catholic social thought and action had not seen their best days. Catholic social teaching, understood as the encyclicals on industrial issues, and most of the theoretical and pastoral approaches associated with these encyclicals, definitely experienced a sharp decline.

Dramatic developments in US society and in the church helped explain this abrupt change in the role of the encyclicals in US Catholicism. First, the issues of industrial relations no longer seemed that significant or important. With greater economic growth and relative prosperity in the post–World War II era, the problems associated with industrial relations had already moved off center stage. Catholics in general moved into the middle class and improved their economic state. Now other pressing issues arose. Race and segregation became a prominent issue. A 1958 statement of the US bishops finally condemned "enforced segregation."[37] The justifiable protest of African Americans came to the fore in the 1960s. Many middle-class white Christians in this country had trouble even with the nonviolent approach of Martin Luther King Jr. Black power advocates, however, could not accept such a gradual and nonviolent approach. The problem of racial segregation and prejudice sparked urban riots across the country in the mid and late 1960s. America's cities were burning. At the same time, opposition to the Vietnam War continued to escalate. The country was seriously divided over the morality of the US involvement in Southeast Asia. Not only the content of the social issues but the way in which they were addressed also changed. The tone of protesters became angrier and more heated. The 1960s ushered in a completely new situation in the United States.

Second, the understanding of how to deal with these new issues also changed. The papal encyclicals, to their credit, called for structural and insti-tutional change. Such change should come about through rational discussion and living out the teaching of the church. Part of the problem for the church in the 1960s, especially in dealing with race and urban problems, came from the fact that Catholics were no longer the poor and the victims. How to help those who were not Catholic and bring about real social change presented new problems and called for new solutions. The US bishops learned some

---

[36] Cronin, "Forty Years Later," 76.

[37] Catholic Bishops of the United States, "Discrimination and Christian Conscience," in Nolan, *Pastoral Letters*, 201–6.

things from their Protestant sisters and brothers. They also learned from the experience of the Catholic Church in the United States in the 1940s and '50s when it had cautiously supported community organizing efforts, as illustrated especially by the support of the Chicago archdiocese for Saul Alinsky's community organizing. The idea was for the poor to organize themselves to work for justice for their neighborhoods. In 1970 the US bishops inaugurated their Campaign for Human Development (CHD), which called for an annual collection in all Catholic churches throughout the country to fund community self-help projects and organizations involving the poor. Notice here that the church did not teach others what to do, but it rather tried to empower the poor to change their own situations. Obviously CHD would not be able to accomplish much, but it definitely indicated a different way for the church to deal with social problems.[38]

Third, significant changes at Vatican Council II contributed to the demise of the importance and influence of the social encyclicals in the United States. Vatican II insisted on the primacy of scripture in the life, liturgy, and theology of the church and especially in the discipline of moral theology. The papal social encyclicals, including the two in the early 1960s written by John XXIII (*Mater et Magistra* in 1961 and *Pacem in Terris* in 1963) employed a natural law methodology and gave practically no importance to the scriptures.

More significantly Vatican II changed the understanding of the church. The laity were no longer second-class citizens who participated in the apostolate of the hierarchy by carrying out in their lives the principles and truths that were taught by the pope and bishops. The church is the whole people of God, not just the hierarchy. All the baptized are called to perfection, not just religious and clergy. The laity should not expect that pastors of the church have answers to all the problems facing the world.[39]

Fourth, a new breed of Catholic social activists appeared on the scene in the light of these dramatic changes in both US society and the church. The old breed insisted on long-term education based on Catholic social teaching and the structural change that could come about as a result. The

---

[38] Lawrence J. Engel, "The Influence of Saul Alinsky on the Campaign for Human Development," *Theological Studies* 59 (1998): 636–61.

[39] For a more popular account of Vatican II and its documents, see Timothy O'Connell, ed., *Vatican II and Its Documents: An American Appraisal* (Wilmington, DE: Michael Glazier, 1986); for an in-depth analysis, see the five-volume study—Giuseppe Alberigo and Joseph A. Komonchak, eds., *The History of Vatican II* (Maryknoll, NY: Orbis Books, 1995–2006).

new breed was impatient and appealed to a scriptural approach, insisted on direct action, prophetic witness, and the need for the church to take stands on these controversial issues and become directly involved in social change. Their primary interests were peace, poverty, and race. In this context the labor encyclicals afforded little or no help.[40]

New Situations and a New Approach

All these reasons help explain why the social encyclical tradition, with its approach to industrial relations that had become a quite prominent aspect of Catholic life in the 1950s, did not really survive after the 1960s. However, a somewhat different focus and role for encyclicals and official church documents on the socioeconomic order began to appear after the 1960s and became important in the life of the Catholic Church in the United States. What brought about this development and renewed interest in Catholic social teaching?

First, the issues confronting US society and the world were truly moral issues affecting the lives of all. The problems were not only national but international. Churches as such had to deal with these issues. Recall the heavy church involvement across the board in the United States on the issues of race and peace. The leaders of the Catholic Church could not and should not be silent in such circumstances.

Second, Vatican II, in its Pastoral Constitution on the Church in the Modern World, insisted that the "split between the faith which many profess and their daily lives deserves to be counted among the more serious errors of our age."[41] Justice in the World, the document from the 1971 Synod of Bishops, maintained: "Action on behalf of justice and participation in the transformation of the world fully appear to us as a constitutive dimension of the preaching of the gospel, or, in other words, of the church's mission for the redemption of the human race and its liberation from every oppressive situation."[42] Thus, after Vatican II the social mission of the church was more central and more important than it had been previously.

Third, as a result of Vatican II, national conferences of Catholic bishops came into existence throughout the world. The United States with its

---

[40] George G. Higgins, "Historical Resumé of the Teaching, Policy, and Action of the Church and Social Mission," in *Metropolis: Christian Presence and Responsibility*, ed. Philip D. Morris (Notre Dame, IN: Fides, 1970), 145–50.

[41] *Gaudium et Spes*, no. 43.

[42] *Justitia in Mundo*, introduction.

NCWC had been a pioneer in this matter, but now many held that the national bishops' conferences had a mandate to teach for the church in their local areas.[43] The US bishops after this time took an even more public role in dealing with social issues.

Fourth, the social encyclical tradition itself developed. The post–Vatican II encyclicals tried to incorporate a more scriptural approach to the issues, although with limited success. Above all, the documents moved away from a primary focus on industrial relations, but even *Quadragesimo Anno* in 1931 talked about a broader reconstruction of the social order and the need for social justice. Beginning with *Mater et Magistra* in 1961, with a strong assist from Paul VI's *Populorum Progressio* in 1967, the documents now recognized that the socioeconomic problem is worldwide. The plight of the third and fourth worlds came in for important consideration in these and subsequent documents. Catholic social teaching now dealt with issues of justice, peace, and poverty in a worldwide perspective.

Fifth, the popes tied their post–Vatican II encyclicals to both the earlier social encyclical tradition beginning with *Rerum Novarum* and into the Pastoral Constitution on the Church in the Modern World. The fact that new documents appeared on anniversaries of the original two documents in 1971, 1981, and 1991 made people more conscious of the tradition as a whole. Pope John Paul II has insisted on calling this tradition the social teaching of the church.[44] Thus, from the viewpoint of the papal magisterium, this body of authoritative teaching, including the earlier documents, constitutes the social teaching of the church and has an important role to play in the life of the church.

Sixth, the ecclesiology of Vatican II changed the role that official hierarchical documents played in the life of the church. In the pre–Vatican II era, the encyclicals were the primary source of such teaching. Theologians commented on the teachings, and the laity put the teachings of the encyclicals into practice in their daily lives. The process was from the top down. After Vatican II, Catholic theologians and commentators on the social scene recognized that Catholic social ethics or Catholic social thought was broader than the documents of Catholic social teaching. Activists often initiated new approaches and movements so that Catholic social action came from the bottom up as well as from the top down. The official docu-

---

[43] Thomas J. Reese, ed., *Episcopal Conferences: Historical, Canonical, and Theological Studies* (Washington, DC: Georgetown University Press, 1989).

[44] Pope John Paul II, *Centesimus Annus*, no. 2.

ments, although still important, did not play the same role they had played in the pre–Vatican II church.

What about the reaction of the rest of the church? The reception of papal and authoritative hierarchical teaching in the Roman Catholic Church, especially after the discussion and dissent occasioned by *Humanae Vitae*, the 1968 encyclical condemning artificial contraception for spouses, has not been as automatic and uncritical as in the pre–Vatican II church. Some US Catholics, in theory and practice, have criticized and disagreed with aspects of this teaching. However, the whole church has received these social documents and given them an important role. Courses in Catholic social teaching now exist in Catholic colleges and universities. Collections of and commentaries on these documents have been published. The whole church has received these documents because they appear to address significant problems in an insightful and convincing manner, but theologians and commentators are more critical in analyzing them. This background sets the stage for a study of the reception of Catholic social teaching after the 1960s in this country.

Teaching of the US Bishops

The US bishops' conference played a much greater role in dealing with social issues as a result of the new emphasis on national conferences of bishops. In addition, on the US scene, many Catholic activists had chided the US bishops for dragging their feet and failing to address in a timely manner the issues of race, urban unrest, and the Vietnam War. Recall that other churches had been involved in these issues in a much earlier and stronger fashion. These two factors help explain the greater involvement of the US bishops in the 1966–80 time frame.

The most innovative involvement of the US bishops in this time frame involves the Call to Action Conference in Detroit in 1976. Pope Paul VI's 1971 Apostolic Letter, *Octogesima Adveniens*, titled in English *A Call to Action*, ended with a fresh and insistent call to action for laity to renew the temporal order. The US bishops led by Cardinal John Dearden called for a national Catholic meeting in Detroit in October 1976, during the US bicentennial, to examine how the church should work for liberty and justice for all in our society. The two-year preparatory period included parish discussions throughout the whole country on the theme of the meeting, six hearings throughout the country in which a committee of bishops listened to experts and people who were involved in community work and social action on the local level, and finally written reports from special committees taking into account the above data and dealing with eight specific issues—church, nationhood, family, personhood, neighborhood, humankind, ethnicity and race, and work. Each of these documents ended with recommendations to be voted on at the meeting in Detroit.[45]

The Detroit meeting involved 1,340 voting delegates, more than 100 of whom were bishops, and many observers. Generally speaking the delegates tended to be people involved in social action in the church and thus tended to have a reform agenda. The resolutions and recommendations passed by the group included the call for change in a number of existing Catholic Church teachings and practices. Although the process itself was far from perfect, the enthusiasm of the delegates was perceptible throughout the hall. However, the US bishops, precisely because of the controversial nature of many resolutions calling for change in existing Catholic teaching and practice, ultimately did not accept much of what the conference had asked for. Never again did the bishops of the United States sponsor a meeting in which Catholics voted on particular issues and resolutions.[46] However, in some of their subsequent teaching documents, they did employ broad and extensive dialogue.

After Vatican II the US bishops issued many statements covering a multitude of social issues and raised some controversy.[47] The bishops were criticized by some for making too many statements, for being too specific, and for adopting too many partisan positions.[48] In the 1980s Cardinal Joseph Bernardin popularized the metaphor of the "consistent ethic of life" to justify the bishops' involvement in a wide variety of social issues such as abortion, human rights, international relations, Central America, poverty, and nuclear war and deterrence.[49] An analysis and criticism of the role of the bishops lie beyond the parameters of this study.

In this context one would expect the bishops to deal with the economic issues facing the country and the world. In 1975, at their annual meeting,

---

[45] "The 1976 Detroit Call to Action," http://cta-usa.org.

[46] For an evaluation of the Call to Action Conference ten years later, see the special issue of *Commonweal*, December 26, 1986.

[47] J. Brian Benestad and Francis J. Butler, eds., *Quest for Justice: A Compendium of Statements of the United States Catholic Bishops on the Political and Social Order, 1966–1980* (Washington, DC: United States Catholic Conference, 1981).

[48] J. Brian Benestad, *The Pursuit of a Just Social Order: Policy Statements of the US Catholic Bishops, 1966–1980* (Washington, DC: Ethics and Public Policy Center, 1982).

[49] Joseph Cardinal Bernardin et al., *Consistent Ethic of Life*, ed. Thomas G. Feuchtmann (Kansas City, MO: Sheed and Ward, 1988).

the bishops issued a short statement titled "The Economy: Human Dimensions." This document justified the church's interest in this subject, explained the pertinent Catholic social teaching of the church, discussed the three issues of unemployment, inflation, and the distribution of income and wealth, and concluded with policy directives in these matters.[50] This statement, like many similar statements and documents coming from the bishops' conference, did not attract much attention either within or outside the church.

1986 Pastoral Letter: Economic Justice for All

At their annual meeting in November 1980, the US bishops were discussing a pastoral letter on Marxism. Some bishops then suggested that the bishops should write a similar letter on capitalism. At that meeting, they decided to write two new pastoral letters—the one on capitalism and one on nuclear war and deterrence, which was ultimately given priority. This chapter does not treat the issue of peace. Archbishop Rembert Weakland of Milwaukee became chair of the five-bishop committee with staff members from the US Catholic Conference and others to draft the pastoral on capitalism. Early on, the committee decided against a theoretical discussion of capitalism as being inappropriate. Because *Octogesima Adveniens* called for local churches to analyze their own situation in the light of Catholic social teaching, the committee adopted that approach. The committee followed closely the successful methodology employed by the committee writing the peace pastoral. The committee held meetings with invited theologians, economists, sociologists, congressional staffers, social justice leaders, business leaders, labor leaders, and farmers. In addition, they welcomed correspondence from any and all. Following the example of the peace pastoral, the committee made public all its drafts so as to broaden the discussion and involve as many people as possible. The committee purposely decided not to issue its first draft before the November 1984 presidential election in order to keep the document out of the partisan political debate.[51]

---

[50]　United States Catholic Conference, "The Economy: Human Dimensions," in Benestad and Butler, *Quest for Justice*, 263–69.

[51]　For the development of the pastoral, see Rembert Weakland, "Church Social Teaching and the American Economy," *Origins* 13 (1983): 447–48; "Where Does the Economic Pastoral Stand"? *Origins* 13 (1984): 753–59; "The Economic Pastoral and the Signs of the Times," *Origins* 14 (1984): 394–96; "The Economic Pastoral: Draft Two," *America* 153 (September 21, 1985): 129–32; "How to Read the Economic

The first draft was issued in November 1984, the second in October 1985, the third in June 1986. The bishops approved and issued the final document in November 1986. Some changes occurred in the drafting process, but these changes were more in the nature of adjustments and refinements and did not reach the level of the substantial. The first draft bore the title *Catholic Social Teaching and the US Economy*. The final version uses this as the subtitle after the title: *Economic Justice for All*. Thus, the bishops gave pride of place to Catholic social teaching and relating the principles of this teaching to the US scene.[52]

Economic Justice for All contains five chapters. The first involves reading the signs of the times and a justification for church involvement in questions of the economy. Chapter 2 develops the Christian view of the economy with a biblical section followed by ethical norms and priorities for the economy. Chapter 3 deals with four economic issues—employment, poverty, food and agriculture, and the US economy and developing nations. Chapter 4 calls for "A New American Experiment" involving the cooperation and participation of all, including the government, in national and international cooperation. Chapter 5 emphasizes the Christian commitment to love and to practice justice in the world and also challenges the church, including in its role as an economic actor (e.g., paying a living wage). In brief, the economic pastoral calls for the just participation of all especially the poor and the marginalized in the economy—what an early draft called economic democracy.[53]

Catholic social teaching is the basis for the pastoral letter and thus heavily influences it. Like Catholic social teaching, the pastoral letter addresses two audiences—the people of the church and the broader public debate about what is good for the country. The approach is reforming rather than radical. Catholic social teaching, while often negative about aspects of capitalism, never condemned it as intrinsically evil. Catholic social teaching claims today not to endorse any one economic system but to propose principles to reform existing systems. The pastoral follows such a "pragmatic

---

Pastoral," *Crisis* 4 (1986): 27–34.

    [52] For the three drafts and the final version of the pastoral, see *Origins* 14 (1984): 337ff.; 15 (1985): 257ff.; 16 (1986): 33ff.; 16 (1986): 410ff.

    [53] *Economic Justice for All* has been published in many places including *Origins* 16 (1986): 410ff.; O'Brien and Shannon, *Catholic Social Thought*, 572–680, and a 1986 publication of the National Conference of Catholic Bishops. Subsequent references in the text will give the paragraph number of the pastoral letter.

and evolutionary" approach that it claims that it is also in keeping with the "American pragmatic tradition of reform" (no. 131).

The pastoral, however, departs from Catholic social teaching in two areas. The drafting committee recognized the need to incorporate a more scriptural approach than that found in the earlier documents of Catholic social teaching with their natural law basis.[54] The document is not entirely successful in integrating scripture into the whole approach, but Catholic ethicists themselves have also been unsuccessful in integrating scripture into Catholic social ethics. In addition, the fact that the bishops also tried to address the broader pluralistic US public means that the document by definition cannot integrate scripture into its whole approach. Second, in keeping with the earlier peace pastoral, the economic pastoral goes beyond the principles found in Catholic social teaching and makes prudential judgments about what should be done. Such judgments in the letter do not carry the same teaching authority as the "statements of universal moral principles and formal church teaching" and are open to debate (no. 135).

According to the pastoral, "The fundamental moral criterion for all economic decisions . . . is this: They must be at the service of *all people, especially the poor*" (no. 24). "Human dignity, realized in community with others and with the whole of God's creation, is the norm against which every social institution must be measured" (no. 25). Such a criterion relies on the universal destiny of the goods of creation to serve the needs of all and the preferential option for the poor. All human beings have a right to a minimally decent human existence.

The pastoral letter develops an anthropology that emphasizes both the dignity of the individual person and the social nature of the person, since we are called by our very being to live together in various communities, such as the family and the political order. (Note these are communities in an analogous sense because the family is quite different from the political order.)[55]

In such an understanding, both society and government are something natural, necessary, and good; but government is also limited. Chapters 1 and 3 also discuss this important foundation of Catholic social teaching. The Catholic approach thus sees itself in opposition to the two extremes of collectivism and individualism. Collectivism so emphasizes the collectivity that it fails to recognize the dignity of the individual person, whereas

---

[54] Weakland, "How to Read the Economic Pastoral," 27–29.

[55] The synthesis proposed in this and the following paragraphs comes from "Chapter 2: The Christian Vision of Economic Life," nos. 28–126.

individualism so emphasizes the individual that it fails to give enough importance to the community.

Based on love, solidarity, and our common humanity, we are called to live in a political community that strives for the common good of the community itself. The common good, by definition, also redounds to the good of the individual person. Thus, clean air is good for the community and good for individual persons. So too not only individual poor people but society as a whole and all other people in society are better off if we can eliminate poverty. Individualism sees only individual goods; collectivism only collective goods; but the common good avoids these two extremes.

Government, however, is also limited. Government is only one part of the political society that includes individual persons, basic natural societies like the family and even the neighborhood, a whole host of voluntary societies such as corporations, nonprofit groups, professional organizations of every type, churches, and finally the government on the local, state, and federal levels. The principle of subsidiarity calls for the higher level to encourage and help the lower level to do everything possible, and the higher level intervenes only to do what the lower level cannot accomplish. Look at housing in the United States. People are encouraged to own their own homes. Habitat for Humanity builds houses for some people. The government intervenes in a number of ways such as the tax break on mortgages that helps families own their own homes, but at times the local government must also intervene and build public housing for others.

Thus the government has a limited but important role to play with regard to making sure the economy exists for the common good that includes the basic good of all individuals. In chapter 4 of the pastoral the bishops propose a "new American experiment" that would feature a partnership of all, including the government, to work for the common good and the need for some planning in order to bring this about.

The common good involves the participation of all in the life of the community, including its economic life as well as justice and human rights for all. Justice in the Catholic tradition involves three types of justice—commutative, distributive, and legal or contributive—corresponding to three different relationships—individuals to individuals, society to individuals, individuals to society (nos. 68–76). Distributive justice deals with how society distributes its goods and burdens to individuals. Individualism claims that we are free to acquire as many material goods for ourselves as we can, provided that all start in a fair position. Distributive justice, according to the pastoral, maintains that society must make sure that all its members have a sufficiency of material goods to live a minimally decent human existence. A basic minimal wage, for example, is not necessarily what employer and employee agree upon but what gives the worker enough to live a minimally decent life. In distributing burdens, those who have more have an obligation to give more to the community, thus the pastoral calls for progressive taxation (no. 202). Legal or contributive justice (this name adds something to the Catholic social teaching approach) involves the obligation of the individual to society, especially in terms of the obligation of the individual to contribute to society and society's need to facilitate that participation. The pastoral remains true to its anthropological foundations in calling not only for civil and political rights, such as freedom of religion, speech, and the press, but also social and economic rights, such as the right to life, food, clothing, shelter, medical care, and basic education (nos. 79–84).

Individualism is very strong in the United States. The pastoral goes against this individualism in its insistence on a more communitarian understanding of human existence, the option for the poor ("the poor have the single most urgent economic claim on the conscience of the nation" [no. 86]), the important but limited role of government in the economy, distributive and contributive justice, and economic rights.

The pastoral wisely recognizes that Catholic social teaching also challenges the church in its educational mission and above all in its life as an economic actor with many different employees. The church should be exemplary in living up to its own principles (nos. 339–58).

Although this essay will not undertake an elaboration of the four specific issues considered in depth in the pastoral letter, a brief overview of the approach to poverty will serve as an illustration of how the other issues are handled (nos. 170–215). At the time of writing, the official governmental definition recognized that one out of every seven Americans is in poverty. In addition, there is great economic inequality and uneven distribution of wealth and income with 28 percent of the total net wealth held by the richest 2 percent of families. Poverty especially affects children, women, and racial minorities. Unfortunately, there are too many misunderstandings and stereotypes of the poor; for example, others in our society receive much greater government subsidies than the poor. The bishops propose the following elements of a national strategy for dealing with poverty: A healthy economy is the best way to prevent poverty; discriminating barriers against women and minorities should be removed; self-help programs for the poor should be supported by both the private and the public sector; the tax system should be reformed in terms of more progressive taxation;

education for the poor must be strengthened; all programs for the poor should support and strengthen the family. A thorough reform of the nation's welfare system and income support program is necessary to ensure adequate levels of support for the poor with a goal of making the poor self-sufficient through gainful employment when possible.

Reaction to the Pastoral

Criticism of the pastoral came from both the left and the right. Gregory Baum, the eminent Canadian theologian and sociologist, lamented that the US bishops were much less radical than the Canadian bishops.[56] Liberation theologians who call into question the capitalist system disagreed with the pastoral. Rembert Weakland, with an obvious twinkle in his eye, puts Cardinal Joseph Ratzinger in the same category as the liberationists because he has a "deep distrust of the capitalist system, especially as manifested in the United States."[57]

Within US Catholicism, the strongest negative reaction from the right came from Catholic neoconservatives such as Michael Novak, George Weigel, and later Richard John Neuhaus (a Lutheran who became a Roman Catholic). The Catholic neoconservative movement began in the 1970s but became stronger and more forceful in the next decade. Catholic neoconservatives describe themselves in terms of their understanding of the church, of the United States system and its role in the world, and of their intellectual predecessors.[58]

With regard to the church, Catholic neoconservatives disagree with the liberal understanding of the church as found in the work of many theologians and even church institutions in the United States with their complaint

---

[56] Gregory Baum, "A Canadian Perspective on the US Pastoral," *Christianity and Crisis* 45 (1985): 516–18.

[57] Rembert G. Weakland, "The Economic Pastoral Letter Revisited," in *One Hundred Years of Catholic Social Thought: Celebration and Challenge*, ed. John A. Coleman (Maryknoll, NY: Orbis Books, 1991), 203.

[58] The following description of Catholic neoconservatives is based on their own self-understanding. See especially Michael Novak, "Neoconservatives," in *New Dictionary of Catholic Social Thought*, ed. Judith A. Dwyer (Collegeville, MN: Liturgical Press, 1994), 678–82; George Weigel, "The Neoconservative Difference: A Proposal for the Renewal of Church and Society," in *Being Right: Conservative Catholics in America*, ed. Mary Jo Weaver and R. Scott Appleby (Bloomington: Indiana University Press, 1995), 138–62.

that the primary problem in the church is a crisis of authority and a recognition of the need for dissent within the church. For the neoconservatives the problem is a crisis of faith. They believe that the liberals claiming to carry on the spirit of Vatican II have gone too far. The neoconservatives strongly supported the pontificate of Pope John Paul II. They claim that even many departments and offices of the US bishops' conference and many bishops themselves have accepted the liberal approach. In the 1980s especially, the neoconservatives emphasized a significant difference between the US bishops and Pope John Paul II. In this light, they strongly criticized both pastoral letters and the positions taken by the US bishops on Central America.[59] Neoconservatives emphasize the need for a new ecumenism embracing a dialogue with the conservative, evangelical, and fundamentalist Protestant churches rather than with the mainline Protestant churches.

Although not completely uncritical, Catholic neoconservatives are supportive of the US political and economic systems. They believe that the Catholic liberal establishment has been too critical of the United States and naïve in its appreciation of movements such as liberation theology, which they associate with Marxism. Catholic neoconservatives emphasize the interconnectedness and necessary linking together of the cultural, political, and economic orders such that they believe that democratic capitalism offers the best hope for overcoming poverty in the world.

From an intellectual perspective, Catholic neoconservatives appeal to the legacy of John Courtney Murray and Jacques Maritain, who strongly defended democracy and the American experiment as well as the realism of Reinhold Niebuhr, who opposed what they see as the progressive illusions of Protestant liberalism. The neoconservatives with their insistence on the intimate connection between the political and economic orders want the US Catholic Church to recognize the benefits of capitalism just as the Catholic Church recognized the value of democracy and religious freedom. They base this in great measure on the work of John Courtney Murray.

Michael Novak, a prolific author, has been the strongest voice for Catholic neoconservatism in the economic realm, beginning with his monograph *The Spirit of Democratic Catholicism* (1982).[60] Novak defends capitalism on theological, philosophical, and economic grounds as the best political economic system for the world today. He criticizes much of the earlier Catholic social

---

[59] George Weigel, "When Shepherds Are Sheep," *First Things* 30 (1993): 34–40.

[60] Michael Novak, *The Spirit of Democratic Capitalism* (New York: Simon and Schuster, 1982).

teaching for emphasizing distribution rather than creativity and the production of wealth. He believes, however, that John Paul II, has corrected this emphasis by insisting on the need for co-creation and entrepreneurship.[61]

Novak was the driving force behind, and primary writer of, *Toward the Future*, an analysis of Catholic social teaching and the US economy, published by a lay group just before the first draft of the bishops' pastoral and proposed as an alternative approach from the one expected from the bishops.[62] Novak also responded to the drafts of the pastoral letter. His criticism of earlier drafts still holds for the final document that did not change substantially from the first draft. He believes that the pastoral letter puts too much emphasis on distribution and not enough on the creation of wealth and that the bishops say too little about the causes of wealth. Novak thought that the pastoral does not give enough importance to individual responsibility at all levels in the economy including the poor. He believed that the letter was too accusatory about the causes of poverty; he thought that the letter implied that wealth rather than poverty was the natural condition of human beings before the advent of capitalism. He believed that the bishops failed to give enough importance to sin and consequently fell into what he calls a soft utopianism. In addition, he felt that they endorsed too many specific proposals.[63]

Novak strongly objected to the concept of economic rights in the first draft because he considered it to undermine the American idea of the limited state. Instead, Novak insisted that the American concept of "equal opportunity for all" is just as effective in actually helping the poor.[64] Later he recognized that John Paul II does have a concept of economic rights, but Novak gave a rather minimal interpretation to such rights.[65] The majority of

---

[61] Michael Novak, "Creation Theology," in *Co-Creation and Capitalism: John Paul II's Laborem Exercens*, ed. John W. Houck and Oliver F. Williams (Washington, DC: University Press of America, 1983), 17–41.

[62] Lay Commission on Catholic Social Teaching and the US Economy, *Toward the Future: Catholic Social Thought and the US Economy* (New York: Lay Commission on Catholic Social Teaching and the US Economy, 1984).

[63] Michael Novak, "Four Views of the Bishops' Pastoral: The Lay Letter and the US Economy: A Panel Discussion," *This World* 10 (Winter 1985): 112–16; "Toward Consensus: Suggestions for Revising the First Draft, Part I," *Catholicism in Crisis* 3 (March 1985): 7–16.

[64] Michael Novak, "Economic Rights: The Servile State," *Catholicism in Crisis* 3 (October 1985): 8–15.

[65] Michael Novak, "The Rights and Wrongs of 'Economic Rights': A Debate Continued," *This World* 17 (Spring 1987): 43–52.

Catholic social ethicists in the United States, however, reject the neoconservative approach.

My own criticisms of the pastoral letter stem primarily from its total acceptance of Catholic social teaching and the failure to add to that tradition from the broader Catholic social ethics tradition and the US Catholic experience. The letter does not deal with some more theoretical but very significant concepts in the US economy, such as the profit motive, the role of markets, and the possible dehumanizing aspects of technology. Catholic social teaching fails to address these issues.

Like Catholic social teaching, the pastoral emphasizes the need for just structures, but it fails to give enough importance to the need for a change of heart and the social justice mission of the baptized in their daily lives. More needs to be said about the spirituality of those working for social change. The virtues and attitudes of the just person receive no in-depth development.

The pastoral letter belongs to the genre of teaching that obviously appeals to the reason and good will of others. Such an approach appeals to the elite and the leaders to put into practice the principles proposed in the teaching. The letter pays little or no attention to the role of power. Power can never be absolutized, but power is an important aspect in changing social structures. In addition, power recognizes that change comes from below as well as from the top down. Here too the US Catholic experience has something to contribute based on its own experience with community organizing and the Campaign for Human Development. Community organizations attempt to bring poor, disaffected, and marginalized people together to work for the betterment of their own neighborhood in terms of schools, public services, job creation, and safety. Here the approach is from the bottom up and often employs some conflictual tactics.[66] In practice the US Catholic Church has recognized a role of power in bringing about structural change but not in the theoretical exposition of the pastoral.

The narrow focus of the letter, in keeping with Catholic social teaching, fails to appreciate the role of what I call prophetic shock minority groups in the church.[67] These groups propose a more radical witness by focusing on one important aspect in human existence. In this case, groups like the Catholic Worker, with a significant influence beyond their small numbers, have contrib-

---

[66] Engel, "Influence of Saul Alinsky on the Campaign for Human Development."

[67] Jacques Maritain used the term "prophetic shock minorities" to refer to those groups which provide and provoke the leaven or energy that political democracy needs. See Jacques Maritain, *Man and the State* (Chicago: University of Chicago Press, 1956), 139–46.

uted much to the life of the Catholic Church by their witness to voluntary poverty. These prophetic shock minorities, by bearing witness to one virtue such as peace or poverty, play a role analogous to religious life in the church. Such an approach reminds the whole church of the danger of materialism and of economic power. Thus, the pastoral letter would have been improved if it had attempted to add to Catholic social teaching from the broader Catholic social ethics tradition and the social experience of the US church.

Effect and Influence of the Pastoral

The pastoral letters of the US bishops in the 1980s on nuclear war and deterrence and the economy had a greater effect on the American public in general and the Catholic Church in the United States than any other documents coming from the US bishops. The primary reason comes from the unique and public way in which these letters were written and discussed. Past episcopal documents were often drafted by one person and after a somewhat pro forma discussion were voted on and accepted by the bishops as a whole. In the case of the two pastorals in the 1980s, the committees held public hearings involving many experts both Catholic and non-Catholic. Also, the drafts were not only discussed by the committee and the bishops but were made public and discussed at large. Such an approach truly involved many more people inside and outside the church in the discussion.

Other factors also contributed to the importance given to these pastoral letters. The quality of the letters gave them credibility in the eyes of many. Although critical of some US positions, they gave a coherent and rational explanation for their criticisms and their proposed solutions. The timing was also good. These two significant issues were high on the agenda and radar screen of the country as a whole. The US Catholic bishops also were taking on a role that mainstream Protestants had played in earlier US society and culture. The social gospel in the early twentieth century and the later Niebuhrian realism had a great influence on US culture and public policy. White Anglo-Saxon Protestant (WASP) culture played an important role in US life, but the WASP influence and the role of mainstream Protestantism were in decline by the 1980s.[68] The economic pastoral thus made people outside and inside the Catholic Church more aware of Catholic social teaching and its application in US life. The broader public debate had a very short life-span, however, since that is the nature of news.

----

[68] William Lee Miller, *The First Liberty: Religion and the American Republic* (New York: Knopf, 1986), 288–89.

The pastoral letter and Catholic social teaching, as well as Catholic social ethics in the United States, have had little effect on philosophical ethics and political science in this country. A number of factors help to explain the lack of the influence of Catholic thought on social and political philosophy and political science. First, the academy in the United States tends to exist behind the walls of academic disciplines. University life has become increasingly driven by individual disciplines and departments. Despite much talk about interdisciplinary approaches, the great complexity of each discipline forces one deeper within the confines of that particular discipline. The academic reward system in the university world tends to emphasize one's standing in the discipline. In many colleges and especially universities today the commitment of the academician to one's discipline is stronger than the commitment to one's institution. Political philosophy and political science, like all academic disciplines, often exist in their own intellectual cocoon. Without doubt, a secularistic antipathy to religion also contributes something to the isolation of the Catholic social tradition from contemporary philosophical social ethics and political science.

However, other problems exist from the viewpoint of the Catholic tradition itself. Many Catholic ethicists (myself included) write primarily for a Catholic audience that at times might expand to a Christian ecumenical or religious interfaith milieu. Many people in the United States see the role of the Catholic Church as a political actor trying to have its positions enshrined in law and public policy and not primarily as an intellectual interlocutor engaged in public dialogue about what is best for the country. Thus, before and even after the pastoral letter on the economy, the Catholic social tradition has had little or no influence on political philosophy and political science.

Christian and religious ethics ever since Vatican II have been more attentive to Catholic social teaching, and the bishops' pastoral letter engaged many other Christian and religious ethicists in their discussion about public policy in the United States.[69] As is to be expected, the greatest influence of the economic pastoral and its application of Catholic social teaching

---

[69] E.g., Charles R. Strain, ed., *Prophetic Visions and Economic Realities: Protestants, Jews, & Catholics Confront the Bishops' Letter on the Economy* (Grand Rapids, MI: William B. Eerdmans, 1989); David Hollenbach, "Liberation, Communitarianism, and the Bishops' Pastoral Letter on the Economy," and Gregory Baum, Ruth Smith, and Robert Benne, "Replies to David Hollenbach," *Annual of the Society of Christian Ethics* (1987): 19–54; Charles P. Lutz, ed., *God, Goods, and the Common Good: Eleven Perspectives on Economic Justice in Dialog with the Roman Catholic Bishops' Pastoral Letter* (Minneapolis: Augsburg, 1987).

was on Catholic scholars. Many Catholic academic institutions, such as Georgetown University, the University of Notre Dame, DePaul University, Catholic Theological Union, and the Woodstock Center at Georgetown University, published books based on symposia held at their institutions.[70] The pastoral on the economy definitely stimulated Catholic theologians and scholars to pay more attention to Catholic social thought in general and Catholic social teaching in particular. The bishops here provided excellent leadership for Catholic theologians and scholars in recognizing the important role of Catholic social teaching.

Since the economic pastoral in 1986, the US bishops have very occasionally issued documents on the economy, but they were in the older format of statements drafted in private and approved at the national meeting of the bishops without much dialogue or discussion. For example, at the 1995 meeting the bishops issued a four-page document marking the tenth anniversary of the economic pastoral with a threefold perspective of looking back, looking around, and looking ahead.[71] A year later at their annual meeting they adopted a very short ten-point "Catholic Framework for Economic Life."[72] These two documents obviously presented Catholic social teaching, but their import was nil as far as both the church and the wider US society are concerned.

Nothing the bishops have done since 1986 has come close to the impact made by their pastoral letters on peace and the economy. What happened to explain this? First, the issue of the economy is not the only social issue facing US society, so one should not expect the bishops to address these issues that often. But deeper problems exist. The US bishops, after 1986, never again

---

[70] R. Bruce Douglass, ed., *The Deeper Meaning of Economic Life: Critical Essays on the US Catholic Bishops' Pastoral Letter on the Economy* (Washington, DC: Georgetown University Press, 1986); John W. Houck and Oliver Williams, eds., *Catholic Social Teaching and the United States Economy: Working Papers for a Bishops' Pastoral* (Washington, DC: University Press of America, 1984); Strain, *Prophetic Visions*; John Pawlikowski and Donald Senior, eds., *Economic Justice: CTU's Pastoral Commentary on the Bishops' Letter on the Economy* (Washington, DC: Pastoral Press, 1988); Thomas M. Gannon, ed., *The Catholic Challenge to the American Economy: Reflections on the US Bishops' Pastoral Letter on Catholic Social Teaching and the US Economy* (New York: Macmillan, 1987).

[71] National Conference of Catholic Bishops, "A Decade after 'Economic Justice for All': Continuing Principles, Changing Context, New Challenges," *Origins* 25 (1995): 389–93.

[72] National Conference of Catholic Bishops, "Catholic Framework for Economic Life," *Origins* 26 (1996): 370–71.

issued a pastoral letter based on the methodology of broad hearings and public drafts. Why did the process not continue?

The bishops attempted to write another pastoral letter following the same format and methodology with regard to the role of women in the church—an obviously controversial issue in the Roman Catholic Church. The committee proposed four drafts, but opposition came from all sides, especially women on the one side and the Vatican on the other. In the end, the bishops scrapped the whole idea of such a pastoral letter. Thus, the last attempt to follow the newer format was an abysmal failure.[73]

Other ecclesial factors have also contributed to a lesser role played by the United States Catholic Bishops' Conference. The Vatican has publicly downplayed the official role of national conferences of bishops as having an official teaching office in the church. There is no doubt that the Vatican has tried to curtail the role that bishops' conferences have played, not only in the United States but also throughout the world.[74] Some maintain that a broad consultation detracts from the teaching authority of bishops. More conservative bishops have been appointed in the last two decades who were more willing to go along with such a policy. In addition, the cardinals in the United States as a body have exercised a much greater public role and thus overshadowed the role of the national conference of bishops. Thus, it is not a surprise that the US bishops in the 1990s issued no pastoral letters following the format of the peace and economic pastorals in the 1980s. Unfortunately, the bishops abandoned what had been their most effective teaching tool.

Theologians

As mentioned, Vatican II introduced significant changes that greatly altered the life of the Catholic Church in general and the approach of Catholic social teaching in particular. These same changes significantly affected Catholic moral theology and Catholic social ethics. Social ethics is a part of moral theology that also includes personal morality, sexuality and marriage, and medical ethics or bioethics. Vatican II called for newer approaches in moral theology with emphasis on a greater role for scripture, the universal call to holiness, a more significant attention to the signs of the times with a corresponding need for a more inductive methodology, and a

---

[73] Marvin L. Krier Mich, *Catholic Social Teaching and Movements* (Mystic, CT: Twenty-Third Publications, 1998), 357–70.

[74] John Paul II, "Motu Proprio: The Theological and Juridical Nature of Episcopal Conferences," *Origins* 28 (1998): 152–58.

recognition of a greater philosophical pluralism with regard to the dialogue partner for theology. As a result, those in the United States who had been leaders in moral theology before Vatican II, both because of age and of these significant changes, no longer played an important leadership role in moral theology. Newer and younger moral theologians had to come along to fill the vacuum. In the immediate post–Vatican II period in the United States (and in the whole Catholic world) the primary moral issue concerned the official Catholic teaching on contraception and other issues of sexuality and marriage. Medical ethics, or bioethics as it was later called, also shared the spotlight. Thus, it took some time for a new generation of Catholic social ethicists and moral theologians in the United States to come to the fore and to begin publishing on matters of social and economic ethics.[75]

It was not until the late 1970s and very early '80s that the first scholarly monographs on Catholic social ethics appeared with the work of David Hollenbach[76] and John Coleman,[77] and in my work.[78] The late '70s also saw an increase in the number of articles dealing with issues concerned with Catholic social teaching. J. Bryan Hehir, as a staff person for the bishops' conference from 1973 to 1992, strongly influenced the social documents and positions taken by the US bishops, and he also contributed many articles and speeches dealing with Catholic social teaching and the broader area of Catholic social ethics.[79] Two centers also contributed to a renewal of Catholic social ethics in general and its relationship to Catholic social teaching—the Woodstock Theological Center started by the Society of Jesus at Georgetown University in 1974[80] and the Notre Dame Center for Ethics and Religious Values in Business founded in 1978.[81] Thus, before the

---

[75] Charles E. Curran, *Moral Theology at the End of the Century*, the Père Marquette Lecture in Theology 1999 (Milwaukee: Marquette University Press, 1999).

[76] David Hollenbach, *Claims in Conflict: Retrieving and Renewing the Catholic Human Rights Tradition* (New York: Paulist Press, 1979).

[77] John A. Coleman, *An American Strategic Theology* (New York: Paulist Press, 1982).

[78] Curran, *American Catholic Social Ethics*.

[79] For Hehir's analysis of the US bishops' social mission, see J. Bryan Hehir, "The Church and the Political Order: The Role of the Catholic Bishops in the United States," in *The Church's Public Role: Retrospect and Prospect*, ed. Dieter T. Hessel (Grand Rapids, MI: William B. Eerdmans, 1993), 176–97.

[80] Available on the Internet at www.georgetown.edu. An early publication of this Center was John C. Haughey, ed., *The Faith That Does Justice: Examining the Christian Sources for Social Change* (New York: Paulist Press, 1977).

[81] Available on the Internet at www.nd.edu. This center has published many

first draft of the economic pastoral, Catholic social ethics was coming to life again, but there can be no doubt that the writing of the economic pastoral contributed greatly to the growth of Catholic social ethics dealing with political and economic issues.

Within the parameters of this essay, one cannot pretend to give a history of Catholic social ethics in the latter part of the twentieth century in the United States or to cover all the people who have contributed to this endeavor. My focus in this short section is how Catholic social ethics has dealt with Catholic social teaching. As has already been pointed out with regard to the neoconservative approach, there are a number of different approaches within Catholic social ethics so that one cannot speak of a monolithic discipline. The contributors to *Modern Catholic Social Teaching: Commentaries and Interpretations* [in which this essay was first published] propose a critical correlation between the gospel and the US ethos involving four different perspectives on Catholic social teaching: a historical critical hermeneutic in discussing Catholic social teaching with a corresponding recognition of great historical development within the body of Catholic social teaching; the realization that Catholic social ethics in the United States involves much more than Catholic social teaching; some criticisms of Catholic social teaching; and the critique of Catholic neoconservatives by the majority of other social ethicists.[82]

First, as mentioned previously, John Cronin, in 1971, perceptively pointed out how he and his earlier colleagues failed to use a critical historical hermeneutic in discussing papal documents.[83] Subsequent Catholic ethicists such as John Coleman have brought such an approach to their understanding of Catholic social teaching. The teaching was very much colored by the European perspective of the papal author as well as the tendency toward triumphalism in the Catholic Church at the time.[84]

Catholic social teaching claimed to be a body of eternal and unchangeable moral principles and truths. In fact, it is a myth to portray the teaching as an unchanging body of truths. Tremendous development has occurred since the time of Pope Leo XIII. Leo had a very paternalistic and even authoritarian

---

symposia dealing with Catholic social ethics edited by John W. Houck and Oliver F. Williams.

[82] Kenneth R. Himes, ed., *Modern Catholic Social Teaching: Commentaries and Interpretations* (Washington, DC: Georgetown University Press, 2004).

[83] Cronin, "Forty Years Later," 73.

[84] John A. Coleman, "Development of Church Social Teaching," *Origins* 11 (1981): 33ff.

notion of society. All recognize the growing importance that Catholic social teaching gave to freedom, equality, and participation in the light of its twentieth-century opposition to communism. The attitude toward socialism and Marxism developed over time with John XXIII fostering an opening to the left with his distinction between false philosophical teachings and historical movements that were originally based on these teachings. This opened the door to the possibility of dialogue with communist countries that differed strongly from the previous anathema of socialism and communism. Many critics have pointed out that Leo XIII's understanding of private property was not a faithful exposition of the teaching of Thomas Aquinas, because it tended to absolutize the individual aspect of private property. However, subsequent popes, without acknowledging error in the previous position of Leo XIII, proposed a more nuanced understanding of private property by insisting on the social as well as the individual aspects of property. Vatican II, as related before, greatly affected the methodological approach to Catholic theology in general and to Catholic social ethics by calling for a greater role for scripture, a close connection between faith or theology and daily life, and a more inductive methodology emphasizing the signs of the times. Later documents of Catholic social teaching have moved in this direction, but commentators have also pointed out how John Paul II moved back from the greater historical-mindedness found in the documents of Paul VI.[85]

Second, Catholic social ethics in the United States no longer sees itself as simply the exegesis and application of Catholic social teaching to the US Catholic scene. Catholic social ethics in the United States is much broader and more inclusive than just considerations of Catholic social teaching. A good number of social ethicists in this country developed their own understandings and approach without being totally dependent on Catholic social teaching. Likewise, on a more practical grassroots level, as Marvin L. Krier Mich has pointed out, many practical movements of different stripes have come into existence in the United States in an attempt to deal with social issues.[86]

The US scene is going to raise issues and require responses that are pertinent to its own historical and social circumstances. What is the proper way for the church to address public issues in the United States in the light of the First Amendment and the US ethos? Theologians have analyzed and critiqued the approach taken by the United States Catholic bishops especially in their period of great activity in the 1980s. One controversy concerns

---

[85]   Charles E. Curran, *Directions in Catholic Social Ethics* (Notre Dame, IN: University of Notre Dame Press, 1985), 5–69.

[86]   Mich, *Catholic Social Teaching.*

the way in which the Catholic Church should address the broader society. Should the church speak a language accessible to all other citizens, as the older natural approach had done, or is a biblical narrative and foundation necessary to sustain a lasting commitment in this area? Most contemporary Catholic social ethicists also disagree with the neoconservative claim that John Courtney Murray's thought is the basis for their neoconservative position.[87] Catholic scholars are in dialogue with philosophers and political scientists about the proper role of religion and the church in public political life.[88] Catholic social ethicists in the United States thus generally recognize that Catholic social teaching involves only one part of the whole of Catholic social ethics in the United States today.

Third, Catholic theologians since Vatican II, despite opposition from the Vatican authorities, have understood their own theological role in terms of analyzing and criticizing papal documents. This also holds for the documents of Catholic social teaching. Catholic feminists have criticized Catholic social teaching from a feminist liberation perspective beginning with the published doctoral dissertation of Christine Gudorf in 1980.[89] Amata Miller,[90] Mary Hobgood,[91] and others have also criticized Catholic social teaching from a feminist perspective, although, of course, feminists do not all take the same approach. Christine Firer Hinze has moved beyond the feminist hermeneutic of suspicion to a hermeneutic of recovery by trying to bring together a feminist approach and the traditional support of Catholic social teaching for a living wage.[92] Many other criticisms have also been developed both from the left and the right.

---

[87] Charles E. Curran and Leslie Griffin, eds., *The Catholic Church, Morality, and Politics: Readings in Moral Theology No. 12* (New York: Paulist Press, 2001).

[88] David Hollenbach, *The Common Good and Christian Ethics* (Cambridge: Cambridge University Press, 2002); Michael J. Perry, *The Idea of Human Rights: Four Inquiries* (New York: Oxford University Press, 2000); Paul Weithman, *Religion and the Obligations of Citizenship* (Cambridge: Cambridge University Press, 2002).

[89] Christine E. Gudorf, *Catholic Social Teaching on Liberation Themes* (Lanham, MD: University Press of America, 1980).

[90] Amata Miller, "Catholic Social Teaching: What Might Have Been If Women Were Not Invisible in a Patriarchal Society," in *Rerum Novarum: One Hundred Years of Catholic Social Teaching*, ed. John Coleman and Gregory Baum (London: SCM, 1991), 21–47.

[91] Mary E. Hobgood, *Catholic Social Teaching and Economic Theory: Paradigms in Conflict* (Philadelphia: Temple University Press, 1991).

[92] Christine Firer Hinze, "Bridge Discourse on Wage Justice: Roman Catholic and Feminist Perspectives on the Family Living Wage," *Annual of the Society of Christian Ethics* 11 (1991): 109–32.

Fourth, many Catholic social ethicists have disagreed with the Catholic neoconservative position already mentioned. Yes, Catholic social teaching recognizes "the fundamental and positive role of business, the market, . . . and human creativity in the economic sector," but in the same encyclical John Paul II calls for economic freedom to be circumscribed within a strong juridical framework pointed toward the common good.[93] Many commentators point to these and other statements of the pope to disprove the neoconservative position of Michael Novak with regard to the pope and capitalism.[94] Daniel Finn has criticized Catholic social teaching for basing the social dimension of property and material goods on the intention of the Creator in making all things. Finn, like the neoconservatives, insists that human creativity has brought about the great increase of material goods in our world, but he strongly argues for the social aspect of material goods produced by such human creativity.[95] Todd Whitmore has maintained that Michael Novak's position differs substantially from that of John Paul II and that Novak actually dissents from the papal teaching especially on such questions as economic rights.[96]

Catholic neoconservatives are not the only ones who have strongly disagreed with the approach taken by the US bishops. A small group of younger scholars has called for the church to be more countercultural.[97]

Thus, Catholic social ethics in the last few decades continues to recognize an important role for Catholic social teaching, but the role of Catholic social ethicists is not simply to repeat and apply that teaching but also to analyze and criticize it in the light of a broader Catholic social ethics.

---

[93] *Centesimus Annus*, no. 42.

[94] E.g., David Hollenbach, "The Pope and Capitalism," *America* 164 (June 1, 1991): 591; Msgr. George Higgins, *Subsidiarity in the Catholic Social Tradition: Yesterday, Today, and Tomorrow*, Albert Cardinal Meyer Lecture (Mundelein, IL: Mundelein Seminary, 1994), 29–39.

[95] Daniel R. Finn, "Creativity as a Problem for Moral Theology: John Locke's 99 Percent Challenge to the Catholic Doctrine of Property," *Horizons* 27 (2000): 44–62.

[96] Todd David Whitmore, "John Paul II, Michael Novak, and the Differences between Them," *Annual of the Society of Christian Ethics* 21 (2001): 215–32.

[97] Michael L. Budde and Robert W. Brimlow, eds., *The Church as Counterculture* (Albany: State University of New York Press, 2000); Michael J. Baxter, "Notes on Catholic Americanism and Catholic Radicalism: Toward a Counter-Tradition of Catholic Social Ethics," in *American Catholic Traditions: Resources for Renewal*, ed. Sandra Yocum Mize and William Portier, College Theology Society Annual Volume 42 (Maryknoll, NY: Orbis Books, 1997), 53–71.

The Practical Influence of Catholic Social Teaching in the Life of the Church

To adequately assess the practical influence of Catholic social teaching in the life of the church would require a broad and deep sociological analysis of what is actually taking place in Catholic parishes and institutions in the United States. Such an analysis is impossible here. Also, such an analysis at this time after Vatican II is more difficult than it was in the pre–Vatican II period with its understanding of Catholic social action as the participation of the laity in the apostolate of the hierarchy. After Vatican II the social mission of the church involves all members of the church working for social justice in their own circumstances and places. Often the initiative comes from below. Perhaps the most significant development in the social mission of the US Catholic Church, as mentioned earlier, has been the support of community organizations and the work of the Campaign for Human Development.

The postconciliar church has recognized that working for justice is a constitutive dimension of the gospel and the mission of the church. Liturgy and preaching should have a strong justice dimension.[98] Justice and peace commissions, human development committees, and similar groups exist in most dioceses and in many parishes. The economic pastoral did more to make Catholic social teaching better known in the church than any other teaching effort by the US bishops. Schools on all levels of Catholic education and also religious education show a concern for social justice. In all these efforts, Catholic social teaching obviously plays a part but only a part in the guidance of such activity. However, one still very often hears the lament that Catholics in the pew on Sunday seldom hear anything about Catholic social teaching.[99]

Catholic social teaching itself has evolved and changed since 1891. This chapter has tried to show the various ways in which this evolving Catholic social teaching has been received and interpreted in the United States in the twentieth century.

---

[98] Anne Y. Koester, ed., *Liturgy and Justice: To Worship God in Spirit and Truth* (Collegeville, MN: Liturgical Press, 2002); Walter J. Burghardt, *Preaching the Just Word* (New Haven, CT: Yale University Press, 1996).

[99] Peter Henriot, Edward De Berri, and Michael Schulteis, *Catholic Social Teaching: Our Best Kept Secret*, centenary ed. (Maryknoll, NY: Orbis Books, 1992).

Chapter 3

George G. Higgins*

Catholic Social Teaching and
Social Action in the United States

The framework for understanding George G. Higgins's contributions to Catholic social teaching and action comes from the role he played and his own personal characteristics.

George Gilmary Higgins (1916–2002), a priest of the archdiocese of Chicago, ordained in 1940, joined the Social Action Department of the National Catholic Welfare Conference in 1944 and became its director in 1954.[1] The National Catholic Welfare Conference came into existence in 1919 with various departments, including the Social Action Department. The general purpose of this department was to disseminate Catholic social teaching and act as a catalyst for Catholic social action in the United States. The department had little or no staff but still accomplished quite a bit over the years. As director, Higgins succeeded the legendary Msgr. John A. Ryan and Father Raymond A. McGowan.[2]

Before his retirement in 1980, the bishops' conference and the Social Action Department were restructured, especially after Vatican II, but Higgins basically continued to do what he had always been doing. In his role as director of the Social Action Department, Higgins became the leading figure in Catholic social action in the United States. His primary field of interest was labor and industrial relations, but in his role he was the primary disseminator of Catholic social teaching and the most visible leader in

---

* Originally published as Charles E. Curran, "George Higgins and Catholic Social Teaching," in *US Catholic Historian* 19, no. 4 (Fall 2001): 59–72. Used with permission.

[1] For bibliographical information on Higgins, see Gerald M. Costello, *Without Fear or Favor: George Higgins on the Record* (Mystic, CT: Twenty-Third Publications, 1984). This book concentrates on the weekly columns for the Catholic Press that Higgins has been writing since 1945. For an analysis of Higgins's work, see "Social Catholicism: Essays in Honor of Monsignor George Higgins," *US Catholic Historian* 19, no. 4 (Fall 2001): 3–118.

[2] Costello, *Without Fear or Favor*, 13–28.

Catholic social action in the United States. After Vatican II, many new and different social action approaches emerged, but Higgins was still recognized as a leading figure.

Higgins's personal characteristics shaped his approach to the dissemination of Catholic social teaching and the structuring of Catholic social action. As pointed out by friend and foe alike, George Higgins was a voracious reader whose interests were quite broad. In addition, Higgins was a controversialist who not only enjoyed a good argument but also liked to needle others. Whenever Higgins began a paragraph, as he often did, by claiming, "I don't pretend to be an expert on the subject, but . . . " his interlocutor would be in for a good argument. Late night bull sessions with Higgins (and a bottle of scotch) were legendary, but all recognized him as a faithful priest of deep spirituality.

Higgins never wrote a monograph or book on the theory and practice of Catholic social teaching. His only book in 1993 dealt with organized labor and the church.[3] He disseminated Catholic social teaching through his column titled "The Yardstick," which appeared weekly in the Catholic press for more than fifty years. In addition, he wrote many articles for popular and intellectual Catholic magazines such as *Ave Maria, Commonweal,* and *America.* Also publications interested in Catholic documents (such as *Catholic Mind,* which is no longer published, and now *Origins*) have frequently published his addresses and speeches. These articles indicate his broad reading, and frequently they are structured as a dialogue with two or three other authors. You never read an article by George Higgins without reading long excerpts from books or articles by other authors with whom he is in conversation. Thus, even his articles tend to be ad hoc observations rather than a systematic development of his own positions.

Thus, Higgins's role, personality, and writing style affected how he dealt with Catholic social teaching and action. He was not primarily a theoretician breaking new ground but rather a disseminator who applied Catholic social teaching to the US scene. Catholic social teaching, as mentioned in the preceding chapter, refers to the body of papal teachings beginning with Leo XIII's encyclical *Rerum Novarum* in 1891. These official documents spawned a broader literature, including commentaries and further discussion of the official teaching. Higgins frequently referred to these papal documents in the "Yardstick" columns, and his other articles included commentaries on all these documents.

---

[3] Msgr. George G. Higgins with William Bole, *Organized Labor and the Church: Reflections of a "Labor Priest"* (New York: Paulist Press, 1993).

In his life and his writings, George Higgins served as a bridge between Catholic social teaching and the US experience. Although he was not primarily a theoretician and an academic, his wide reading on Catholic social teaching and on the US political and economic scene gave a strong intellectual foundation to his approach. He read commentaries and discussions about Catholic social teaching in many foreign languages. Thus, he was more than just a popularizer of Catholic social teaching. For example, George Higgins called to the attention of both academics and general readers in the United States the important work of Marie-Dominique Chenu soon after its French publication in 1979.[4] In this work, Chenu addressed the important methodological shift, especially in the writings of Pope Paul VI, to a more inductive approach, as contrasted with the deductive approach of the earlier documents of Catholic social teaching.[5]

In discussing Pope John Paul II's attitude to capitalism, Higgins cites what he calls "an extraordinarily frank interview" the pope gave to the Italian newspaper *La Stampa* on September 9, 1992. The pope criticizes the negative results of socialism as lived out in Eastern Europe, but he recognizes there are seeds of truth in socialism that should not be destroyed. The proponents of capitalism in extreme forms tend to overlook the good things achieved by communism, such as the efforts to overcome unemployment and their concern for the poor.[6] To my knowledge, no other Catholic writer in this country has referred to this interview.

On the US scene he frequently cites philosophical, political, economic, and cultural works. The "Yardstick" columns often dialogue with a book dealing with the US scene. Thus, for example, in June 1947 he discusses two different books coming from the Harvard School of Business.[7] An article on the sixtieth anniversary of *Rerum Novarum* and the twentieth anniversary of *Quadragesimo Anno* reevaluates the two encyclicals in the light of the economic history of the past sixty years. In the process Higgins then

---

[4] Marie-Dominique Chenu, *La "Doctrine Sociale" de l'Eglise comme Idéologie* (Paris: Cerf, 1979).

[5] George G. Higgins, "Religion and National Economic Policy," in *The Formation of Social Policy in the Catholic and Jewish Traditions*, ed. Eugene J. Fischer and Daniel F. Polish (Notre Dame, IN: University of Notre Dame Press, 1980), 80–82.

[6] Msgr. George Higgins, *Subsidiarity in the Catholic Social Tradition: Yesterday, Today, and Tomorrow*, Albert Cardinal Meyer Lectures (Mundelein, IL: Mundelein Seminary, University of St. Mary of the Lake, 1994), 30.

[7] Rev. George G. Higgins, "Yardstick," June 2 and June 9, 1947.

dialogues with many economic theorists.[8] Higgins brings a wide-ranging intellect and broad background reading to his application of Catholic social teaching in the United States.

Interpretation of Papal Documents

In his role of urging Catholics and others to apply Catholic social teaching to the United States, one would naturally expect him to strongly support and praise that teaching even somewhat uncritically. Such was the case in the earlier years. Commenting on *Rerum Novarum* and *Quadragesimo Anno*, he quotes from an official statement by Archbishop Patrick O'Boyle, the episcopal chair of the Social Action Department, claiming that "history will undoubtedly record" these two encyclicals as being "among the most important moral pronouncements of recent centuries."[9] (Higgins here seems to be quoting himself as he in all probability wrote that official statement.) *Mater et Magistra*, published in 1961, "may well prove to be one of the most important ecclesiastical documents ever issued in modern times."[10] On another anniversary of *Rerum Novarum* and *Quadragesimo Anno* he refers to the "timeless social principles to guide us in our life in society" given by "these great pontiffs."[11] Such statements belong to a pre–Vatican II triumphalism and a very uncritical interpretation or hermeneutic of the social encyclicals themselves.

However, in the light of subsequent scholarship, Higgins had a more nuanced and critical view of the encyclicals. A 1981 article addressed the question: Are the social encyclicals out of date? His conclusion is that, even granting that the encyclicals deal only with the distribution of national income, they still apply in varying ways not only to the economically developed countries of the world but also to the developing nations. Then he hastens to add that encyclicals date rather quickly and are culturally conditioned to a greater degree than the documents of revelation. Higgins here adopts a historically critical hermeneutic for interpreting the documents of the hierarchical magisterium and cites many authors, including Chenu, who advocate such an approach. In the process Msgr. Higgins recognizes

---

[8] Rev. George G. Higgins, "After Sixty Years," *Catholic Mind* 49 (1951): 606–17.

[9] Ibid., 608.

[10] Rt. Rev. George G. Higgins, "The Meaning of *Mater et Magistra*," *Ave Maria* 94 (August 26, 1961): 6.

[11] Rt. Rev. Msgr. George G. Higgins, "Toward a New Society," *Catholic Mind* 54 (1956): 629.

the European background and perspective of the pre–Vatican II encyclicals. In keeping with Chenu and others, Higgins also acknowledges the
more dialogical and inductive approach of *Octogesima Adveniens*, the 1971
apostolic letter of Pope Paul VI. In addition, Higgins appears to favor the
position that papal documents in the future should be developed through
a process of open debate and dialogue in a structured way The papal encyclicals no longer hand down principles from on high from the source of all
truth, but rather these documents should emerge through dialogue in a
more structured way. However, Higgins does not see this newer approach
as denigrating the older more deductive documents but rather as updating
and refining the older principles in the light of changed social conditions.[12]

In my judgment greater discontinuity exists between the two
approaches. In other places Higgins seems to recognize such discontinuity.
He explicitly points out that the documents of John XXIII and Paul VI not
only have a changed style and tone, but they also introduce a quite new note
of hesitancy based on the call for dialogue not only with Catholics but with
all people of good will.[13] This hesitancy to claim great certitude definitely
comes from the changed methodology of the later documents. But there
can be no doubt that in the course of time Higgins himself adopted a more
critical hermeneutic with regard to papal encyclicals.

Role of Government

Within the broad category of Catholic social teaching, Higgins gives
primary attention to the proper role of government. Such an emphasis
coheres with his role of applying the documents to many different social
issues in the United States. What is common to all these issues is the role that
government should play in dealing with them. Msgr. Higgins accepts the
general understanding that papal social teaching opposes the two extremes
of socialistic collectivism and individualistic liberalism or capitalism. The
Catholic position, stressing both the dignity and the social nature of the
person, is in the middle opposing both collectivism and individualism.
The Washington-based priest insisted on this point since his earliest writings in the 1940s. He quotes Pope Pius XI, "First so as to avoid the reefs of
individualism and collectivism, the twofold character that is individual and

---

[12] George G. Higgins, "Issues of Justice and Peace," *Chicago Studies* 20 (Summer
1981): 191–206.

[13] Rt. Rev. Msgr. George G. Higgins, "Commentary on *Octogesima Adveniens*,"
Catholic Mind 69 (November 1971): 59–60.

social, both of capital or ownership and of work or labor must be given due and rightful weight."[14] In the United States the primary tendency emphasizes individualism and leans toward a laissez-faire approach by government. Higgins in the early 1940s strongly opposed this very prevalent approach in the United States and insisted that *"Quadragesimo Anno*, if effectively implemented, will give us in time an economic system which will differ almost as radically from the system proposed by socialism as it will from the anarchic system which we have in the United States today."[15]

The working person in the United States might not be able to assimilate in every detail the philosophical reasoning behind the pope's opposition to "Manchester liberalism," but the worker knows from bitter experience and personal suffering the problems created by laissez-faire. But in the 1940s Higgins was not optimistic that American industry will go along with *Quadragesimo Anno*. In this context he cited a leaflet distributed by the Committee for Constitutional Government that tried to equate laissez-faire economics (freedom of the marketplace) with freedom of speech and freedom of religion. The Committee for Constitutional Government included some important and influential members, but maybe we should not take them too seriously. Their leaflet claims that Mr. Truman derives his economic philosophy from Russia and is determined to undermine the American republic. If Mr. Truman is subversive, what shall we say of Pope Pius XI![16] However, the young George Higgins also recognized that many Catholics have the same inclination toward individualism and laissez-faire economics. According to Pius XI, social justice is a virtue that demands from the individual all that is necessary for the common good. This is a big order and one that even the best of Catholics can rather habitually fail to carry out without any noticeable twinge of conscience.[17]

Pope Paul VI, in *Octogesima Adveniens,* makes the point even more emphatically that economic activity must be subject to legitimate political power—a position that will be more widely contested in the United States than any other part of the document. *Octogesima Adveniens* also breaks new ground in pointing out some legitimate aspects of Marxism and socialism.[18]

---

[14] Rev. George G. Higgins, "Catholic Tests of the Social Order," *Catholic Mind* 46 (1948): 566.

[15] George G. Higgins, "Socialism and Socialism," *Commonweal* 43 (1945–46): 307.

[16] Rev. George G. Higgins, "Who Is More Subversive?" *Catholic Mind* 44 (1946): 336.

[17] Rev. George G. Higgins, "What Is Social Justice?" *Catholic Mind* 45 (1947): 561.

[18] Higgins, "*Octogesima Adveniens*," 63.

Higgins recognizes that socialism holds little or no attraction for people in the United States, but he wants citizens of the United States to understand why so many people in the world are attracted to socialism.[19]

Subsidiarity and Socialization

Catholic social teaching develops and fills out its teaching on the role of the state with the principle of subsidiarity and the principle of socialization. The principle of subsidiarity as enunciated in *Quadragesimo Anno* and developed in chapter 1 understands society as made up of individuals and intermediary groups of all types (e.g., family, neighborhood, all varieties of voluntary associations, and finally the state). This principle (the Latin word *subsidium* means "help") maintains that the larger and higher grouping should help the individual and smaller groupings to do all they can for the common good, and the state should do only what the lower associations and individuals cannot do even with the state's help.[20]

John XXIII in *Mater et Magistra* introduced the concept of socialization, referring to the multiplication of social relationships and the complex interdependencies of contemporary human existence, which call for a growing intervention of larger associations and public authorities in human life. The pope recognized advantages and some disadvantages with the greater role for government.[21]

George Higgins frequently appealed to these two principles for a proper understanding of the role of government. The principle of subsidiarity does not mean that the best government is the least government. On the contrary, although government should not arbitrarily usurp the role of individuals or voluntary associations in social and economic life, neither should it hesitate to adopt such programs as are required by the common good and are beyond the competence of individual citizens or groups of citizens.[22] Notice how this interpretation refutes the conservative position of greatly reducing the role of government. But according to Higgins, extreme liberals who do not accept subsidiarity misinterpret what John XXIII said about socialization.

---

[19] Higgins, "Justice and Peace," 203–6.

[20] Pope Pius XI, *Quadragesimo Anno*, nos. 78–80, in *Catholic Social Thought: The Documentary Heritage*, ed. David J. O'Brien and Thomas A. Shannon (Maryknoll, NY: Orbis Books, 1992), 60.

[21] Pope John XXIII, *Mater et Magistra*, nos. 59–67, in *Catholic Social Thought*, ed. O'Brien and Shannon, 93–95.

[22] Higgins, "Religion and National Economic Policy," 92.

Socialization does not mean the same as socialism, nor does it equate socialization exclusively with government action.[23]

Industry Council Plan

Especially in his earlier years up through the 1960s, George Higgins
emphasized more than anything else the Industry Council Plan (ICP),
which serves as a good illustration of his understanding of the proper role
of intermediary institutions and the state in the light of the principles of
subsidiarity and socialization. No fewer than thirty separate "Yardstick"
columns in the 1950s deal with the ICP.[24] The ICP is based on the principle
of an organic society as outlined in *Quadragesimo Anno*. All the people
engaged in a given industry or profession, workers and employers alike, are
intended by nature to cooperate for the good of their own industry and
for the common good of the entire economy. These self-governing associations would regulate economic life according to the requirements of social
justice. Each industry would have a separate organization or association (or
industry council), and all the various industry councils would work coop-
eratively with each other and with the government to achieve the common
good. This plan disagrees with government dictatorship of the economy
but also with management dictatorship and even with labor dictatorship, if
that were possible. All three have to work together for the common good.
Labor thus should be interested in more than the bread and butter issues of
wages, benefits, and working conditions. Higgins himself was quite confi-
dent in the 1950s that there were signs of progress toward this goal despite
some obstacles along the way.[25] Thanks to Catholic influence, with Higgins
playing a very central role, many in the CIO agreed with such a role for
labor. However, some Protestants saw in the CIO's support for the ICP
the nefarious role of the Catholic Church in proposing what they called a
fascist plan.[26]

In working toward the establishment of the ICP in 1956, Higgins
distinguished between the reforming aspects of Catholic social teaching
and the reconstruction aspects. The principal reform measures advocated
by Leo XIII and Pius XI are legislation and organization. In the United

---

[23] Higgins, "*Mater et Magistra*," 9.

[24] Costello, *Without Fear or Favor*, 170.

[25] Higgins, "After Sixty Years," 610–17; "New Society," 629–35.

[26] Kermit Eby, "The Catholic Plan for American Labor," *Christianity Today* 1
(April 29, 1957): 12–15.

States we have made some progress in social legislation moving away from the one-sided laissez-faire approach of the nineteenth century and likewise in organization thanks to the strengthening of labor unions. Thus, legislation and organization have done much to balance the individual and social aspects of economic life. But these reforming aspects are not the final answer but rather steps toward the reconstruction of the economic order in accord with the ICP.[27]

However, despite Higgins's own hard work and his seeing some signs of progress toward such reconstruction, the reconstruction has never come about in the United States. In fact, the later popes themselves moved away from explicitly supporting this specific plan. In my judgment the problem comes from the deductive nature of *Quadragesimo Anno*, which deduced this plan in an abstract way and did not work from the existing realities. Higgins hints at such an explanation by claiming that John XXIII was more flexible than Pius XI in terms of the reconstruction of the social order. However, Higgins continued to insist on some form of codetermination and comanagement between capital and labor.[28] Throughout most of the 1950s and into the '60s Higgins saw the ICP as a good illustration of the principles of subsidiarity and socialization at work.

Differences with Neoconservatives

In the 1980s and afterward, George Higgins used his understanding of the proper role of government, intermediary bodies, and individuals to criticize the approach of Catholic neoconservatives in the United States. The three names most associated with Catholic neoconservatives in the United States are Michael Novak, Richard John Neuhaus, and George Weigel.[29] Our author has expressed strong disagreement with all of these writers on different occasions.

The primary difference comes from Higgins's understanding of the need for a bigger role for government, although he would agree with

---

[27] Higgins, "New Society," 629–35.

[28] Higgins, "Justice and Peace," 202–3.

[29] For succinct statements of Catholic neoconservatives' own self-understanding, see Michael Novak, "Neoconservatives," in *The New Dictionary of Catholic Social Thought*, ed. Judith A. Dwyer (Collegeville, MN: Liturgical Press, 1994), 678–82; George Weigel, "The Neoconservative Difference: A Proposal for the Renewal of Church and Society," in *Being Right: Conservative Catholics in America*, ed. Mary Jo Weaver and Scott Appleby (Bloomington: University of Indiana Press, 1995), 138–62.

neoconservatives on the role of intermediary groups in society. Thus, for example, in commenting on *Laborem Exercens*, Pope John Paul II's 1981 encyclical, the Washington-based monsignor points out against the neoconservatives that the encyclical explicitly calls for national and international planning with some role for the state but not in a collectivist manner.[30] Higgins himself served as a consultant to the draft committee of the US bishops' pastoral letter on the economy, which devoted an entire chapter to the need for planning with the title: "A New American Experiment: Partnership for the Public Good."[31]

Msgr. Higgins defended the draft of the bishops' pastoral on the economy as being a balanced approach to the US economy against the charge of the neoconservatives that the US bishops and most of the contemporary Catholic intellectuals and scholars have been too negative about the US economy. The bishops rightly praise some aspects of the US economy, but they also point out its shortcomings. On the present scene [as written in 2001] there is no shortage in the media or in the nation at large of complimentary assessments of the US economic situation. Our problem is that too few people of prominence are speaking out loud enough for the need to improve the system with a preferential option for the poor in the manner that the bishops have done.[32] Higgins claims that Neuhaus in *The Catholic Moment* (1987) fails to uphold his own method about the need to hold in tension the Christian proposition and the American proposition. Neuhaus overreacts to criticism of the American system.[33]

Our author Higgins faults the neoconservatives for not being critical enough of democratic capitalism and the American system. Especially when we are trying to convince people in the third world about the advantages of the US system, we must also recognize its shortcomings and problems.[34]

The neoconservatives have been quite critical of the positions taken by the US bishops and claim they have been too influenced in their social teachings by their staff, especially J. Bryan Hehir, who served as the staff person for the bishops' pastoral letters on peace and the economy. Higgins

---

[30] Higgins, *Subsidiarity in the Catholic Social Tradition*, 27–29.

[31] US Catholic Bishops, *Economic Justice for All*, nos. 295–325, in *Catholic Social Thought*, ed. O'Brien and Shannon, 646–53.

[32] George G. Higgins, "The US Bishops and Their Critics," *Doctrine and Life* 35 (1985): 221–22.

[33] George G. Higgins, "The Catholic Moment," *America* 159 (June 25–July 2, 1988): 15.

[34] Higgins, *Subsidiarity in the Catholic Social Tradition*, 26.

accuses Neuhaus and Weigel of "a sweeping and highly pejorative general-ization" and "a polemical line of argument" with regard to their criticism of the US bishops' social policy teachings.[35] Weigel maintains that through the work of J. Bryan Hehir the US bishops have abandoned the heritage of John Courtney Murray. Higgins staunchly defends Hehir "as one of the most gifted and well-balanced priest-scholars in the United States," who has been badly treated by his critics. Higgins sees Weigel's comment about Hehir as an insult not just to Hehir but also to the American bishops whom Weigel thinks were apparently duped by this one person.[36] There has been much discussion among Catholic scholars today about the Murray project in the light of the criticism from neoconservatives that the bishops and liberal Catholic scholars have misinterpreted Murray and thus moved away from his approach and project. However, Higgins does not go into this in any depth.

The neoconservatives loudly praised John Paul II's 1991 encyclical *Centesimus Annus* for its condemnation of the welfare state and for its support of democratic capitalism. Higgins strongly disagrees. One must interpret *Centesimus Annus* in a larger context. At the University of Latvia the pope emphasized that Catholic social teaching "is not a surrogate for capitalism" and recognized that "there was a kernel of truth" in Marxism. The pope described the ideal state as one "which offers everyone the legal guarantees of an orderly existence and assures the most vulnerable the support they need in order not to succumb to the arrogance and indiffer-ence of the powerful." In the same context Higgins cites similar remarks from the pope's interview with *La Stampa*. Our author needles his oppo-nents by pointing out that even the *Wall Street Journal*, "the flagship daily of American capitalism," had a front-page article reporting that the leaders of the anticommunist revolution throughout Eastern Europe are "now its victims, exposed to capitalism's survival of the fittest competition."[37]

In his lifelong comments about the proper role of government, Higgins's penchant for liking a good fight and needling his opponents (as well as his friends) often colors his approach. But at the same time the realist and the pragmatist come through. He is interested in getting things done. Even in his strongest comments against the neoconservatives, Higgins called for a temporary moratorium on the use of ambiguous and ideologically

---

[35] Higgins, "Catholic Moment," 15.

[36] Ibid., 17.

[37] Higgins, *Subsidiarity in the Catholic Social Tradition,* 29–30.

loaded terms such as "democratic capitalism" and "socialism" so all of us can concentrate on trying to reconcile in a very practical, nonideological, North American way the principle of solidarity and the principle of socialization, or in Novak's terms, the twin values of the inimitable person and the common good.[38]

Other Issues

Especially in the "Yardstick" George Higgins touched on most of the issues of the day without being able to develop his approach in any depth, but two significant issues also treated in other writings are of great importance. Higgins was an early and constant promoter of interracial justice. From the 1940s he advocated justice for African Americans, supported the NAACP, belittled those who claimed that African American organizations were tied to the Communist Party, and frequently reminded white, American Catholics that they too had experienced prejudice and discrimination in this country.[39] More academic Catholic moral theologians in the United States (such as myself) have rightly been criticized for ignoring the issue of racial justice.[40] But the more practically oriented Higgins recognized early on that racial discrimination constituted an unconscionable blot on the American record. He frequently chided the labor movement for its failure with regard to racial justice. One column of the "Yardstick" also reprinted in the *Catholic Mind* responds vehemently to a critic who accused Higgins of never mentioning the discriminatory practices of some unions. Our author cites the record to disprove the accusation.[41]

In the late 1970s and early '80s, Msgr. Higgins was deeply troubled by the Catholic prolife movement's relationship to the New Right.[42] He agreed

---

[38] Ibid., 28–29.

[39] Costello, *Without Fear or Favor*, 145–68.

[40] Bryan N. Massingale, "The African American Experience and US Roman Catholic Ethics: Strangers and Aliens No Longer?" in *Black and Catholic: The Challenge and Gift of Black Folk: Contributions of African American Experience and Thought to Catholic Theology*, ed. Jamie T. Phelps (Milwaukee, WI: Marquette University Press, 1997), 79–101.

[41] Higgins, "Yardstick," June 17, 1963; "Setting the Record Straight," *Catholic Mind* 61 (December 1963): 32–34.

[42] George G. Higgins, "The Prolife Movement and the New Right," *America* 143 (1980): 107–10.

with the goal and position of the Catholic right-to-life movement but very strongly warned them about their tactics. First, he maintained in no uncertain terms that the Catholic right-to-life movement should have nothing to do with the New Right. One can readily see why Higgins and the leadership of Catholic social teaching would be strongly opposed to the New Right with its positions on capital punishment, disarmament, gun control, national health insurance, welfare reform, foreign aid, inflation, full employment, and agricultural policy. But Higgins goes much further and argues, based on the very words of leaders of the New Right, that they are not really interested in the abortion issue as such but are using it for their own political purposes of trying to elect very right-wing candidates and defeat liberal political candidates. Those in the New Right are not conservatives but radicals trying to overturn much of what Catholic social teaching stands for. For all these reasons, the Catholic prolife movement should dissociate itself from the New Right.

Practical considerations also come to the same conclusion. To pass a human life amendment one needs the support of the majority of citizens and legislators. This is a basic principle of democracy. But the New Right, with its narrow right-wing political agenda and with many of its adherents supporting a Christian political movement, remains a small and isolated group that will never constitute a majority and will actually prevent the Catholic right-to-life movement from ever being successful.

Higgins also chides many in the Catholic prolife movement who forget about the other aspects of Catholic social teaching on the dignity of life. We cannot wait until a human life amendment is passed to face the problems of capital punishment, massive poverty, starvation, high unemployment, and severely inadequate housing. In this context Higgins praises a statement of the administrative board of the United States Catholic Bishops that lists more than a dozen issues that the church addresses, thus emphasizing the interrelated nature of the respect life agenda. We need a "consistent commitment" to the sanctity of human life. The bishops themselves would later accept the need for a consistent ethic of life as illustrated especially in the many writings of Cardinal Joseph Bernardin addressing these issues beginning in 1983.[43]

---

[43] Joseph Cardinal Bernardin et al., *Consistent Ethic of Life*, ed. Thomas G. Fuechtmann (Kansas City, MO: Sheed and Ward, 1988).

Practical Involvements

Msgr. Higgins's primary practical involvement was in support of the labor movement and unions. He was often recognized as a "labor priest" and even "the labor priests' priest." He strongly advocated the cause of labor in his "Yardstick" column. He was close to the major figures in American unions and attended their annual meetings. Higgins criticized corruption and racism in the unions, but he did not tell the labor unions how to go about their business. He always had a great respect for the role of the professionals in their own fields. One indication of his public role was as a member and longtime head of the United Auto Workers Public Review Board, which monitored the union's conduct toward its individual members and protected the due process rights of all the members.[44]

Higgins also played a key role in support of César Chávez and what came to be called the United Farm Workers (UFW).[45] Chávez himself was a devout Catholic; the workers were Catholic; but so were almost all the growers in California. Chávez twice asked the Catholic bishops for help. After some hesitation, the Catholic bishops in 1969 established a Committee on Farm Labor to investigate the situation and to take appropriate action. Higgins was appointed as a consultant to the committee, but for four years he was heavily involved in the day-to-day operations. On July 29, 1970, with the bishops playing a key mediational role, an agreement was reached between the growers and the union. But lettuce growers in the Salinas Valley wanted nothing to do with Chávez and made sweetheart deals with the teamsters' union. The teamsters' union finally made an agreement with Chávez but then reneged. Chávez called for a strike and a boycott. At this stage, the bishops committee now moved from its mediational role to total support for Chávez and his union. Through Higgins and others, a papal audience was arranged for Chávez. The AFL-CIO strongly supported Chávez, and Higgins with his many connections there worked in concert with the AFL-CIO. With the election of Jerry Brown as governor of California in 1975, the state enacted the California Agricultural Relations Act, which gave unions the right to strike and boycott. Unfortunately due to many circumstances, the influence of the UFW dwindled. Chávez himself said in 1980, "I doubt that anyone has done as much for us as Msgr. Higgins has." [46]

---

[44] Higgins with Bole, *Organized Labor and the Church.*

[45] Marco G. Proty, *César Chávez, the Catholic Bishops, and the Farm Workers' Struggle for Social Justice* (Tucson: University of Arizona Press, 2006).

[46] Costello, *Without Fear or Favor*, 33.

A second important involvement arising out of the labor movement had to do with Jewish–Catholic relations. The Jewish and Catholic communities in the twentieth century were immigrant communities; both experienced discrimination; both were interested in the defense of justice for workers. Through the labor movement, Higgins met many Jewish leaders who shared his social agenda. In his "Yardstick" column, Higgins strongly disagreed with some Catholics who, as he put it, used Jewish suffering to support their understanding of the Catholic agenda. In these columns, he also praised the positive aspects that took place in Catholic–Jewish relations. Since Higgins was well known by Jewish American leaders, he played a significant behind-the-scenes role at Vatican II to work for a strong positive statement on Jewish–Catholic relations. After the council, he was instrumental in having the US bishops establish a Committee for Ecumenical and Interreligious Affairs with one of three secretariats devoted to Jewish relations. In a sense, the secretariat took over the work that Higgins himself had begun. He continued to work in Catholic–Jewish dialogue over the years. In June 2001, the International Catholic–Jewish Liaison Committee sponsored by the Vatican and the International Jewish Committee for Interreligious Consultations named Higgins one of eight great pioneers in this dialogue.[47]

Higgins's many involvements made him quite well known even outside the Catholic community. In August 2000, President Clinton bestowed on Higgins the Presidential Medal of Freedom, the nation's highest civilian honor. The citation referred to his work for social and economic justice for working Americans.[48]

Social Mission of the Church

George Higgins, as the bridge builder between Catholic social teaching and the US scene, was a participant-observer for almost sixty years of the social mission of the church. How should the church structure and implement its social teaching? Higgins reflected on this question both from his theoretical knowledge and his practical involvements and experiences.

In my judgment, four basic concepts for structuring the social mission of the church emerge from Higgins's many writings. I shall try to synthesize here his most recent understanding of this issue.

---

[47] Eugene J. Fischer, "Catholic–Jewish Relations," *US Catholic Historian* 19n4 (2001): 41–49.

[48] O'Brien and Shannon, *Catholic Social Thought*, xii.

First, the primary, though not exclusive, function of a church-related, social-action organization is to prepare the laity to engage in social action on their own initiative in the secular arena. The social action of the church, especially since Vatican II and perhaps somewhat ironically so, has tended to be too churchy, too institutional, and too clerical. We have tended to overemphasize the role of church professionals, be they clerical or lay, in the social mission of the church. For many people the primary concern has been to have the hierarchical church take positions on certain issues rather than having the primary emphasis on empowering and motivating the laity to carry on the social mission of the church in their daily lives and work. Higgins, as is obvious, strongly supported official Catholic social teaching and the pastoral letters of the United States bishops on peace and the economy, but the primary place where Catholic social teaching touches the road is in the daily lives of Catholic laity who should thus be prepared for their role in the temporal sphere. This point was well made by the Chicago Declaration of Christian Concern in 1978. Secular action by the laity is more important than churchy actions by hierarchy and church professionals, but both are necessary.[49]

Second, hierarchy, clergy, and church professionals must respect the legitimate autonomy of the temporal sphere and the expertise of those who work in all dimensions of the temporal sphere.[50] Msgr. Reynold Hillenbrand convinced Higgins as a young seminarian of the important role of the laity and their expertise in the social mission of the church.[51] Especially in the 1960s and early '70s, he reacted strongly against the self-righteousness and moralizing of many of the "New Breed" who too glibly claimed to have all the answers to complex societal problems.[52]

Higgins followed just such an approach in his dealings with unions and labor leaders. He respected their expertise. It was not his function or his role to tell them how to run a union. However, when moral issues were involved, such as racial discrimination or corruption, Higgins was very willing to speak out.

---

[49] George G. Higgins, "The Social Mission of the Church after Vatican II," *America* 155 (July 26, 1986): 25–27; Higgins, *Organized Labor and the Church*, 208–16.

[50] Higgins, "Social Mission," 27.

51 Higgins, *Organized Labor and the Church*, 19–24.

[52] George G. Higgins, "Historical Resumé of the Teaching, Policy, and Action of the Church in Social Mission," in *Metropolis: Christian Presence and Responsibility*, ed. Philip D. Morris (Notre Dame, IN: Fides, 1970), 145–50.

Respect for professional expertise characterizes Higgins's whole approach. He abhorred moralizing and rhetoric.[53] When Higgins retired from the bishops' conference in 1980, the late Father Carl Peter and I convinced the administration of Catholic University to offer George a position as an adjunct lecturer in theology with a residence on campus so he could stay in the Washington area. We had a tougher job selling George on this idea. He protested that he had no experience as a teacher and could not start to learn the profession at age sixty-five. However, we finally convinced him that he could be a real help to many of our seminarians and priest students. In a sense, George was right. He really was not a good teacher in the classical approach, but dialogue and personal contact with him, with his quick and broad mental powers, and with his voracious reading encouraged many of our better students. It was this same respect for professional expertise that was behind his opposition to the self-righteous rhetoric of some clergy, religious, and church professionals with regard to what should be done in the temporal order.

Third, how should church professionals and also the teaching office of the church address the moral issues facing society? Higgins recognized an important role for such teaching and involvement, but it was not the primary aspect of the social mission of the church. A comparatively long 1971 article addresses how the preacher should deal with social issues. Higgins, like many, argues for a middle position, avoiding the extremes of reducing the gospel just to the personal realm or politicizing the gospel and losing its own distinctive and transcendent aspects. In keeping with some of the points mentioned above, Higgins recognizes the complexity of social issues, the need for expertise and professional knowledge, the many different prudential judgments that are possible amid such complexity, and the freedom of the individual believer. The preacher must not impose one's personal or political opinions on a captive audience. The danger of moralizing is ever present for the preacher. Higgins argues against what many called the need for the preacher to be prophetic and take clear and certain stands on complex issues such as the Vietnam War. Instead, the preacher should, above all, stress the moral principles involved, and when making applications to particular cases, the preacher must be careful to propose

---

[53] In a eulogy for Dorothy Day, Higgins, who followed a very different approach to the social mission of the church, praised her for not being judgmental, moralistic, or self-righteous. She was not disposed to examine other people's consciences. See George G. Higgins, "Dorothy Day: A Sign for the Times," *Origins* 10 (February 1981): 545–50.

his solutions as personal positions. Such an approach is dialogical and not dogmatic.[54] The United States bishops in their two 1980 pastoral letters on peace and the economy basically followed the same approach.

Fourth, Higgins makes a distinction between activism and social action. Proponents of "activism" in the post–Vatican II period have put too much emphasis on prophetic witness.[55] Elsewhere he refers to the "Selma syndrome"—participation in demonstrations especially by clergy and religious—as the most important way to advance the social mission of the church.[56] However, social action recognizes the need for long-range social education and structural reform for bringing about social change. Various groups in society, for example African Americans, cannot go it alone. They need to form coalitions with others because structural reform comes about in a democracy only through a majority of citizens and legislators.

I basically agree with most of his understanding of the social mission of the church. However, Higgins himself in the 1960s and early '70s, tended to be somewhat more polemical and less nuanced in his approach to the social mission of the church.

The '60s and early '70s witnessed great social change and even upheaval in the United States. The civil rights movement with Martin Luther King Jr., and later Black Power, dominated the civil rights scene. As noted, Higgins had always been a strong advocate for interracial justice and passionately supported the 1964 Civil Rights Act. The Washington-based monsignor, however, vehemently opposed the rhetoric and tactics of Black Power with its advocacy of black racism and violence. He strongly defended Roy Wilkins and A. Philip Randolph against Black Power attacks. These two black leaders, like Higgins, saw social action primarily in terms of long-term education and structural reform. Here again he recognized the importance of coalitions because structural reform could come about only through a broader approach. In one column he even strongly castigated the rhetoric of Martin Luther King himself.[57]

Higgins for a long time strongly supported President Lyndon Johnson and the American involvement in the Vietnam War. Recall that US labor organizations held a very similar position. In addition, he thoroughly

---

[54] George G. Higgins, "Preaching and Social Development," *American Ecclesiastical Review* 167 (1973): 121–33.

[55] Higgins, "Social Mission," 26; *Organized Labor and the Church*, 214.

[56] Higgins, "Historical Resumé of the Teaching, Policy, and Action of the Church," 166.

[57] Costello, *Without Fear or Favor*, 154–63.

disagreed with the tactics and approach of most of the Catholic war protesters.[58]

George Higgins recognized a new approach to Catholic social action associated with the civil rights movement and the antiwar protests. He distinguished between the "New Breed" and the "Old Breed." He contrasted the approach of the New Breed and the Old Breed, which he identified with himself and many of those who had gone before him in Catholic social action. The New Breed he considered too churchy, too interested in seeing the problem in terms of pushing the church hierarchy to take a particular position rather than recognizing the role of the laity in the secular realm as primary, too enthralled with the efficacy of marches and demonstrations rather than recognizing the need for long-term education and structural reform, too moralizing and quick to make prophetic denunciations without recognizing professional expertise and the complexity of most moral issues, such as the Vietnam War. He admired many of the qualities of the New Breed, but their approach would go only so far; he felt that it would not solve the social issues the country was facing at the time. However, in the same article he cautioned the reader that the New Breed–Old Breed distinction is somewhat of a rhetorical ploy.[59]

In my judgment, his later understanding of the social mission of the church, as reflected in the opening part of this section, is more nuanced. His later position assumes more of a both-and approach rather than the somewhat either-or approach of the late 1960s and early '70s. The acrimonious milieu of the '60s and early '70s, together with Higgins's own penchant for liking a good fight and the very genre of column writing, obviously contributed to his tendency to emphasize a more either-or approach at that time.

George Higgins has been the most important figure in US Catholicism dealing with the practical application of Catholic social teaching to the cultural, economic, and political scene in the United States in the second half of the twentieth century. This chapter has tried to synthesize and assess Higgins's great contributions in this regard.

---

[58] Ibid., 228–38.

[59] Higgins, "Historical Resumé of the Teaching, Policy, and Action of the Church," 144–72.

Chapter 4

HUMAN RIGHTS IN THE
CHRISTIAN TRADITION*

The aim of this chapter is twofold. The first aim is to substantiate briefly the thesis that the Christian churches, primarily Roman Catholic and Protestant in the Western world, have moved from hostility to, or reluctance about, human rights to acceptance and even to a leadership role in the struggle for human rights in the world today.[1] Second, a much longer section will try to explain how this development occurred. A brief conclusion will reflect on what the churches can learn from this development.

From Hostility/Reluctance to Acceptance

Human rights in the Western tradition are primarily associated with the seventeenth- and eighteenth-century philosophy of the Enlightenment, especially that of Thomas Hobbes and John Locke, and with the political systems that emerged from this approach, which toppled the older political order. Some scholars have proposed that human rights as such arose only with the Enlightenment.[2] Both human rights and the Enlightenment are associated with opposition to religion in general and to Christianity in particular. Human rights have often been seen as coming from a growing secularism with its emphasis on human reason, the primacy of the individual, science, and a skepticism with regard to religious and Christian truth claims.[3]

---

* Originally published as Charles E. Curran, "Churches and Human Rights: From Hostility/Reluctance to Acceptability," *Milltown Studies* 42 (1998): 30–58. Used with permission.

[1] Note the problem in speaking in general about Catholicism and Protestantism. The problem is less in dealing with Catholicism because of the role of the hierarchical teaching office. The discussion of Protestantism that follows generally refers to mainstream Protestant churches and in the twentieth century to the worldwide Protestant ecumenical movement.

[2] C. B. Macpherson, *The Political Theory of Possessive Individualism: Hobbes to Locke* (Oxford: Clarendon Press, 1962).

[3] Richard Ashcroft, "Religion and Lockean Natural Rights," in *Religious Diversity and*

Opposition to the Enlightenment

Roman Catholicism disagreed with the Enlightenment precisely because of its emphasis on the individual and its secularism, which denied our relationship to God. Almost until the Second Vatican Council in the 1960s, Roman Catholicism strongly opposed the Enlightenment and its teaching on human rights. One of the primary rights proposed by the Enlightenment was the right to religious liberty, but it was only at Vatican II that Roman Catholicism accepted such a right.[4] A defensive and ultramontanist Roman Catholicism saw the Enlightenment as its primary opposition. Nineteenth-century papal documents, including the famous Syllabus of Errors, condemned and excoriated the theory and practice of the Enlightenment.[5] Gregory XVI's encyclical *Mirari Vos* of 1832 well illustrates the Catholic Church's intransigent opposition to Enlightenment ideas. The pope strongly condemned liberalism, individualism, freedom of conscience (it is a *deliramentum*—a madness), freedom of opinion and of the press, democracy, and the separation of church and state. The remedies of these evils are found in the recognition that all authority comes from God, and the church has the role to teach the truth to all.[6] Hierarchical Catholic teaching only accepted democracy as the best form of government in the pontificate of Pius XII in the 1940s.[7]

In general, Protestantism was much more open to religious freedom and a role for freedom in human society, but it strongly opposed the rationalism and secularism associated with the Enlightenment and its emphasis on natural and human rights. Erich Weingärtner, who served as executive secretary of the Commission of the Churches International Affairs (CCIA), an

---

Human Rights, ed. Irene Bloom, J. Paul Martin, and Wayne L. Proudfoot (New York: Columbia University Press, 1996), 195–97. Ashcroft here summarizes this generally accepted thesis which he then refutes.

[4] Declaration on Religious Liberty, in *Vatican Council II: The Conciliar and Post-Conciliar Documents*, ed. Austin Flannery, rev. ed. (Collegeville, MN: Liturgical Press, 1992), 799–812.

[5] For a historical overview of this period see Roger Aubert et al., *The Church in the Age of Liberalism* (New York: Crossroad, 1981).

[6] Pope Gregory XVI, *Mirari Vos*, nos. 14–21, in *The Papal Encyclicals, 1740–1878*, ed. Claudia Carlen (Wilmington, NC: McGrath, 1981), 238–39.

[7] Paul E. Sigmund, "Catholicism and Liberal Democracy," in *Catholicism and Liberalism: Contributions to American Public Philosophy*, ed. R. Bruce Douglass and David Hollenbach (New York: Cambridge University Press, 1994), 226.

important arm of the World Council of Churches (WCC), has recognized that for most of their history the Protestant churches opposed human rights "as the product of humanistic philosophy."[8] Calvinist theologians associated with the Free University of Amsterdam in the nineteenth century and the first part of the twentieth century fiercely criticized the idea of human rights even though they were often willing to accept the content of human rights. The idea of human rights basically repudiated the strong Calvinist belief in the sovereignty of God, since it derives these rights from human reason and human beings.[9]

To make historical generalizations about Protestantism as a movement is quite difficult. Yes, there was opposition to the human rights movement, but this opposition in general was considerably less than the Catholic opposition and in many areas much quicker to change. As will be pointed out, many Protestants came to appreciate the content of the political and civil rights associated with the Enlightenment but had problems with the grounding and concept of human rights. I have chosen the word "reluctance" to refer to the general Protestant approach to human rights before the twentieth century.

The Contemporary Scene

Great change has occurred in the last fifty years. Obviously the churches were influenced by the 1948 Universal Declaration of Human Rights of the United Nations. As will be mentioned, other significant contemporary realities also influenced a decided change in the churches' attitude toward human rights. The churches have not only accepted human rights, but they have exercised significant leadership in the theoretical understanding of rights and the practical struggle for human rights around the globe. Max Stackhouse claims that the WCC "has done more for human rights among the peoples of the world than any other single international body."[10] Some might claim that Stackhouse as a Protestant theologian is somewhat

---

[8] Erich Weingärtner, "Human Rights," in *Dictionary of the Ecumenical Movement*, ed. Nicolas Lossky et al. (Grand Rapids, MI: Eerdmans, 1991), 486.

[9] Aad van Egmond, "Calvinist Thought and Human Rights," in *Human Rights and Religious Values: An Uneasy Relationship?* ed. Abdullah An-Na'im, Jerald D. Gort, Henry Jansen, and Hendrik M. Vroom (Grand Rapids, MI: Eerdmans, 1995), 192.

[10] Max L. Stackhouse, "Public Theology, Human Rights, and Mission," in *Human Rights and the Global Mission of the Church*, ed. Arthur Dyke (Cambridge, MA: Boston Theological Institute, 1985), 16.

triumphalistic in the matter, but the subsequent pages will give some indication of the significant leadership role taken in this area by the WCC.

Human rights have also become central in the contemporary approach of Catholic social teaching. The first systematic development of human rights in hierarchical Catholic social teaching occurred only in 1963.[11] The Second Vatican Council and subsequent popes continued to insist on the importance of human rights for human existence on this globe. John Paul II in his social encyclicals and in his many trips throughout the world made human rights the focus of his appeal to provide greater justice for human beings on our earth today. Pope John Paul's special relation to Eastern Europe and the dramatic changes that took place there attracted great attention to his human rights approach.[12] The American political scientist Samuel P. Huntington has highlighted the important role of Catholicism in supporting democracy and human rights during the global struggles of the 1970s and '80s.[13] Thus the Protestant and Catholic Churches have moved from their opposition to human rights to a leadership role in promoting and defending human rights throughout the globe since the latter part of the twentieth century. Perhaps even more startling than the dramatic changes in the churches' acceptance of, and leadership in defending, human rights is the often mentioned argument that religion, and in this case Christianity, provides the best ground for the support and defense of human rights throughout the world.[14]

Catholic and Protestant thought today also share a general agreement about the content of human rights. Historically, the Enlightenment identified human rights with civil and political rights to freedom from external coercion in matters of religion, speech, assembly, opinion, press, and so on. Those who gave more importance to the social aspect of human existence stressed the social, economic, and cultural rights, such as the right to food,

---

[11] Pope John XXIII, *Pacem in Terris*, nos. 11–27, in *Catholic Social Thought: The Documentary Heritage*, ed. David J. O'Brien and Thomas A. Shannon (Maryknoll, NY: Orbis Books, 1992), 132–35.

[12] J. Bryan Hehir, "Religious Activism for Human Rights: A Christian Case Study," in *Religious Human Rights in Global Perspective: Religious Perspectives*, ed. John Witte and Johan D. van der Vyver (The Hague: Martinus Nijhoff, 1996), 97–119.

[13] Samuel P. Huntington, "Religion and the Third Wave," *National Interest* 24 (Summer 1991): 30.

[14] Max L. Stackhouse and Stephen E. Healey, "Religious and Human Rights: A Theological Apologetic," in *Religious Human Rights in Global Perspective*, ed. Witte and van der Vyver, 485–516.

clothing, shelter, and health care. These rights have been called the second stage of the human rights movement since they came to the fore after the civil and political rights associated with the Enlightenment and philosophical liberalism and were often associated with the socialist world. Some refer to a third stage in the human rights development, associated with the rights of new nations especially in the south—nations that had been under the thumb of European colonizers. However, for our purposes this aspect can be included under social, economic, and cultural rights, provided they are seen also in light of the two-thirds world.[15] The Protestant and Catholic churches have generally accepted the need for both kind of rights.

Protestant and Catholic theorists, as perceptively pointed out by Joseph L. Allen, often recognize the same basis and grounding for human rights—the equal dignity and worth of the human person. This dignity itself is ultimately seen in terms of the person's relationship to God.[16] In explaining the relationship some theological differences come to the fore in the different approaches of Catholics, Reformed Protestants, and Lutheran Protestants.[17] However, these different theological approaches to the grounding of human dignity do not detract from the acceptance of human dignity as the basis for human rights.

As might be expected, many factors have played a role in the changed understanding of Protestant and Catholic churches as they moved from reluctance or hostility to acceptance and leadership with regard to human rights. If we look at the development, it is obvious that the opposition to human rights was never absolute or total. There have been aspects of the Christian tradition that could be appealed to in defense of human rights. But the belated recognition of human rights and their acceptance came to life in the intellectual, historical, cultural, and economic developments with regard to human existence and human rights. This chapter will try to answer the question of change by concentrating on three different but interrelated aspects of the question—human rights in general, civil and political rights, and finally social, cultural, and economic rights.

---

[15] Weingärtner, "Human Rights," 485. For some, the fourth generation of human rights refers to the rights of future generations and the environment.

[16] Joseph L. Allen, "Catholic and Protestant Theories of Human Rights," *Religious Studies Review* 14 (1988): 347–48.

[17] Ibid. See also Jürgen Moltmann, "Christian Faith and Human Rights," in *Understanding Human Rights: An Interdisciplinary and Interfaith Study*, ed. Alan D. Falconer (Dublin: Irish School of Ecumenics, 1980), 182–223.

Change with Regard to Human Rights in General

Historically, Roman Catholicism and Protestantism, to a lesser degree, have been seen in opposition to the human rights movement which is usually associated with the Enlightenment and its aftermath. But history also shows some continuity with the churches' contemporary acceptance of human rights.

The Catholic Approach

Scripture gives strong support to the dignity of human beings, which became the ecumenical basis for the contemporary acceptance of human rights. The Christian understanding of creation based on the Genesis narrative sees the human being as created in the image and likeness of God. The hierarchical notion of creation found in Genesis recognizes the human being as the crown and glory of all that God made—the one who was to have dominion over all other creatures. Some have even accused Christianity of being too anthropocentric.[18]

Thomas Aquinas insisted on the concept of the human being as the image of God and made this anthropology of image and participation the cornerstone of his ethical considerations. Aquinas begins the discussion of morality by recalling that the first part of the *Summa* has considered God and so the second part would consider the human being, who is an image of God, precisely because like God the human being has intellect, free will, and the power of self-determination. Thus the greatest of the medieval theologians continued the Christian tradition of supporting the dignity of human beings and seeing the human being primarily in her or his rational and volitional aspects as an image of God.[19]

Aquinas also gave great importance to the concept of *ius*—the Latin word for right. Such an emphasis was in keeping with the Thomistic acceptance of natural law. However, *ius* in Aquinas did not mean a subjective right but rather a system of objectively right relationships. *Ius* in Aquinas often signifies "the just thing itself" or the object of justice.[20] Aquinas had not

---

[18] James M. Gustafson, *Ethics from a Theocentric Perspective*, 2 vols. (Chicago: University of Chicago Press, 1981, 1984).

[19] Thomas Aquinas, *Summa theologiae*, 4 vols. (Rome: Marietti, 1952), I–II, prologus.

[20] Brian Tierney, *The Idea of Natural Rights: Studies on Natural Rights, Natural Law, and Church Law* (Atlanta, GA: Scholars, 1997), 22–27, 256–65.

made the turn to the subject. The other cardinal virtues include a relationship to the agent, but the relationship involved in justice is not to the agent but to the equality of one thing to another as, for example, in salary for the work done.[21]

Most scholars, including Catholics, have seen the early seventeenth-century Enlightenment as the most significant place for the development of subjective rights. The Enlightenment emphasized the freedom and consequently the rights of the individual. It then had enormous ramifications in cultural, political, and economic life. The American Revolution and the French Revolution of the eighteenth century are clearly associated with Enlightenment ideas. As time went on, Roman Catholicism became the implacable foe of the Enlightenment and the liberalism associated with it. By the nineteenth century, as illustrated in the pontificates of Popes Gregory XVI and Pius IX, Roman Catholicism saw itself as strongly opposing liberalism in all its forms. Theoretically, liberalism emphasized the freedom and rights of the individual person, whereas Catholics emphasized the law of God as mediated through the natural law and the duty to obey God's law. Individualistic liberalism strongly opposed the Catholic understanding of the individual as belonging to many different communities. Practically and politically, the Catholic Church vehemently resisted political changes from the old order and castigated the concept of democracy. The Catholic Church insisted on the union of church and state.[22] In the first part of the nineteenth century, some Catholic liberals tried to be more supportive of democratic regimes and the autonomy of the political and social orders, thus recognizing rights even for religious freedom. However, by the middle of the century this incipient liberal movement was squelched. As a result, the Catholic Church was seen by others and by itself as strongly opposed to liberalism. In a defensive and polemical posture, Catholicism failed to recognize the different shades of liberalism and some of its significant human aspirations.[23] In the Catholic approach associated with this nineteenth-century understanding, religious liberalism began when Luther insisted on the freedom of conscience and broke the bond between conscience and the teaching of the church. Philosophical liberalism, by insisting on autonomous human reason, cut people off from the law of God. Political

---

[21] Aquinas, *Summa theologiae*, II–II, q. 57 a. 1.

[22] See footnotes 5–7.

[23] Peter Steinfels, "The Failed Encounter: Catholic Church and Liberalism in the Nineteenth Century," in *Catholicism and Liberalism*, ed. Douglass and Hollenbach, 19–44.

liberalism rejected God's law by making the will of the majority determinative. However, this approach also condemned the economic liberalism of capitalism.[24] Without doubt the Catholic Church constituted a strong opposition to individualistic liberalism in the nineteenth century.

Change in the Twentieth Century

How did this staunch opposition change? As the twentieth century developed, the Catholic enemy (or to employ more ecumenical terms, the dialogue partner) changed. In the twentieth century totalitarianism came to the fore with its attempt to subordinate the individual to the good of society. In the light of Catholicism's defense of monarchies and denial of religious freedom, Catholicism was often somewhat tolerant of right-wing authoritarianism but strongly disagreed with Marxism and communism on the left. As the twentieth century progressed, Roman Catholicism little by little came to give much greater emphasis to the freedom, dignity, and rights of the human person. In this context the first cautious acceptance of democracy by the hierarchical magisterium came in the 1944 Christmas message of Pope Pius XII with his recognition that many people see a democratic form of government as a postulate of human reason.[25] One of those supporters of democracy was the Catholic neo-Thomist philosopher Jacques Maritain, who advocated democracy and human rights on the basis of his approach to Thomism and who later played a significant role in the 1948 United Nations' Universal Declaration of Human Rights.[26] As time went by, the Catholic commitment to democracy became stronger.

The first full-blown development of human rights in hierarchical social teaching appeared in Pope John XXIII's 1963 encyclical *Pacem in Terris*. Here John developed both political and civil rights as well as economic and social rights. These approaches to human rights are accompanied by a recognition of duties and found within a communitarian framework that still opposes the individualism often associated with

---

[24] See, for example, William J. Engelen, "Social Reflections VI: Deuteronomy versus Liberalism," *Central-Blatt and Social Justice* 15 (March 1923): 407–9; "Social Observations VII: The Saviour's Social Principles and Liberalism," *Central-Blatt and Social Justice* 16 (April 1923): 3–5.

[25] Sigmund, "Catholicism and Liberal Democracy," 226.

[26] John W. Cooper, *The Legacy of Jacques Maritain and Reinhold Niebuhr* (Macon, GA: Mercer University Press, 1985), 108–9.

Enlightenment liberalism.[27] From this time on, human rights have been developed in theory and in practice to become the primary way in which the contemporary papacy has addressed the social issues of our world.

Yes, there has been a dramatic change in the position of the Catholic Church with regard to human rights. However, this change does not mean that the Catholic Church has totally accepted the classical liberal approach associated with Enlightenment thought. Contemporary hierarchical Catholic teaching still insists on a communitarian basis for human rights and recognizes both political and civil rights as well as social and economic rights.[28]

Changed Understanding of Historical Development

The Catholic understanding of the historical development of human rights has also changed dramatically in the last two centuries. Evidence indicates that the understanding of this historical development was heavily influenced by the attitude taken to human rights. Catholic scholars in the nineteenth century who were strongly opposed to political and civil rights generally identified the origin of human rights with the Enlightenment tradition and the individualistic liberalism associated with it.

In the twentieth century Michel Villey wrote extensively on the history of human rights and its development. Villey sees a Catholic move toward the acceptance of subjective human rights in the work of the fourteenth-century philosopher and theologian William of Ockham. Thus the concept of human rights was not something unknown to Catholicism before the Enlightenment.[29]

Villey, who wrote about the historical development of human rights for almost forty years, strongly opposed the concept of subjective human rights, for he insisted on the Thomistic understanding of an objectively just order where everyone possesses her or his just share. There was no need for egoistic

---

[27] John XXIII, *Pacem in Terris*, nos. 8–37, in *Catholic Social Thought*, ed. O'Brien and Shannon, 132–37.

[28] David Hollenbach, "A Communitarian Reconstruction of Human Rights: Contributions from Catholic Tradition," in *Catholicism and Liberalism*, ed. Douglass and Hollenbach, 127–50. See also his earlier study, David Hollenbach, *Claims in Conflict: Retrieving and Renewing the Catholic Human Rights Tradition* (New York: Paulist Press, 1979).

[29] For an overview of his position, see Michel Villey, *Leçons d'histoire de la philosophie du droit*," rev. ed. (Paris: Dalloz, 1977).

clamoring for one's rights in the Thomistic approach. But the move to subjective human rights first appeared in the voluntarism and nominalism of William
of Ockham. As a voluntarist, Ockham gave great importance to God's power
and our power, not to rational ordering. As a nominalist, he insisted that only
individuals have real existence, so law must begin with the individual's claims.
Thus it was the fourteenth-century Catholic nominalist who gave birth to the
monstrous infant of understanding *ius* as a subjective power of the individual—
a concept that paved the way for the excesses of the Enlightenment.[30]

Villey's approach well illustrates the neoscholasticism that Leo XIII
authoritatively imposed on Catholic philosophy and theology in the last
quarter of the nineteenth century and which remained the primary Catholic approach to philosophy and theology until Vatican II. Thomas Aquinas
was considered the high point of philosophical and theological development. Thus it was thought that periods of decline in Catholic intellectual
life occurred when Aquinas was not acknowledged. In my judgment Leo
XIII used Aquinas to prevent any dialogue with modern philosophies, especially those in any way associated with the Enlightenment. Neoscholasticism
generally identified Ockham as one of the first villains whose nominalism
and voluntarism destroyed the synthesis of Aquinas. However, Thomistic
revivals in the sixteenth century and again in the nineteenth and twentieth centuries, thanks to Leo XIII's intervention, once again recognized
the perennial philosophy of Thomas Aquinas, which was so opposed to the
concept of subjective human rights.[31]

In the last few years Brian Tierney and his student Charles Reid have
convincingly challenged Villey's thesis.[32] Yes, Thomas Aquinas did not have
an understanding of subjective rights, but the thirteenth-century canon
lawyers known as the Decretalists possessed a well-developed, explicit
understanding of subjective rights. In this view the Catholic legal system
developed the theoretical and practical understanding of subjective rights
before Ockham. Thus historically the concept of human rights did not begin
with the Enlightenment or with Ockham, but these subjective rights are

---

[30] Michel Villey, "La genèse du droit subjectif chez Gillaume d'Occam," *Archives
de Philosophie du Droit* 9 (1964): 97–127.

[31] For a very significant study of nineteenth-century neoscholasticism, see Gerald
A. McCool, *Catholic Theology in the Nineteenth Century: The Quest for a Unitary
Method* (New York: Seabury, 1977).

[32] Tierney, *Idea of Natural Rights,* 1–203; Charles J. Reid Jr., "The Canonistic
Contribution to the Western Rights Tradition: An Historical Inquiry," *Boston College
Law Review* 33 (1991): 37–92.

found in thirteenth-century canon lawyers. Yes, significant developments occurred with Ockham and later with Grotius and the Enlightenment, but the idea of subjective rights was not foreign to the earlier Catholic tradition.

The Protestant Approach

The mainstream Protestant churches also had their problems with the concept of human rights. In general, Protestantism was more open to the concept of freedom associated with the first generation of civil and political rights than was Roman Catholicism. Protestantism never saw itself in total opposition to the Enlightenment as did Roman Catholicism. However, Protestantism had problems with the concept of human rights and the anthropological foundation for these rights. According to Erich Weingärtner, for much of its history, mainstream Protestantism opposed human rights as the product of a humanistic philosophy.[33] Even after the United Nations' Declaration in 1948 many Protestants still had problems with the term and concept of human rights even though they agreed with the basic content involved.[34]

The problem with the term and concept of human rights comes from theological concerns. Human rights, natural rights, or the rights of man (to use the term often employed to describe the same reality) emphasize the rational and human perspective, whereas many Protestants insisted on a distinctively theological foundation and basis for these realities in God's actions. However, since 1950 Protestant theologians and churches have come to propose such a theological foundation (God's gracious act of creation grounds human dignity and rights) and have become stalwart champions of human rights. Ironically, Roman Catholicism never had the same problem with the concept of human rights. The Catholic natural law theory was quite open to seeing human reason and human nature as the foundation for moral realities.

Change with Regard to Political and Civil Rights

In discussing political and civil rights this section will concentrate on religious liberty, which from the viewpoint of the churches has been the most important and/or problematic of political rights. Here too the historical

---

[33] Weingärtner, "Human Rights," 486.
[34] Egmond, "Calvinist Thought and Human Rights," 193.

development shows the fascinating and tortuous path that led from reluctance or hostility to acceptance, but once again some elements in the Christian tradition from its very beginning were not necessarily hostile to religious liberty.[35]

The gospels insist that Jesus freely calls disciples to follow him. Both the freedom of God in giving the gift and the freedom of the disciple in responding are emphasized. The free will of human beings is seen in the rejection of Jesus by many. The possibility of accepting or rejecting Jesus recognizes the fundamental importance of human freedom with regard to religious belief.

A very significant development that profoundly influenced subsequent church teaching occurred with Augustine at the end of the fourth century. In the struggle with the Donatist dissidents, Augustine moved from his earlier position that the church should only use persuasion and justified the church's asking the state to use force to punish heretics and schismatics. Augustine argued from two New Testament passages. God used force to convert St. Paul; and, in the parable of the prepared banquet with no guests, the servants were sent out to compel people to come into the banquet (Luke 14:16–24). The famous Latin phrase "*compelle intrare*" set the tone for much of the subsequent Christian approach. Augustine maintained that if the state can prevent people from killing themselves physically, it can prevent them from killing themselves spiritually. Thus began the long history of the Catholic Church's using force and violence against heretics in the name of the gospel.[36]

The Catholic Approach

Thomas Aquinas in the thirteenth century well summarizes the teaching and practice of the Catholic Church in the Middle Ages. Those who have never accepted the Catholic faith, such as gentiles and Jews, should not be forced to believe because to believe is an act of the free will. However, if these infidels impede or persecute the true Christian faith, then the faithful can make war against them. The treatment of Native Americans by the

---

[35] For an excellent essay on the historical development of religious liberty, see Brian Tierney, "Religious Rights: An Historical Perspective," in *Religious Liberty in Western Thought*, ed. Noel B. Reynolds and W. Cole Durham Jr. (Atlanta, GA: Scholars, 1996), 29–57. This entire volume is most helpful on the topic of religious liberty.

[36] René Coste, *Théologie de la liberté religieuse: Liberté de conscience—Liberté de religion* (Gembloux, France: J. Duculot, 1969), 286–91.

Spanish conquistadors shows how this teaching could be abused in practice. However, it was believed that heretics and schismatics should be physically forced to fulfill what they have promised and to hold on to what they had received. An important difference was maintained between those who once accepted the Catholic faith and those who had never accepted it.[37]

However, since the beginning of the second millennium, popes have insisted on the freedom of the church vis-à-vis the state. The church has to be free from the state in order to carry out its proper mission. The Catholic Church strongly insisted on the freedom of the church down through the years. However, this freedom of the church was not extended to the freedom of the believer until the second part of the twentieth century.[38]

The defensive posture of the Counter-Reformation only made Catholics insist all the more that the Catholic Church was the one true church and that there was a need for the union of church and state. It seemed even more apparent, especially in the light of the Constantinian heritage of the union of church and state, that civil peace and unity could exist only in a country with religious unity.

The opposition to the Enlightenment only intensified the Catholic opposition to religious freedom. The excesses of the French Revolution and the attempt of European liberals to remove the church from public life and the public square heightened the Catholic opposition to the freedoms and rights of liberalism, especially religious liberty. The Catholic Constantinian history and tradition, an authoritative or at least paternalistic notion of the state, and the subordination of freedom to truth, especially the religious truth of the Catholic religion, grounded the Catholic opposition to religious liberty until Vatican II.[39]

However, some changes were developing. The first change, as is often the case, was pragmatic. After Pope Pius IX's Syllabus of Errors, Bishop Felix Dupanloup of Orléans, France, interpreted the strong condemnation of religious liberty in the light of the distinction between thesis and hypothesis. The thesis is the ideal which should exist. The hypothesis is the historically necessary acceptance of something less than the ideal. Thus in religiously pluralistic

---

[37] Aquinas, *Summa theologiae*, II–II, q. 10, a.8.

[38] Tierney, "Religious Rights," 34–36. Note that the Russian Orthodox Church today insists on the freedom of the church but has difficulty accepting the religious liberty of all citizens.

[39] For the development from these arguments to the acceptance of religious liberty, see John Courtney Murray, *The Problem of Religious Freedom* (Westminster, MD: Newman, 1965).

countries one could tolerate the existence of religious freedom as a means of obtaining greater goods or avoiding greater evils.[40] Many Catholics including popes accepted this distinction, which in practice managed to moderate somewhat the strong opposition to religious liberty in Catholic hierarchical teaching. However, the implication of the distinction was still clear. If Catholics ever became the predominant religious group, the ideal of the union of church and state and the corresponding denial of religious liberty should come into play. The solution proposed by the distinction between thesis and hypothesis was a pragmatic way of living with the reality of a pluralistic society, but it fell far short of accepting a concept of religious liberty.

The second development, as detailed in preceding chapters, concerned the Catholic opposition to collectivism and totalitarianism, especially of the left, as the twentieth century developed. Papal teaching began to recognize and even emphasize the dignity, freedom, and rights of the person over against the state. In this movement toward accepting political and civil rights, religious liberty was the major obstacle and the last holdout.

Finally Vatican II, in 1965, accepted religious liberty. However, the acceptance of religious liberty, especially in terms of its grounding, still differed in many ways from secular and Protestant justifications. Yes, the freedom of the act of faith and the role of conscience are important, but the justification of religious liberty shows the influence of John Courtney Murray in seeing religious liberty primarily as an article of peace and not an article of faith. Religious liberty in society is not primarily a theological or moral issue but a juridical or constitutional issue, which has foundations in theology, ethics, and political philosophy. A limited constitutional government has no role to play in directing the religious lives of its citizens.[41]

Thus only in 1965 did the Roman Catholic Church come to the acceptance of religious liberty after this long and somewhat tortuous development in which it obviously learned from many others the significance and importance of civil and political rights, especially the right to religious liberty. With religious liberty finally in place, the Catholic Church could then accept and propose the importance of these civil and political rights

---

[40] Roger Aubert, "Mgr. Dupanloup et le syllabus," *Revue d'Histoire Ecclésiastique* 51 (1956): 79–142, 471–512, 837–915.

[41] Murray, *Problem of Religious Freedom*, 17–31. For an overview of Protestant approaches to human rights, see Robert Traer, *Faith in Human Rights: Support in Religious Traditions for a Global Struggle* (Washington, DC: Georgetown University Press, 1991), 19–31.

originally associated with liberalism. However, Catholicism sees these rights existing together with social and economic rights and both types of rights grounded in the community and not in an isolated individual.

The Protestant Approach

Protestantism has been much more open to freedom in general than Catholicism. Mainstream Protestantism accepted religious liberty long before Catholicism, but again the first step in the direction of religious liberty was pragmatic as it was much later for Catholicism.[42] Martin Luther[43] and John Calvin[44] did not accept religious liberty. Roland Bainton, an influential American Protestant historian, uses Calvin to illustrate the peak of Protestant intolerance and persecution.[45]

The first movement toward religious liberty came from the left wing of the Protestant Reformation with such groups as the Mennonites, the Baptists, and the Quakers. These minority groups had often been the object of persecution, and hence they strongly defended religious liberty against the majority religion. From 1500 into the 1700s religious wars wracked Europe. Some religions were again persecuted, and they called for religious liberty. As a result of these wars, stronger national states arose, which commanded the loyalty of people of different religions. Religious liberty in the United States resulted from the pragmatic fact that many different religions already existed in the colonies. Pennsylvania, with its Quaker origins, had accepted religious liberty in a theoretical manner and not simply as a pragmatic adjustment to existing reality. As time went on, seventeenth-century Protestant thinkers gradually moved to seeing religious liberty as compatible with and even based on their faith and theology. By the end of the seventeenth century the theory of religious liberty was proposed as

---

[42] J. Robert Nelson, "Human Rights in Creation and Redemption: A Protestant View," in *Human Rights in Religious Traditions*, ed. Arlene Swidler (New York: Pilgrim, 1982), 1–12.

[43] Steven E. Ozment, "Martin Luther on Religious Liberty," in *Religious Liberty in Western Thought*, ed. Reynolds and Durham, 75–82.

[44] John Witte Jr., "Moderate Religious Liberty in the Theology of John Calvin," in *Religious Liberty in Western Thought*, ed. Reynolds and Durham, 83–122. There are aspects of Calvin's theology that were later used to justify religious liberty.

[45] Roland H. Bainton, *The Travail of Religious Liberty: Nine Biographical Studies* (Philadelphia: Westminster, 1951), 54–71.

grounded in Protestant theology, but implementing religious liberty took some time.[46]

Protestantism thus accepted religious liberty much earlier than Catholicism and was also more open to the content of political and civil rights than was Catholicism. Protestantism put much more stress on conscience and its freedom. Protestant theology saw the church as a gathered community or voluntary association of individuals in contrast to the Catholic organic notion of the church as God's community of salvation, which was necessary for all those who were to be saved. Thus it was much easier for Protestants to see religious liberty for all as an implication of their own faith. Catholic understanding of the one true church as the only means of salvation made it much harder to accept religious liberty for other faiths. The greater Protestant emphasis on the individual and freedom of conscience together with the more democratic quality of Protestant churches resulted in a strong affinity between Protestantism and democracy as it developed in the Western world.[47] The famous thesis of Max Weber, which continues to be hotly debated, saw Protestantism as the ripe soil for capitalism.[48] However, Protestantism did not lose sight of the Christian concern for the poor and the needy. Despite problems with the concept or term of human rights or natural rights, mainstream Protestantism long before the twentieth century became sympathetic to and supportive of religious liberty and the concepts behind political and civil rights.

Religious liberty was a significant topic in the modern Protestant ecumenical movement in the twentieth century. The International Missionary Council explicitly raised the religious liberty issue in the context of Protestant missionaries in colonial lands at its 1928 meeting in Jerusalem. Subsequent years saw the topic of religious liberty become quite significant in the international ecumenical movement. The Commission of the Churches on International Affairs (CCIA) played a significant role in the final drafting of the article on religious liberty in the United Nations' Universal Declaration of Human Rights in 1948. The WCC from its first meeting in Amsterdam in 1948 gave great importance to religious liberty as the primary human right. The CCIA was also instrumental in bringing about the United Nations Commission on Human Rights and actively

---

[46] Tierney, "Religious Rights," 46–55.

[47] Graham Maddox, *Religion and the Rise of Democracy* (New York: Routledge, 1996).

[48] Max Weber, *The Protestant Ethic and the Spirit of Capitalism* (New York: Charles Scribner's Sons, 1958).

participated in the composition of the two 1966 International Covenants on Human Rights.[49] Thus the Protestant churches were comparatively very early and strong supporters of religious freedom, the freedom of conscience for all, and the content of civil and political rights despite some problems with the terminology of human or natural rights.

Change with Regard to Social and Economic Rights

The Christian church from its inception has insisted on the care and concern for the poor, the needy, the sick, the outcast, the marginalized. The church has tried to provide for people in need as evidenced by the origin of hospitals and places to care for the sick. Concern for the poor was very clear in the scriptures and exemplified in the work of deacons in the New Testament. Concern for orphans and widows has been rather constant in the Judeo-Christian tradition.

The Catholic Approach

As mentioned, eighteenth- and nineteenth-century Catholicism strongly opposed liberalism and the rights movement associated with the Enlightenment, but Catholics were more open to social and economic rights. Pope Leo XIII, in his 1891 encyclical *Rerum Novarum* marking the beginning of modern papal social teaching, explicitly recognized such social and economic rights. The purpose of the encyclical in the light of the misery and wretchedness affecting the majority of the poor is to "define the relative rights and mutual duties of the wealthy and of the poor."[50] Leo XIII recognizes both duties and rights, bases these rights on the transcendent dignity of the human being, and recognizes the right to possess what is necessary for life—rights to food, clothing, and shelter, and the right to free association so that workers can protect themselves. The encyclical insists on the right to private property but wants that right extended in a wider way to the poor. The state should give special consideration to protecting the rights of the poor and the helpless.[51]

---

[49] Jerald D. Gort, "The Christian Ecumenical Reception of Human Rights," in *Human Rights and Religious Values*, ed. An-Na'im et al., 206–7; N. Koshy, "Religious Liberty," in *Dictionary of the Ecumenical Movement*, ed. Lossky et al., 859–63.

[50] Pope Leo XIII, *Rerum Novarum*, nos. 1–2, in *Catholic Social Thought*, ed. O'Brien and Shannon, 14–15.

[51] Ibid, nos. 30–38, in *Catholic Social Thought*, ed. O'Brien and Shannon, 28–34.

As mentioned, the first full-blown discussion of human rights in modern papal teaching occurred in *Pacem in Terris* with its insistence on duties and rights as well as political and economic rights. The primary difficulty for the Catholic tradition had been political and civil rights. There was no great controversy or dispute in accepting social and economic rights. However, social and economic rights occasioned serious tensions and divisions for Catholics in the subsequent years. After Vatican II greater emphasis shifted to national and local churches. In Latin America, liberation theology came to the fore. In many countries the local Catholic Church was identified with the struggle on behalf of the poor and often opposed political oligarchies and dictators defending the status quo. Catholics could generally agree in theory about social and economic rights, but great disagreements centered on the concrete way of securing these rights. In Latin America, for example, some insisted on the need for a democratic socialist form of government while others emphasized the need to reform capitalism. The tensions and struggles were very serious.[52]

The Protestant Approach

Mainstream Protestantism showed the same concerns with the poor and the needy. The modern Protestant ecumenical movement in the twentieth century recognized many social problems in the first part of the twentieth century, some of which were associated with colonialism—economic justice, peace, racism, social change—but none of these were viewed from the concept or language of human rights. At the first meeting of the WCC at Amsterdam in 1948 and in subsequent years, the primary emphasis in human rights was given to religious liberty as the first and most important of political and civil rights.[53]

Developments on many fronts occurred in the 1960s and '70s.[54] The Cold War, the invasion of the Dominican Republic by the United States in 1965 and that of Czechoslovakia by Russia in 1968, the Vietnam War, the

---

[52] Margaret E. Crahan, "Catholicism and Human Rights in Latin America," in *Religious Diversity and Human Rights*, ed. Bloom, Martin, and Proudfoot, 262–77; Hehir, "Religious Activism for Human Rights," 111–17.

[53] Gort, "Christian Ecumenical Reception of Human Rights," 204–7.

[54] The following overview of the work of the WCC is based on José Zalaquett, *The Human Rights Issues and the Human Rights Movement: Characterization, Evaluation, Propositions* (Geneva: WCC, 1981); Erich Weingärtner, *Human Rights on the Ecumenical Agenda: Report and Assessment* (Geneva: WCC, 1983).

rise of repressive regimes in many areas, the struggle of oppressed people for liberation, the Helsinki Accords, and many other significant events were occasions for the discussion of human rights. The WCC itself knew the tensions existing among the churches of the first world, of the second world, and of the third world. Human rights and their vindication became a burning issue in both theory and in practice.

The WCC sponsored a meeting at St. Pölten in Austria in 1974 to deal with human rights. Some, especially from the first world, saw political and civil rights as primary and the only true human rights with singular importance given to religious liberty. The second approach emphasized the social nature of human beings and insisted on social and economic rights as well as what has been called the third generation of human rights—the rights of oppressed people and cultures to achieve their own identity and just desserts. Proponents of political and civil rights stressed denunciation and advocacy as the best strategies to promote human rights. But the second group logically called for political action to deal with the root causes of poverty, oppression, and exploitation. The St. Pölten consultation and the subsequent work of the Fifth Assembly of the WCC in Nairobi in 1975 achieved a remarkable consensus by recognizing the broad concept of human rights embracing all human rights with no primacy given to religious liberty in particular or to political and civil rights in general. Likewise, the WCC from that time took a more active role in enabling oppressed people to secure their rights. Many practical tensions and divisions continued to erupt, but there was general agreement about the content of human rights and the strategies to implement these rights around the globe. The WCC's Program to Combat Racism established in 1968 occasioned many tensions by contributing small amounts of money for humanitarian purposes to resistance groups in the third world, some of whom advocated the use of violence.

This section has shown that the WCC experienced many more tensions in arriving at an acceptance of social and economic rights, including rights in the third world, than had papal social teaching. This is explained by the nature of the WCC with member churches representing the different perspectives of first world countries, second world countries, and third world countries and with their rightful insistence on practical ways of dealing with the root causes of the abridgment of social and economic rights. The Catholic papal tradition did not experience many tensions in arriving at the theoretical insistence on social and political rights, but subsequently national and local Catholic churches experienced similar divisions in trying to protect and promote social and economic rights for the poor and the oppressed.

Problems and tensions continue to exist with regard to understanding human rights and to implementing them. For example, on the theoretical level some now speak of the rights of future generations and of environmental rights as a fourth generation of rights. However, mainstream Protestantism and Roman Catholicism have come to a remarkable agreement on the theory, content, and practical promotion of human rights in our world.

This concluding section focuses on what the Roman Catholic Church can learn from the development of its approach to human rights. The section discusses four important points—methodology of theological social ethics, the learning church, dialogue, and development with real change.

Moral methodology. The history shows the various elements that have entered into this change in the Catholic understanding of human rights. Scripture, tradition, theological concerns, historical and cultural realities, human experience, philosophical concepts, and pragmatic needs—all have played a role in fashioning the development of the understanding of human rights in the Roman Catholic tradition. At its best the Catholic theological tradition has recognized such a methodology in theory, but it has not always applied it in practice.

This development shows the importance of two traditional methodological approaches in Catholic moral theology—the importance of tradition and a proper role for the human. The Catholic approach has recognized that the scripture alone is not sufficient for theology and the life of the church. The historical insistence on scripture and tradition often resulted in a poor understanding of both of these realities, but the recognition of the need for tradition is significant. From a theological perspective tradition is based on the fact that the community of the church exists in time and space and continues to live under the inspiration of the Holy Spirit. The church must understand, live, and appropriate the word and work of Jesus in the light of the ongoing historical and cultural circumstances of time and place.

Catholic methodology has also recognized human reason and human nature as sources of moral wisdom and knowledge for the Christian. The Roman Catholic natural law theory has been criticized from many perspectives, but its insistence on the human as a source for moral wisdom is most important and helpful. The history of the development of the Catholic Church's understanding of human rights shows how much the church has learned from human sources of moral knowledge. The earlier Catholic tradition with its lack of historical consciousness did not give that much importance to human experience, but in the light of historical change and development, such as the one on human rights, we are very conscious of how important a role human experience plays in the church's understanding. Of course, critical questions need to be raised to test human reason and human experience in order to determine if they are true and not erroneous. The development with regard to human rights thus illustrates the basic sound-ness of the Roman Catholic theological method with its acceptance of the human but also shows the importance of human experience as well as human reason as sources of wisdom and knowledge.

Dialogue as a way of learning. The development of the teaching on human rights together with the need for multiple sources of moral wisdom and knowledge underscores the importance of dialogue for learning about morality. Dialogue does not mean that one simply accepts the position expressed by others; these positions must also be tested. But dialogue recog-nizes the need to be open to learn from others. There is no doubt that the Catholic Church has learned from others the importance of religious liberty and of all the political and civil rights. However, here too the Catholic Church has not merely accepted in an uncritical way all that has been said by others. The Catholic position correctly insists on civil and political rights today, but it sees them as rooted in the realty of human society and commu-nity and not simply based on the rights of individuals seen as isolated monads. Likewise, the acceptance of religious liberty is not based on a reli-gious indifferentism, which has often characterized the approach of others. True dialogue will always be open to learn from others but also is prepared at times to criticize them when necessary.

Church as learner. The Roman Catholic tradition has often insisted on the role of the church as a moral teacher, but the developing understanding of human rights shows the importance of seeing the church as a learner as well. Without doubt the church has learned much from many sources to arrive at its contemporary understanding of human rights. The method of dialogue mentioned above and the learning process illustrated in the under-standing of human rights point out that the church must learn even before it can teach. An older understanding of the deposit of faith thought that the church already had all that it needed in order to teach. However, even on questions of doctrine, the church itself has learned, as illustrated in the very fundamental question of the understanding of God as Trinity. This doctrine was not found explicitly in the scripture but was only learned in the tradition through the community reflecting on its faith under the inspiration of the Holy Spirit. It is even more true in moral matters that the church has to learn before it can teach because the Catholic Church now recognizes that its moral teaching depends heavily on human reason and experience.

Development with real change. No one can deny the tremendous development and change that has occurred in the Roman Catholic Church's teaching on human rights. Development properly understood includes both continuities and discontinuities, as is well illustrated in this particular case.

The Roman Catholic tradition has had a tendency to overemphasize the continuities and downplay the discontinuities in its understanding of development with regard to its own teaching. Nowhere is this clearer than in its official understanding of the development that took place with regard to religious liberty. At the Second Vatican Council the question of religious liberty raised the even more basic question of change and development in official church teaching. Nineteenth-century papal teaching strongly condemned religious liberty. How could the Roman Catholic Church teach in the twentieth century what it had denied in the nineteenth century? Proponents of the newer teaching maintained that changing historical circumstances explained the development. The nineteenth-century teaching was correct at its time, but in changed historical circumstances a different teaching was required. The proponents of religious liberty at Vatican II did not explicitly recognize that the earlier teaching in any time or place had been wrong.[55]

The Vatican II Declaration on Religious Liberty skips very quickly and loosely over the reality of past teachings on religious liberty. "Throughout the ages she has preserved and handed on the doctrine which she has received from her Master and the Apostles. Although in the life of the People of God in its pilgrimage through the vicissitudes of human history there has at times appeared a form of behavior which was hardly in keeping with the spirit of the gospel and was even opposed to it, it has always remained the teaching of the church that no one is to be coerced into believing."[56] At best this statement is disingenuous. The document recognizes some error or problem with regard to occasional forms of behavior but not with regard to official church teaching. However, many papal documents justified the

[55] Emile-Joseph de Smedt, "Religious Freedom," in *Council Speeches of Vatican II*, ed. Yves Congar, Hans Küng, and Daniel O'Hanlon (London: Sheed and Ward, 1964), 160–68; Murray, *Problem of Religious Freedom*, 47–84.

[56] Declaration on Religious Liberty, no. 12, in *Vatican Council II*, ed. Flannery, 809.

use of force in religious matters and denied religious liberty. Although the Catholic tradition recognized even in the Middle Ages that no one was to be coerced into believing the first time as the Vatican document explicitly recognizes, the official teaching also accepted the use of force against heretics and schismatics—part of the teaching not mentioned in the Declaration on Religious Liberty. It is much too simplistic to explain the development by simply saying that the historical circumstances had changed and that the teaching was always right in the light of the circumstances. At the very minimum in a number of different areas, church teaching was wrong and should have changed much earlier than it did.

The history of the church's attitude toward human rights shows that development involves both continuities and discontinuities. Too often hierarchical Catholic teaching has been unwilling to admit the discontinuities and has seen development almost solely in terms of evolution and continuities. Development is much messier and more complicated than a simple evolutionary theory is willing to recognize.

The shift in the Christian churches' understanding of human rights from reluctance or hostility to acceptance is a remarkable story that not only calls for an explanation of its development but also contributes to our understanding of the way in which the church learns and teaches morality.

Chapter 5

THE CATHOLIC TRADITION IN DIALOGUE WITH THE BLACK THEOLOGICAL ETHICS OF J. DEOTIS ROBERTS*

To my knowledge no real dialogue of Catholics with J. Deotis Roberts's theological writings has taken place, and that is unfortunate. Catholic theology and ethics, to its shame, in the past has not been in much conversation with black theology in this country. Recently, however, some dialogue has taken place, especially with the work of James Cone. Cone himself has explicitly addressed the Catholic Church and the Catholic theological tradition.[1] Black Catholic theologians in response have engaged in important dialogue with Cone.[2] The thesis of this essay maintains that strong affinities exist between the theology of J. Deotis Roberts and theology in the Roman Catholic tradition. Consequently, dialogue between the two will be helpful and constructive, and the Catholic tradition can learn significant insights from Roberts's work.

J. Deotis Roberts and Catholics

Although Roberts has not addressed the Catholic tradition and community as explicitly and directly as James Cone, he is quite familiar with the Catholic approach. I first had contact with J. Deotis Roberts in

---

*   Originally published as Charles E. Curran, "J. Deotis Roberts and the Roman Catholic Tradition," in *The Quest for Liberation and Reconciliation: Essays in Honor of J. Deotis Roberts,* ed. Michael Battle (Louisville, KY: Westminster John Knox Press, 2005), 82–92. Used with permission.

[1]   James H. Cone, *Speaking the Truth: Ecumenism, Liberation, and Black Theology* (Grand Rapids, MI: W. B. Eerdmans, 1986).

[2]   The December 2000 issue of *Theological Studies* is dedicated entirely to "The Catholic Reception of Black Theology," with articles by Diana L. Hayes, M. Shawn Copeland, Cyprian Davis, Jamie T. Phelps, and Bryan N. Massingale and a final piece by James H. Cone. See *Theological Studies* 61, no. 4 (December 2000).

the middle and late 1960s when he was teaching at Howard University and I was a young assistant professor of theology at the Catholic University of America. In fact, we invited him to teach at Catholic University in the 1968–69 school year. Later I recall recommending that a white religious woman student who had worked in the inner city visit Professor Roberts at Howard to see if she could take courses with him. I believe she took two courses with him and frequently talked with him about her own ministry. She has often told me that she remains ever grateful for the help and the knowledge that Professor Roberts so graciously gave her. In the 1970s I assigned his book, *Liberation and Reconciliation*, as required reading for my course in social ethics at Catholic University, which was directed primarily, but not exclusively, to Catholic seminarians.

Deotis Roberts's first venture into black theology came at a conference titled "Black Church/Black Theology," which was sponsored jointly by the Graymoor Ecumenical Institute and the Georgetown University Department of Theology in 1969. The coordinator of the conference was a young white Graymoor priest, Father James Gardiner, who had been a student of Deotis Roberts at Catholic University.[3] From that beginning in 1969, Deotis Roberts has gone on to develop his understanding of African American theology and ethics in many significant publications and books. In the process, he has read and appreciated the work of Catholic liberation theologians in South America. He has also dialogued with a few other Catholic theologians, such as Avery Dulles.[4]

Professor Roberts has only occasionally commented on the Roman Catholic Church, but his comments have been both strong and perceptive. He has pointed out and forthrightly criticized the racism in the Catholic Church. Black Catholics have experienced powerlessness in a powerful church. The move by Father George Stallings to launch his Imani Temple for disenchanted black Catholics in 1989 was both logical and inevitable.[5] No honest Catholic can deny that charge. We white Catholic theologians have also contributed to the problem. I personally have never written

---

[3] James J. Gardiner and J. Deotis Roberts, eds., *Quest for a Black Theology* (Philadelphia: Pilgrim Press, 1971), xi.

[4] J. Deotis Roberts, *Black Theology in Dialogue* (Philadelphia: Westminster, 1987), 48–51; J. Deotis Roberts, *The Prophethood of Black Believers: An African-American Political Theology for Ministry* (Louisville, KY: Westminster/John Knox, 1994), 9, 49.

[5] J. Deotis Roberts, "Status of Black Catholics," *Journal of Religious Thought* 48 (1991): 74–75; see also J. Deotis Roberts, *Black Theology Today: Liberation and Contextualization* (New York: Edwin Mellen, 1983), 153.

anything substantial on racism despite the oppression and injustice suffered by African Americans in my church and in our society.

Roberts has been both appreciative and supportive of black Catholics. Despite his recognition of the inevitability of the Stallings church, Roberts affirms that a black Catholic layperson who is a friend of his who appreciated the African American culture of the Imani Temple elected to stay in the Catholic Church despite its racism.[6] Professor Roberts has often been called on to be a retreat leader among black Catholics and was pleasantly surprised to find them seeking to recover their African roots.[7] He realistically recognizes the need for black Catholic leadership. Unfortunately, clerical celibacy together with racism discourages many blacks from becoming priests. Some black bishops have been appointed, but Roberts points out with wry wisdom that bishops of whatever race or denomination are cautious and conservative. The Catholic Church desperately needs to develop good black theologians. He was disappointed that a black Catholic theologian, Father Edward K. Braxton, was more interested in metaphysics as a basis for black theology than in black history and culture. (Braxton is now the bishop of Belleville, Illinois.) Roberts also perceptively recognizes that some of the best minds among black Catholics today are black Catholic women scholars.[8]

Affinities between Roberts and Roman Catholic Theology

But I want to move beyond Roberts's familiarity with Catholic theology and his sharp and perceptive comments on racism in the Catholic Church and the plight of black Catholics. The bulk of this essay will demonstrate strong and significant affinities between Roberts's theology and the Roman Catholic theological tradition.

Ironically, one can apparently cite J. Deotis Roberts as disagreeing with my thesis. Roberts has recognized that much of Latin American liberation theology comes out of the Roman Catholic theological tradition. He also points to a developing black Catholic theology in Francophone Africa. But he explains "the similarity of Roman Catholic and Protestant Afro-American theology more on cultural grounds than on theological foundations."[9]

---

[6] J. Deotis Roberts, *Africentric Christianity: A Theological Approach for Ministry* (Valley Forge, PA: Judson, 2000), 81–82.

[7] Ibid., 100.

[8] Roberts, "Status of Black Catholics," 77; Roberts, *Black Theology Today*, 23ff.

[9] Roberts, *Black Theology in Dialogue*, 47.

In one sense I agree with Roberts. The communality of Catholic liberation theology and African American theology stems directly from the analogous situation of oppressed people who are victims of injustice and sinful social structures. But at a deeper level there exist strong affinities between Roberts's own theology and theology in the Roman Catholic tradition. I now want to prove this point.

The Roman Catholic Theological Method

Roman Catholic is also catholic with a small "c." Catholic is universal, all-embracing, and all-inclusive. The theological thesis for this universality and inclusivity comes from the belief that God is creator and redeemer, and thus all reality is related to God.

Two significant theological methodological approaches follow from this all-inclusive catholicity. First, the Catholic approach has insisted on a "both-and" approach. Karl Barth has said his greatest problem with Roman Catholicism was its "and." At the very minimum, Barth has put his finger on what is characteristic of the Catholic theological approach. This "catholic and" figured prominently in the classical Protestant and Catholic polemics which in the last decades have happily been transformed. Protestants emphasized the scripture alone; Catholics insisted on scripture and tradition. Protestants stressed faith alone; Catholics, faith and reason. Protestants insisted on grace alone; Catholics, on grace and works. Protestants emphasized Jesus alone; Catholics insisted on Jesus, and Mary, and the saints.[10] In my judgment at times, the Catholic tradition puts the two aspects together rather poorly. In the above both-and approaches, the first aspect is the more significant and the second is the junior partner and in some way dependent on the first. But for some Catholics tradition became more important than scripture, reason more important than faith, works more significant than grace, and Mary more important than Jesus. But properly understood, the both-and approach, in my judgment, makes great theological sense.

A second characteristic of Catholic theological method, following from the all-inclusive attitude and the recognition of both creation and redemption, is analogical thinking based especially on the analogy of being.[11]

---

[10] From a Roman Catholic perspective, see Hans Urs von Balthasar, *The Theology of Karl Barth* (New York: Holt, Rinehart, and Winston, 1971), 40ff.

[11] Andrew M. Greeley, *The Catholic Imagination* (Berkeley: University of California Press, 2000); David Tracy, *The Analogical Imagination: Christian Theology and the Culture of Pluralism* (New York: Crossroad, 1981).

The shadow of the creator is found in all of creation. From what we see in creation, we can learn something about God. The danger in the Catholic tradition was to forget that an analogy is partly the same and partly different. Too often the Catholic tradition has claimed to know more than is possible about God. Contemporary Catholic theology uses different words and concepts here but still frequently insists on an analogical approach by which we can go from the human to the divine, even though we must be careful in the process. Here again Karl Barth explicitly opposes the analogy of being. For Barth, one cannot go from the human to the divine; one must always start with God and God's revelation in Jesus Christ.[12]

I believe the Christian tradition from its very beginning has used such an analogical approach. For example, why do we celebrate Christmas on December 25? We have no idea what day or even what year Jesus was born. December 25 falls during the darkest part of the year. It seems most fitting (this is the word the Catholic tradition uses in developing analogy—the Latin word is *conveniens*) to celebrate the coming of salvation and light into the world at this time. In addition, there were pagan feasts at the same time that Christians took over and transformed in the light of their own faith. Yes, it is most fitting that we celebrate Christmas at that time of year, but there is also a problem that is inherent in analogical thinking. This makes great sense from the perspective of one in the northern hemisphere. But what about one in the southern hemisphere? Here too there is a danger of the northern hemisphere imposing its own views and perspective on the southern hemisphere. We must constantly be conscious of the danger of making God into our image and likeness, but still analogical thinking about God is most helpful if one is conscious of the dangers.

Roberts's Theological Methodology

J. Deotis Roberts frequently describes his own methodology as both-and and as holistic. "It is important to remind ourselves that the black perspective is 'holistic.' Even our way of thinking is 'both-and.'"[13] No reader of Roberts can deny his insistence on a holistic and both-and approach.

In the course of all his writings, going back over a period of almost fifty years, Roberts consistently and often disagreed with the neoorthodox

---

[12] Will Herberg, introduction to Karl Barth, *Community, State, and Church: Three Essays* (Garden City, NY: Doubleday Anchor, 1960), 22–38.

[13] Roberts, *Prophethood of Black Believers*, 110.

theology of Karl Barth. There is no doubt that he disagrees with Barth more than with any other white theologian he has discussed. Roberts's first two books were in the area of philosophical theology, and he returned to this topic in his 1991 *A Philosophical Introduction to Theology*. "In Protestant theology we find a powerful challenge to the philosophical approach to theology in neoorthodoxy under the leadership of Karl Barth. Theology turned anti-intellectual and advocated biblical revelation as the sole source of religious knowledge."[14] He wrote the 1991 book because his holistic understanding of religion requires and deserves the best that our intellects have to offer in the service of faith. Philosophy has been an instrument for theological interpretation throughout Christian history. Today faith continues to seek understanding in philosophy. Faith has priority, but "reason is the means by which we enrich and enhance our understanding of faith. We love God from the top of our minds as well as from the bottom of our hearts."[15]

In addition, Roberts's corpus on black and African American theology and ethics also frequently disagrees with Karl Barth. Very often this disagreement comes out in his early criticism of the influence of Barth on the liberation theology of James Cone.

The beginning of the very first chapter of *A Black Political Theology* published in 1974 deals with foundations and method. For Roberts, "James Cone will need to break with Barthianism if he is to enter into meaningful dialogue with African theologians who are taking seriously their pre-colonial religious traditions." A narrow Christological view of revelation based on Karl Barth is inadequate. "Black theology requires an understanding of revelation sufficiently comprehensive to deal with the pan-African context of the black religious experience.... What would be helpful is an understanding of the revelation of God as manifest in all creation and all history as measured by the supreme revelation of God in the incarnation."[16] Roberts frequently criticizes Barth and his influence on Cone while recognizing some movement of Cone away from a Barthian approach.[17] Our author also criticizes Jürgen

---

[14] J. Deotis Roberts, *A Philosophical Introduction to Theology* (Philadelphia: Trinity Press International, 1991), 14.

[15] Ibid., 6–7.

[16] J. Deotis Roberts, *A Black Political Theology* (Philadelphia: Westminster, 1974), 19–20.

[17] Ibid., 122–24; Roberts, *Black Theology Today*, 38–42, 118; J. Deotis Roberts, "Black Theological Ethics: A Bibliographical Essay," *Journal of Religious Ethics* 3 (1975): 69–109; J. Deotis Roberts, *Roots of a Black Future: Family and Church* (Philadelphia: Westminster, 1980), 12–14.

Moltmann's approach to human rights as being too Barthian. Such a narrow and exclusive Christological approach cannot guarantee human rights for all human beings, the majority of whom are not Christian.[18]

Perhaps the most central aspect in the Catholic theological and ethical methodology concerns the insistence on faith and reason. This Catholic approach is well illustrated in the work of Thomas Aquinas (d. 1274), the foremost figure in the Catholic historical tradition. Contemporary Catholic theologians still continue to follow his insistence on faith and reason. In his 1991 book, Roberts is quite sympathetic to the Thomistic harmony of revelation and reason. According to Aquinas, faith and reason grow into an organic unity because they both spring from the same source. Roberts's description of Aquinas also describes himself—"He was a person of faith before he became a philosopher."[19] His own position is similar to Aquinas's—"I assume that faith has priority and reason is a means by which we enrich and enhance our understanding of faith."[20]

Thus, there can be no doubt of the similarity between the Roman Catholic theological method and that followed by Deotis Roberts.[21] Roberts insists on a method that is inclusive, both-and, analogical, and based on the primacy of faith but also the harmony between faith and reason. The basis for this approach in Roberts is not cultural but theological.

Method as the Basis for His Contributions

In my judgment, this method is behind the two most significant contributions made by J. Deotis Roberts to black and African American theology and ethics—his holistic understanding of black theology and his ethical approach to the situation of African Americans in the United States.

First, his approach to black and African American theology. Our author has always insisted on the primacy of Christian faith and the Bible in his approach to black theology and has also given great importance to the experience of blacks in the United States in the light of slavery and the later white racism that created such sinful social structures. But from the

---

[18]   Roberts, *Black Theology Today*, 118.

[19]   Roberts, *Philosophical Introduction to Theology*, 110–12.

[20]   Ibid., 7.

[21]   On one occasion (*Black Theology in Dialogue*, 28), Roberts criticizes an older Catholic theology for being too exclusive based on its axiom of no salvation outside the church. However, the traditional recognition of baptism by desire and of the universal salvific will of God gave a universalizing interpretation to this axiom.

very beginning, Roberts has insisted on the need to root black theology in the African cultural and religious traditions. One cannot understand the African American experience without knowing the roots of the black experience in Africa, even though this experience is quite different from that of an enslaved people in the United States. Roberts has also learned much from other liberation theologies, especially the liberation theology coming from Latin America. Our author has brought to his understanding of African American theology his study of world religions. And, as mentioned above, he also continues to use his philosophical knowledge to understand better and explain more adequately the meaning of African American theology. He frequently calls for an interdisciplinary approach. *A Black Political Theology* published in 1974 already insists on such an approach in its very first chapter on foundations, and subsequent writings have continued to use the same holistic methodology to develop his African American theology.

Black Theology in Dialogue published in 1987 by its very title recognizes such a holistic method. The first chapter insists on an interdisciplinary, ecumenical, contextual, and historical approach with the Bible at the center of theological reflection. The following chapters put special emphasis on the African roots of black theology and an Afro-American/African theological dialogue. Later in the book Roberts also dialogues with Minjung theology, which was then just developing in South Korea, and with the Palestinian liberation theology proposed in the United States by the Jewish scholar Marc Ellis. Roberts's *Africentric Christianity*, published in 2000, continues and deepens this dialogue with African roots. He believes African American theology can learn much from Africentrism, but the Christian faith for him must always be the primary and deciding criterion. This broad, holistic, and interdisciplinary approach to black theology, with a special emphasis on its African roots, is a most significant and lasting contribution of Professor Roberts.

An equally important and lasting contribution concerns his insistence on both liberation and reconciliation in describing the struggle of African Americans in the United States. The 1960s were tumultuous times. Black Power replaced the integrationist approach of Martin Luther King Jr. A great number of blacks abandoned the Christian church, accusing it of failing to support true black liberation. Roberts, the Christian theologian, called on the church to play a central role but insisted on both liberation and reconciliation. Some black communities insisted on liberation alone and called for a separate black nationalism. Whites in general, including liberal whites, wanted reconciliation without liberation. In their perspective, reconciliation and integration were based on the existing white power structure. Our author insisted that the Christian understanding definitely calls for reconciliation, but reconciliation can truly occur only in the light of a full liberation of blacks so that blacks and whites could come together as equals and not with dependent and inferior blacks being integrated into the already existing white structures. Looking back from the vantage point of the present, one can appreciate both the wisdom and the courage behind Roberts's insistence on both liberation and reconciliation.[22] Unfortunately, his agenda has not yet been accomplished and still faces us. Without doubt, his both-and rather than an either-or approach was the most adequate one in the 1970s and remains the most proper answer to our problems today.

Agreement on Substance and Content

Anthropology constitutes a most fundamental concept for Christian ethics and social ethics. Here again, Professor Roberts and the Catholic tradition share the same basic understanding. Catholic tradition has built on the biblical, Aristotelian, and Thomistic approaches to insist that the human person is social and political by nature. This tradition, as pointed out in earlier chapters, has recognized and strongly opposed the tendency to individualism and materialism that is so prevalent in the United States. On the basis of such an anthropology, the Catholic tradition has developed its understanding of the state as being natural, necessary, and good but limited. The state has as its function securing the common good, which involves many aspects, such as justice and human rights. This tradition precisely because of its both-and approach to anthropology (personal and social) constitutes a middle position avoiding the two extremes of individualism and collectivism. Individualism is interested only in individual goods and does not give enough importance to the community. Collectivism emphasizes the collectivity but fails to give enough importance to the individual person. The common good ultimately redounds to the good of the individual persons living in that society.[23]

Roberts's concern has been with the real issues facing African Americans, and so he has not developed in a systematic way a social, political, and

---

[22] J. Deotis Roberts, *Liberation and Reconciliation: A Black Theology* (Philadelphia: Westminster, 1971), 13–48.

[23] Charles E. Curran, *Catholic Social Teaching 1891–Present: A Historical, Theological, and Ethical Analysis* (Washington, DC: Georgetown University Press, 2002), 137–59.

economic ethics. However, what he has said on these issues basically agrees with the Catholic tradition because he starts with the same fundamental anthropology. According to Roberts, the human person is social because God made us for fellowship. No person is an island. We are all persons in community. Our well-being as persons depends on a healthy group life in families, communities, and nations. Social consciousness is built into the very nature of Christian anthropology.[24] In his writings, Roberts frequently refers to the East African concept of *ujamaa*, or familyhood and the extended family, and also to the Swahili concept of *harambee*, or social solidarity.[25] Our author favorably cites Aristotle in describing humans as "political animals" and in calling for government to promote justice and equity.[26]

Roberts insists that the state is the broadest expression of full community life apart from humanity itself, and in this respect it is necessary for a complete satisfaction of human sociability. The state or government has its chief roots in the need of citizens for justice, and it is for that reason that the state has its power.[27] In his realism, our author recognizes that the state is also subject to human sinfulness and can readily support an unjust status quo or wishes of the majority. But the state also has the constructive role of promoting justice and the common good. Here too Professor Roberts, like Catholic social teaching, sees capitalism and socialism as direct opposites. Capitalism is too tied to individual selfishness and greed. Socialism is too concerned with the collectivity and downplays the dignity and worth of persons. Like Catholic social teaching, he recognizes what he calls "an acceptable 'communalism' inherent in the Christian ethic that is authentically human."[28]

Roberts recognizes a role for the church as "servant critic of the state." Such a role requires both critical and supportive functions. At times the church must protest the injustice of the state and work to overcome sinful structures such as racism, but at other times it supports the public structures in the struggle for justice, human rights, and the common good. Roberts also recognizes the complexity of political problems with the realization that no agreement will often exist among good Christians about what should be done.[29] Catholic theology agrees with such approaches.

---

[24] Roberts, *Black Political Theology*, 91–92.

[25] Roberts, *Roots of a Black Future*, 90–93.

[26] Roberts, *Prophethood of Black Believers*, 104, 91–92.

[27] Ibid., 104.

[28] Ibid., 97.

[29] Ibid., 107–8.

The Catholic social tradition has consistently recognized the family as the basic and fundamental unit of society. However, I doubt if there is a general theologian discussing primarily other matters who has paid as much attention to the family as Professor Roberts. He recognizes problems stemming from what slavery, discrimination, and white racism have done to the black family in this country. In his analysis of the family, Roberts emphasizes the African roots of the family and its importance. Special attention is paid to the extended family. He also develops the important role of the church with regard to the family, which again combines a both-and aspect— a priestly and prophetic ministry of the black church to the family.[30]

Another strong affinity between Professor Roberts and the Roman Catholic tradition concerns the importance and general understanding of the church. Roberts primarily does his theology for the church. He is a theologian in the service of the black church but also recognizes the broader church universal. At first glance, it would seem that a black Baptist theologian and the Roman Catholic tradition would have very diverse views of church. But such is not the case. Professor Roberts correctly recognizes that the Catholic Church has always given special attention to the institutional aspect of the church.[31] I think he would have been justified in pointing out that at times Roman Catholic theology has given such great importance to the institutional aspect of the church that it has failed to see the institution as a means for carrying out the transformative ministry of the church. But Roberts's basic understanding of the church, including some institutional aspects, shares much with contemporary Catholic understanding.

Our author sees the church as connected with his own both-and approach. One of his chapters is titled "Jesus and the Church"[32] and another, "Jesus, the Church, and Ministry."[33] In practically every one of his books he addresses the role of the church, and some of his books concentrate almost exclusively on the role and ministry of the church.[34] Jesus established the Christian church as an extension of the incarnation to be a community that carries on his saving mission in the world. The metaphors that Roberts uses to understand the church are very similar to those in contemporary Catholicism. He develops at some length the metaphors of the church as the family

---

[30] For his most developed discussion of the family, see Roberts, *Roots of a Black Future*.

[31] Roberts, *Black Theology in Dialogue*, 51.

[32] Ibid., 43–52.

[33] Roberts, *Prophethood of Black Believers*, 1–10.

[34] Roberts, *Roots of a Black Future* and *Africentric Christianity*.

of God, the communion of saints, the body of Christ, and the people of God.[35] Professor Roberts and the Roman Catholic tradition share a primary concern for the church and its transformative life and ministry as a corporate and communitarian assembly of the people of God.

Lessons the Roman Catholic Tradition
Can Learn from Roberts

The affinities and similarities between Professor Roberts and the Roman Catholic tradition are more significant and central than most people would realize. As a result, fruitful dialogue can and should take place between these two theologies. Above all, from Roberts and others, the Catholic Church must learn to confront its own racism. In addition, I will conclude this essay by pointing out two important aspects that the Catholic tradition can learn from Professor Roberts. Obviously, Deotis Roberts is not the only one saying these things, and even some Catholics themselves are already moving in this direction, but in the context of a dialogue between Roberts and the Catholic tradition, the Catholic tradition can and should incorporate these two emphases.

Emphasis on the Particular

First, the Catholic tradition can learn from Roberts a greater emphasis on the particular. Roberts emphasizes the particular but also holds onto the importance of the universal aspect. Roman Catholicism has often so emphasized the universal that it has failed to give enough significance to the particular. Roberts insists that Christians must do their own theological reflection based on their understanding of the Bible, Jesus Christ, and their own histories and experiences. Such a theology should be contextual and particular but not provincial. Theology needs to combine a concrete contextual orientation with a universal vision that takes biblical revelation and authority seriously.[36]

In his own work, Roberts stresses the importance of the particular and the contextual without denying the universal. His great contribution in insisting on both liberation and reconciliation well illustrates an insistence on the particular while still holding on to the universal. The liberation aspect

---

[35] Ibid., 80–109.
[36] Roberts, *Black Theology in Dialogue*, 15–19.

for blacks is obvious. But reconciliation is an integral part of the gospel, the very essence of the good news. Reconciliation involves a cross both for racist whites and for oppressed blacks. The cross for whites is repentance; the cross for blacks is forgiveness. There is no cheap grace. But reconciliation cannot take place without liberation. Reconciliation must involve equals.[37] Roberts approaches the concept of the black Messiah in a similar way. The universal Christ is particularized for the black Christian in the black Messiah; but the black Messiah is at the same time universalized in the Christ of the gospels who meets all believers in their particular situations.[38]

Just as Jesus Christ is Lord and Redeemer of each people and of all people, so too Jesus Christ is judge of each and of all. He judges in history and beyond history. He stands outside and above black culture as well as in it.[39] No culture, however oppressed and sinned against, is itself completely without sin.

While holding on to the need for a universal vision, Professor Roberts also recognizes the dangers of a false universalism in which a particular perspective has claimed to be universal. There is no completely universal perspective. Too often white Western Christian theologians have been guilty of a theological neocolonialism. The cosmic Christ must always stretch the limited boundaries of every particular Christian perspective.[40] The Catholic tradition can and should learn from Roberts and others to give more emphasis to the particular and the contextual while holding onto a proper universalism.

Emphasis on Power

Second, the Roman Catholic tradition can learn from Roberts's understanding of the importance and role of power in social life and ethics. Liberation theologies in the Roman Catholic tradition often refer to power, but the papal and hierarchical teaching known as Catholic social teaching fails to recognize the importance of power and conflict in social ethics and life.[41]

A number of factors contribute to the failure of Catholic social teaching to discuss power. (One must also note the abject failure to address racism in these documents.) The approach heavily depends on

---

[37] Roberts, *Black Political Theology*, 221–22.
[38] Roberts, *Liberation and Reconciliation*, 137–40.
[39] Roberts, *Black Political Theology*, 127–29.
[40] Roberts, *Black Theology Today*, 106–8.
[41] Curran, *Catholic Social Teaching*, 85–91.

an organic understanding of society based on the organism of the human body. Each part has its own role to play for the good of the whole. Later documents in the tradition recognize sinful social structures, but Catholic theology and ethics have not given enough recognition to the power of sin and the conflicts brought about by it in social life. The Catholic tradition has emphasized human reason and appeals to all people of good will, but unfortunately evil and evil people exist in our world. Even the Catholic emphasis on both-and often tends to bring the two different elements together into a harmonious whole.

Professor Roberts has dealt with power in all his writings. Black Power came to the fore in the 1960s. Roberts recognized the importance and need for Black Power from a Christian understanding. No change could be brought about without it. However, together with Vincent Harding and others he opposed "the religion of Black Power." Such an understanding tended to substitute this religion for Christianity, emphasized total black separatism, and accepted and even promoted violence.[42] *A Black Political Theology* devotes a chapter to "The Gospel of Power," which insists on the radical change needed in our society that can come about only through power, confrontation, and conflict. But still all this is a means to reconciliation.[43]

Roberts's most extensive treatment of Black Power comes in three chapters in *Black Theology in Dialogue* that were originally three lectures delivered at Brite Divinity School. Here he uses Paul Tillich in developing separate chapters on love, justice, and power. Power is deeply rooted in the Judeo-Christian understanding of God—almighty and all-powerful God. But with Tillich, Reinhold Niebuhr, and Martin Luther King Jr., he insists that power is neutral and must always be used in the service of love and justice. Power is not an end in itself. Power is to be used to realize the highest human values: personal, social, and institutional.[44]

Catholic social teaching can learn much from Roberts about power. Power is absolutely necessary in social life and social ethics, but it must always be in the service of love and justice. Conflict and confrontation are legitimate means against the forces of evil, but they are strategies that must serve Christian values and always aim at ultimate reconciliation.

This chapter has studied the writings of Professor Roberts from the perspective of the Roman Catholic theological tradition. Our author has

---

[42] Roberts, *Liberation and Reconciliation*, 20–25.
[43] Roberts, *Black Political Theology*, 139–55; *Black Theology Today*, 151–61.
[44] Roberts, *Black Theology in Dialogue*, 65–92.

worked with Roman Catholics over the years and has been familiar with the Catholic tradition. But more important, significant similarities and affinities exist between his theology and Roman Catholic theology. In the context of this dialogue, the Catholic Church must confront its own racism, and the Catholic tradition can learn significant lessons from the writings of J. Deotis Roberts.

Chapter 6

White Privilege*

This chapter, an autobiographical narrative reflecting on my awareness of racism and white privilege in my theological journey, has not been easy to write. In the last few years, I have become somewhat educated about racism and white privilege. I have to face the reality that I barely recognized the problem of racism in my own somewhat extensive writings and was blithely unaware of my own white privilege.

Racism

The references to racism in my writings are very few, and there is never any concentrated discussion of the issue. This lack is especially telling in a moral theologian who often dealt with social ethics. Other theologians because of the focus of their discipline might not have had the same opportunities to discuss and evaluate racism.

In my 1982 monograph, *American Catholic Social Ethics: Twentieth-Century Approaches*, I analyzed and offered critiques of the writings of five figures in Catholic social ethics. The index has seven references to race discrimination and racism. The two most extended discussions (at best, a few pages each) deal with Paul Hanly Furfey and John A. Ryan. Looking back now on what I wrote then, I am very embarrassed and uncomfortable.

Paul Hanly Furfey, the Catholic University of America sociologist, in the 1930s, developed a Christian personalist approach to ethics based on the Catholic Worker model. The radical gospel ethic strongly criticizes the social ethos in the United States. Personalist action calls for the twofold strategy of separation and nonparticipation on the one hand and bearing witness on the other hand. Furfey, in his writings, emphasizes three significant issues—poverty, racism, and war. He strongly condemns Catholic conformity in all

---

   * Originally published as Charles E. Curran, "White Privilege: My Theological Journey," in *Corrupting White Privilege: Catholic Theologians Break the Silence,* ed. Laurie M. Cassidy and Alex Mikulich (Maryknoll, NY: Orbis Books, 2007). Used with permission.

these areas. Furfey, the sociologist, points out the grave evils in racial segregation and discrimination in all aspects of life. For Catholics this is a serious moral obligation—a matter of eternal life or death.[1]

I disagreed somewhat with Furfey's approach but praised his recognition of the three deep problems facing our country—poverty, race, and war—issues that have remained very important in our society. Catholic liberals tend to overlook these deep problems, "but the radical possesses a methodological approach which makes one sensitive to the real problems facing our society."[2] In later writings, I have addressed issues of poverty and peace, but I have never dealt the same way with racism. I did not follow up on what I had written and recognized in 1982!

The other comments in this book refer to John A. Ryan, the premier Catholic social ethicist in the first half of the twentieth century. In the 1920s, Ryan urged his student, Fr. Francis Gilligan, to write a pioneer doctoral dissertation under his direction titled *The Morality of the Color Line*.[3] But Ryan himself did not discuss racism in any depth, and I negatively criticized two of his comments about racism. With regard to interracial marriages, Ryan mentioned that the church prudently urges its pastors to conform to such laws, and few if any priests or bishops have been accused of violating these laws. My reaction was, "His comments on the issue were totally conforming without a hint of the prophetic."[4]

I described as "disappointing" a lecture he gave in 1943 at Howard University in Washington. After identifying many of the existing problems of racial discrimination, he called for active leadership and the avoidance of violence, urged patience, and recommended working with people of good will in the white community. Ryan's great contribution to social ethics was his insistence on the need for government intervention. But there was no mention of law or government intervention in the area of racism.[5] Thus, I criticized Ryan, but I am open to even deeper negative criticism.

Only in the last few years have I become somewhat conscious of my failure to recognize the problems of racism in the United States and in the Catholic Church. My friend and would-be student, Bryan Massingale,

---

[1] Charles E. Curran, *American Catholic Social Ethics: Twentieth-Century Approaches* (Notre Dame, IN: University of Notre Dame Press, 1982), 149–58.

[2] Ibid., 166.

[3] Francis James Gilligan, *The Morality of the Color Line* (Washington, DC: Catholic University of America Press, 1928).

[4] Curran, *American Catholic Social Ethics,* 83.

[5] Ibid.

correctly pointed out the failure of contemporary Catholic moral theology, myself included, to deal with the evil of racism.[6]

Massingale has also pointed out two windows of convergence of black theology and racism with Catholic theology—the Catholic recognition of social or structural sin and solidarity with the poor.[7] Margaret Pfeil uses the option for the poor to attack white privilege.[8] I have made many references in my writings to these three aspects but have never connected them with racism beyond an occasional word or phrase. So despite having the tools that should have made me more aware of the problem of racism, I never really addressed racism in my writings.

I could offer many excuses, but they would be only excuses. Actually, I did pay a little attention to racism in my classes. In the late 1960s, as I mentioned in the preceding chapter, I worked on occasion with J. Deotis Roberts, who was then teaching at Howard University. We were involved in one or two projects together, and he graciously accepted one of my students into his classes at Howard. I assigned his book on liberation and reconciliation in my classes on social and political ethics.[9] A few years later I also used *A New American Justice*, by my friend Dan Maguire.[10] I continued my association with Deotis Roberts in both the Society of Christian Ethics and the American Theological Society. I was invited to contribute an article to a festschrift in his honor that I have republished in this volume. I was most grateful for the opportunity that provided me the occasion for writing my first article dealing with racism and black theology, which was finally published only in 2005.[11]

---

[6] Bryan Massingale, "The African American Experience and US Roman Catholic Ethics: 'Strangers and Aliens No Longer?'" in *Black and Catholic: The Challenge and Gift of Black Folks*, ed. Jaime T. Phelps (Milwaukee: Marquette University Press, 1997), 79–101.

[7] Ibid., 94–95.

[8] Margaret Pfeil, "Option for the Poor: Dismantling White Privilege as Part of the Theological Vocation," paper presented at the Annual Meeting of the Catholic Theological Society of America, Cincinnati, Ohio, 2003.

[9] J. Deotis Roberts, *Liberation and Reconciliation: A Black Theology* (Philadelphia: Westminster, 1971).

[10] Daniel C. Maguire, *A New American Justice: Ending the White Male Monopolies* (Garden City, NY: Doubleday, 1980).

[11] Charles E. Curran, "J. Deotis Roberts and the Roman Catholic Tradition," in *The Quest for Liberation and Reconciliation: Essays in Honor of J. Deotis Roberts*, ed. Michael Battle (Louisville: Westminster/John Knox, 2005), 82–92. This essay appears as the preceding chapter in this volume.

White Privilege

Acknowledging my failure as a Catholic theologian to recognize and deal with the problem of racism in society and the church is only the first step toward a recognition of white privilege. Shawn Copeland has rightly challenged us white theologians to recognize the omnipresent reality of white privilege and how it has affected our understanding of and approach to theology. White privilege functions invisibly and systemically to confer power and privilege.[12] Only very recently have I been educated to realize the extent and power of white privilege and my participation in it.

Here too I now realize the inadequacies and errors in some of my earlier approaches. I have tried to be supportive of minority colleagues in theology. At Catholic University, I encouraged the African American women who were working on their doctorates. I often went to sessions of professional societies when African Americans and other minorities were presenting so that I could show my support for them.

On one occasion at a Call to Action conference, I went to a session given by an African American woman theologian who was a former student. I was somewhat embarrassed because I embarrassed her. She saw me come in and sit in the last row and almost immediately told her audience that she was nervous because I had come to her session. She graciously thanked me publicly for the support I had already given her from the time that she was in graduate school.

Yes, I supported African Americans and other minority Catholic theologians, and I was quite satisfied that I was doing what I could for the cause. But only recently have I become aware of the problem with such an approach. "I" was the subject; "they" were the object. "I" was graciously doing what I could to help and support "them."

In reality, the problem was "I" and not "them." I was blithely unaware of how white privilege had shaped my understanding of what was going on. The invisible and systemic nature of white privilege came through in my absolutizing my own limited privileged position and making all others the object of my good will. My perspective was the normative perspective from which all others were to be seen. My white theology was the theological standpoint from which all others were to be judged. I finally realized to some extent that I was the problem.

---

[12] M. Shawn Copeland, "Racism and the Vocation of the Christian Theologian," *Spiritus* 2, no. 1 (2002): 15–29.

Three Conversions

White privilege is invisible, structural, and systemic. Borrowing from Bernard Lonergan, Shawn Copeland describes white privilege as biased common sense.[13] Lonergan used the term "scotosis" to describe this reality.[14] There is a need then to shed light on this evil and to overcome its invisibility to the person. White privilege is a structural sin that has to be made visible and removed. Borrowing from Lonergan and Copeland, I believe that there is need for conversion and especially continuing conversion to overcome white privilege. I have just begun to recognize white privilege as the problem, and I have to continually strive to uncover it in my own life and work. On the basis of what I have read and experienced, there are three types of conversion involved—personal, intellectual, and spiritual.

Personal Conversion

With regard to the first conversion, Peggy McIntosh's important 1988 article is an eye-opener on the road to personal conversion.[15] I have to see myself as the oppressor and as the problem. She lists about fifty different ways in which I, as a white person, am privileged because of being white. This privilege exists in practically every aspect of my life. Making matters worse, this privilege comes at the expense of others. I have to become much more aware of the role of white privilege in my daily life brought about by the systemic injustice of racism.

I became somewhat aware of white privilege two years ago when I was teaching a course in moral theology for the Perkins School of Theology at Southern Methodist University in their Houston program. Most of the students were older and second-career folks studying for ministry. There were twenty-one students in the class, including five African Americans. In the exams and papers, the African Americans received the lowest grades. But I also broke the class down into four groups to role-play different cases of quandary ethics. In this role-playing, four of the African Americans truly excelled. They understood exactly what was involved,

---

[13] Ibid.

[14] Bernard J. F. Lonergan, *Insight: A Study of Human Understanding* (New York: Philosophical Library, 1957), 191–203.

[15] Peggy McIntosh, "White Privilege and Male Privilege: A Personal Account of Coming to See Correspondences through Work in Women's Studies" (1988). This paper is available through Wellesley Centers for Women on line at www.scwonline.org.

went to the heart of the case, and presented the whole issue with intelligence and humor.

The African American students in this role-playing showed themselves to be just as intelligent, and perhaps even more so, than the others in the class. But they did not have the same skills with regard to reading texts and writing papers. Obviously, they were products of a poor educational system that had never prepared them to read and write that well.

In light of that experience, I reflected on my own privilege with regard to education. I was born to a family that took reading and education very seriously. My parents encouraged us to read and to get a good education. I went to good schools and had some excellent teachers. To this day I still know the names of the sisters who taught me in the eight grades of grammar school. As a seminary student and priest, the church paid for all my college, theology, and doctoral studies. I did not have to work, to take out loans, or to worry in any way about how my expensive education was paid for. This was not all due to white privilege, but it obviously was a privilege that very few others have had.

Intellectual Conversion

The second conversion is intellectual. Early on I learned from Bernard Lonergan the importance of historical consciousness. The person as subject is embedded in one's own cultural and historical environment. No one can claim to be the neutral, objective, value-free knower. Liberationist and feminist theologies made me all the more aware of social location with its limits and biases. I learned about the hermeneutic of suspicion and the need to recognize that the strong and powerful create the structures and institutions of our world. But I did not see black racism and its connection to my white privilege until I was prodded by recent writings. I was trying to help and encourage African American theologians to do their work. But I never realized how they could and should help me and my theology. My failures here indicate the need for both a stronger moral imagination and for the other conversions to affect the intellectual conversion.

Spiritual Conversion

The third conversion is spiritual conversion. In reading the literature, I was taken by how many theologians dealing with white privilege emphasize spiritual conversion. At first I was fearful that this was an escape to reduce the invisible, structural, and systemic reality of white privilege to the realm of the spiritual. The flight to the spiritual might be a dodge for avoiding the structural and institutional realities of life.

Yes, the flight to the spiritual can be an escape but not for one who sees the spiritual as the primary area that affects all other aspects of human existence. In moral theology, I have emphasized the role of a fundamental option that gives direction to all aspects of life. But I have purposely not embraced a transcendental understanding of the fundamental option precisely because in my judgment it does not give enough importance to the historical and the concrete. The spiritual thus influences the other two conversions—the intellectual and the personal.

Here I remembered what I had forgotten for so long. In my praise of Furfey's approach, I pointed out that his Christian perspective clearly recognized the deep problems existing in American society—poverty, race, and nationalistic violence. The spiritual conversion of the radical Furfey made him see what others did not see.

What effect will these beginning conversions have on my doing moral theology? At this stage of my life as a "senior" theologian, I am not going to become an expert on racism and white privilege. The best analogy for the future is what I have done with regard to feminist theology. I am not an expert in feminist theology, but I recognize the problem of pervasive patriarchy. I dialogue with feminism, and I have appropriated many of its insights into my work. I hope to do the same with regard to racism and white privilege.

A spirituality that prays to a God who is black and female can and should help open my eyes to white male privilege.

Part II

BIOETHICAL AND SEXUAL PERSPECTIVES

Introduction

Part II considers the bioethical and sexual traditions in Catholic moral theology. Chapter 7, "The Catholic Moral Tradition in Bioethics," provides an overview of the topic. The Catholic tradition was interested in medical ethics long before others were and made some lasting contributions, especially the recognition that people do not have to use extraordinary means to preserve human life. The new approach associated with Vatican II brought about some tensions in the tradition, especially with regard to issues involving sexuality. In looking to the future, the chapter points out that issues such as euthanasia will come to the fore in discussions of public policy and law. In light of the teaching of Vatican II on religious freedom it is possible at times on these issues for Catholics to recognize that their moral teaching does not necessarily have to be incorporated into law.

Chapter 8, "An Appraisal of Pope John Paul II's Teaching on Sexuality and Marriage," focuses on the theology of the body that the pope developed in his weekly public audiences immediately after his election. The very topic indicates that the pope wanted to give a more positive appraisal of the body, recognizing the body as part of God's good creation, affected by sin, but also sharing in God's redeeming love. Pope John Paul's approach throughout is heavily scriptural, but he sees in the scriptural approach of Genesis a metaphysical understanding of the body that is true for all times. Here he also develops the indissolubility of marriage and proposes a more biblical and personalist approach to support the teaching of Paul VI's encyclical *Humanae Vitae* condemning artificial contraception for spouses. The primary negative criticism raised against his approach is its lack of historical consciousness.

Chapter 9, "The Long Shadow of *Humanae Vitae* on the Tradition," discusses the teaching of *Humanae Vitae* with regard to contraception, natural law, and papal teaching authority. The understanding of the meaning of natural law and the role of authoritative papal teaching have cast a long shadow affecting especially the approach to sexual norms. The end of the chapter briefly notes for further consideration that these two approaches differ from what is found in the tradition of Catholic social teaching. There has been little or no disagreement or dissent within the Catholic theological community on the use of natural law in the social tradition. The reason for the difference between the two traditions is the fact that the understanding of natural law in the sexual tradition suffers from the problem of physicalism by identifying the human moral act with the physical structure of the act. The problem of physicalism does not appear in the natural law employed in the social tradition. Likewise, despite the pluralism of theological approaches in the Catholic social tradition, there has been practically no dissent from papal teaching, whereas dissent has frequently been discussed in terms of the sexual tradition. The reason is that in the social tradition the papal teaching generally proposes principles only and does not get into concrete specifics, whereas in the sexual tradition the teaching condemns very specific, concrete acts. In addition there has been much more growth and change in the social tradition than in the sexual tradition. The hierarchical magisterium in the last fifty years has recognized the role of historical consciousness in the social tradition but not in the sexual tradition.

Chapter 7

THE CATHOLIC MORAL TRADITION IN BIOETHICS*

This chapter proceeds in three stages—the prehistory of bioethics with special attention to medical ethics in the Roman Catholic perspective; my approach to bioethics in the early 1970s; and a reflection looking back on what has developed in Catholic bioethics since that time and looking forward to what might transpire in the future.

André Hellegers, the esteemed founder of the Kennedy Institute at Georgetown University in 1971 and a good friend, invited me to spend the 1972 calendar year as a senior research scholar at the institute. That year I wrote a monograph—*Politics, Medicine, and Christian Ethics: A Dialogue with Paul Ramsey.*[1] My colleagues that year at the Kennedy Institute were, in addition to André Hellegers, the founder, and LeRoy Walters, the director of the institute, Francisco Abel, John Connery, Richard McCormick, Gene Outka, and Warren Reich. These were all scholars with a background in Christian ethics, and five of the seven come out of the tradition of Catholic moral theology. Many might expect a predominance of Catholic scholars in a Catholic university in 1972, but the fact of Georgetown's being a Catholic university does not adequately explain the strong Catholic presence and interest in medical ethics in 1972.

Prehistory of Bioethics

By 1960, medical ethics was a well-developed subdiscipline of moral theology in the Roman Catholic tradition. Books on medical ethics existed in the major European languages (e.g., Bonnar, Healy, Kelly, Kenny, Niedermeyer,

* Originally published as Charles E. Curran, "The Catholic Moral Tradition and Bioethics," in *The Story of Bioethics: From Seminal Works to Contemporary Explorations,* ed. Jennifer K. Walter and Eran P. Klein (Washington, DC: Georgetown University Press, 2003), 113–30. Used with permission. www.press.georgetown.edu.

[1] Charles E. Curran, *Politics, Medicine, and Christian Ethics: A Dialogue with Paul Ramsey* (Philadelphia: Fortress, 1973).

O'Donnell, Payen, Paquin, Pujiula, Scremin).[2] Periodicals devoted to medical ethics existed in many of the same countries—*Arzt und Christ, Cahiers Laënnec, Catholic Medical Quarterly, Linacre Quarterly,* and *Saint-Luc Médicale.* Catholic medical ethics was strong in the United States especially because of the courses on medical ethics in Catholic medical and nursing schools and the textbooks used for these courses. With the exception of a very few Protestants, both religious ethicists and philosophical ethicists were not interested in medical ethics at this time.

This historical situation raises three questions: (1) Why were Roman Catholic scholars interested in medical ethics? (2) Why were other ethicists not interested in medical ethics? (3) What explains the great interest in medical ethics and the tremendous growth of bioethics since?

Why Were Roman Catholics so Interested in Medical Ethics before 1960?

Historically, Roman Catholicism has insisted on the need to respond to the gift of God's love with a change of heart and to show such a change in good actions in daily life. The Catholic tradition has insisted on both faith and works. The Catholic emphasis on works at times went too far even to the point of Pelagianism—the heresy that human beings save themselves by their own works and are not saved by God's gift. The sacrament of penance in the Catholic tradition underscored the importance of works. From the time of the Fourth Lateran Council in 1215, Catholics were obliged to confess their mortal sins at least once a year.[3] Appropriate books came into existence to describe the good actions required in life and to point out the wrong or sinful actions. The most famous of these texts in

---

[2] Alphonsus Bonnar, *The Catholic Doctor,* 2nd ed. (London: Burns, Oates, 1939); Edwin F. Healy, *Medical Ethics* (Chicago: Loyola University Press, 1956); Gerald Kelly, *Medico-Moral Problems* (St. Louis: Catholic Hospital Association, 1958); John P. Kenny, *Principles of Medical Ethics* (Westminster, MD: Newman, 1952); Albert Niedermeyer, *Pastoralmedizinische Propädeutik* (Salzburg: Pustet, 1935); Thomas J. O'Donnell, *Morals in Medicine* (Westminster, MD: Newman, 1956); Jules Paquin, *Morale et médecine,* 2nd ed. (Montreal: Immaculée Conception, 1957); P. G. Payen, *Déontologie médicale d'après le droit naturel* (Zi-Ka-Wei: T'ou-se-we, 1935); Jacobus Pujiula, *De medicina pastorali,* 2nd ed. (Turin: Marietti, 1953); Luigi Scremin, *Dizionario di morale professionale per i medici,* 5th ed. (Rome: Editrice Studium, 1953).

[3] Henricus Denzinger et al., eds., *Enchiridion Symbolorum Definitionum et Declarationum de Rebus Fidei et Morum,* 32nd ed. (Barcelona: Herder, 1963), no. 812, 264.

the fifteenth century was the *Summa* of St. Antoninus, the archbishop of Florence (1389–1459). In the third volume of a huge four-volume work, Antoninus considers the duties and obligations of people according to their different states in life—married people, virgins and widows, temporal rulers, soldiers, lawyers, doctors, merchants, judges, craftworkers, and many others. The duties and obligations of physicians include the following: competence, diligence, care for the patient, the obligation to tell the dying patient of his or her condition, the proper fee or salary for the doctor, the duty to care for the sick even when they cannot pay, and the obligation not to prescribe things against the moral law such as fornication and abortion.[4]

One illustration will show the very realistic practical wisdom of Antoninus. How do we know if a physician is competent? Some claim that degrees from a university are a proof of competence. (Think of every doctor's office you have ever been in with the diplomas hanging on the wall.) But Antoninus realistically points out there are many people in universities, both students and professors, who are not competent. For him the best criterion of competence is judgment by one's peers.[5]

Casuistry played a significant role in Catholic moral theology as Professors Jonsen and Toulmin have pointed out.[6] Casuistry often became a pejorative term because some casuists, who became known as *laxists*, used casuistry to weaken or avoid moral obligation. One moral theologian was ironically described as "the lamb of God who takes away the sin of the world"! However, at its best, casuistry is a helpful and creative way of perceiving and trying to solve moral problems, as illustrated in the case of care for the dying.

Early on, the Catholic moral tradition had come to the conclusion that human beings do not have to do everything possible to keep human life in existence, based on the recognition that positive obligations can often conflict with other positive obligations. As a result, the tradition maintained that one has to use ordinary means but not extraordinary means to preserve life. A very widely accepted understanding of extraordinary means describes these as all medicines, treatments, and operations that cannot be obtained

---

[4] Sanctus Antonius Archiepiscopus Florentini, *Summa, Pars Tertia* (Verona: Typographia Seminarii, 1740; Lithographic reprint, Graz, 1959), *titulus septimus*, 277–92.

[5] Ibid., 281. See Louis Vereecke, "Médecine et morale chez Saint Antonin de Florence," in his *De Guillaume d'Ockham à Saint Alphonse de Liguori: Etudes d'historie de la théologie morale moderne 1300–1787* (Rome: Collegium S. Alfonsi de Urbe, 1986), 259–82.

[6] Albert R. Jonsen and Stephen Toulmin, *The Abuse of Casuistry: A History of Moral Reasoning* (Berkeley: University of California Press, 1988), 137–265.

without excessive expense, pain, or other inconvenience, or that, if used, would not offer a reasonable hope of benefit.[7] In the light of developing technology, the major problem faced in the middle of the twentieth century concerned the continued use of means such as the respirator or the nasogastric tube that would only prolong the dying process and not offer any reasonable hope of success. For many this seemed to be a new question. However, in the seventeenth century, the Jesuit casuist, Juan de Lugo, creatively raised the issue of no hope of success or benefit. His imaginative case was this. A person condemned to death by burning at the stake can manage to get some water to douse the flames and prolong one's life. But there is no obligation to do so because the captors will just light the fire again.[8] Here one sees the best of creative casuistry at work imagining a problem that only became quite prominent with the development of modern technology.

In addition to the significant ethical dimension, the Roman Catholic tradition had other reasons for staying in contact with developing medical and biological sciences. Catholic canon law dealt with many aspects of life, including the laws governing marriage. To enter marriage, a couple had to be able to perform the marital act. The tradition thus recognized the distinction between impotency (the inability of the couple to perform the marital act) and sterility (the inability to have children). This important distinction called for Catholic canonists to be conversant with the medical knowledge of the time to determine the difference between impotency and sterility.[9] Beginning in 1621, Paolo Zacchia published a multivolume work, *Quaestiones Medico-Legales*, dealing with subjects impinging on the relationships among medicine, law, and theology that became a standard reference book for Catholic moral theologians even as late as the nineteenth century.[10] Also in the seventeenth century, books appeared on the question of baptizing the fetus in the womb and on the morality of cesarean sections.[11] Franciscus Emmanuel Cangiamila's eighteenth-century book on sacred embryology

---

[7] Kelly, *Medico-Moral Problems*, 129.

[8] Joannes de Lugo, *Disputationes Scholasticae et Morales* (Paris: Vives, 1868–69), vol. 6, chap. 10, sec. 1, no. 30. For further elaboration see Daniel A. Cronin, *The Moral Law in Respect to the Ordinary and Extraordinary Means of Conserving Life* (Rome: Pontificia Universitas Gregoriana, 1958), 64.

[9] Josephus Antonelli, *Pro Conceptu Impotentiae et Sterilitatis Relate ad Matrimonium* (Rome, 1901).

[10] Paolo Zacchia, *Quaestiones Medico-Legales*, 3 vols. (Lyons: Posuel, 1701).

[11] Girolamo Florentinus, *De Hominibus Dubiis Baptizandis* (Lyons, 1658); Theophilus Raynaudus, *De Ortu Infantium* (Lyons, 1637).

was published in four different languages.[12] In the nineteenth and twentieth centuries, a subdiscipline called pastoral medicine came into existence with the purpose of providing the priest with the medical knowledge needed to carry out one's ministry and the doctor with the moral principles to ensure that the doctor's actions are in accord with Christian morals.[13] In the United States as the twentieth century developed, courses in medical ethics existed for nurses and doctors in Catholic colleges and universities, and textbooks were written for these courses.[14] At the same time, the many addresses on medical moral issues by Pope Pius XII, who spoke not only to Catholics but often to international meetings of medical specialists in Rome, gave further impetus to Catholic interest in medical ethics.[15] All this explains why and how the Catholic tradition developed a strong interest in and concern for medical ethics long before 1960.

Two Other Questions

The second question naturally arises: Why were not other Christian ethicists, philosophical ethicists, and legal scholars interested in medical ethics before 1960? The primary reason was that there were not that many controversial issues, because for all practical purposes good medicine and good morality had the same basic criterion—what is for the good of the patient. Whatever is for the good of the patient is morally, medically, and legally good. Consequently, there were no real tensions between good medicine and good morality.

One major difference between Catholics and other approaches to marriage and medical morality before 1960 concerned contraception and sterilization. Why did official Catholic teaching condemn direct sterilization

---

[12] Hugo Hurter, *Nomenclator Literarius Theologiae Catholicae Theologos Exhibens Aetate, Natione, Disciplinis Distinctos*, vol. 4 (New York: B. Franklin, 1962), col. 1646. The Bridwell Library of Southern Methodist University has the second French edition: Francesco Emmanuele Cangiamila, *Abregé de l'Embryologie Sacrée*, 2nd ed. (Paris: Nyon, 1766).

[13] Carolus Capellmann, *Medicina Pastoralis*, 7th ed. (Aachen: R. Barth, 1879); Josephus Antonelli, *Medicina Pastoralis*, 2 vols. (Rome: Pustet, 1905); Albert Niedermeyer, *Handbuch der speziellen Pastoral-Medizin*, 6 vols. (Vienna: Herder, 1948–52).

[14] See the books published in the United States in footnote 2.

[15] John P. Kenny, *Principles of Medical Ethics*, 2nd ed. (Westminster, MD: Newman, 1962), 272, lists in the index forty topics in medical ethics that Pope Pius XII addressed.

So what happens when the air goes out

while most others in society accepted it? The official Catholic teaching rested on the understanding that the sexual organs had a twofold purpose or finality—the good of the species and the good of the individual.[16] One could not subordinate the good of the species to the good of the individual. Most others rejected the absolute good of the species argument and justified contraception and sterilization if it were for the good of the individual or the marriage. Thus the distinctive Catholic position on contraception and sterilization did not accept the criterion in this area that the moral good depends on what is good for the individual person. But in all other cases outside sexual issues the Catholic position endorsed the moral criterion of what is for the good of the individual patient.

Third question: Why the growth of bioethics since 1970? In many ways technology occasioned the great interest and growth in bioethics. First, technological developments made possible new realities that questioned the established criterion that good morality and good medicine depended on what was for the good of the patient. Transplants of organs such as kidneys became possible in the 1950s. Now, for the first time, medicine did harm to one patient in order to help another. Experimentation fueled the tremendous growth in medical procedures and drugs. But the researcher as such was not primarily interested in the good of the individual patient, but rather the good of science and the knowledge that could be used to help others in the future. Thus, the most fundamental principle of traditional medical ethics—do no harm to the patient—no longer held.

Technology developed significantly new ways of bringing human life into existence, whereas previously the only known process was the natural process of the sexual act. Even in the 1960s people talked about the possibilities of cloning. Developments in genetics and technology obviously raised a whole slew of new questions. These very significant issues not only faced many people in their daily lives but also became matters of legal interest and public policy. Thus, technology constitutes the primary occasion for the tremendous development of bioethics since 1970.

My Perspective in 1972

Vatican Council II (1962–65) introduced new understandings in Catholic thought and life. Catholic moral theology in general underwent significant developments after Vatican II. So significant were these develop-

---

[16] Kelly, *Medico-Moral Problems*, 149–217.

ments that the leading Catholic moral theologians before Vatican II were not comfortable with the Vatican II approaches. I tried to approach moral theology and Catholic medical and bioethics in the light of my understandings of the council.

Historical Consciousness

First, the shift to historical consciousness. Bernard Lonergan, the Canadian theologian who taught in Rome, pointed out that the primary change at Vatican II was the shift from classicism to historical consciousness. Classicism emphasized the eternal, the immutable, and the unchanging and employed a deductive methodology. Historical consciousness recognizes the subject, the historical, the particular, and the contingent, and employs an inductive methodology.[17] In my judgment a more inductive methodology recognizes that our understanding of anthropology is not something fixed forever but develops somewhat over time. Consequently, Catholic moral theology has to be open to learn some things about the human from all other interested perspectives and disciplines, including science and technology. In a sense, the relationship should be dialogical, but this does not mean that moral theology cannot and should not at times criticize the scientific and technological—an aspect that will be developed later.

A more inductive approach can never claim the same certitude that the pre–Vatican II deductive Catholic moral theology claimed. The syllogism, the characteristic logical device of deduction, maintains that the conclusion is just as certain as the premises provided that the logic is correct. An inductive moral method has to be tentative in its specific conclusions without, however, failing to take positions.[18]

The Pastoral Constitution on the Church in the Modern World employed a historically conscious methodology by beginning its discussion of particular issues with an examination of the signs of the times. The classicist approach always began with the definition that was true at all times and in all places.

The best illustration of historical consciousness at work in the area of moral theology at Vatican II came from the Declaration on Religious

---

[17] Bernard Lonergan, "A Transition from a Classicist Worldview to Historical Mindedness," in *Law for Liberty: The Role of Law in the Church Today*, ed. James E. Biechler (Baltimore: Helicon, 1967), 126–33.

[18] Charles E. Curran, "Absolute Norms and Medical Ethics," in *Absolutes in Moral Theology?* ed. Charles E. Curran (Washington, DC: Corpus, 1968), 109–53.

Freedom. As mentioned earlier, in this document the Catholic Church changed its teaching and recognized the universal right of all people to religious freedom. Discussions about this document in the council focused especially on how the church could change its teaching in this particular area. The generally accepted approach maintained that historical conditions had changed and the church in these new historical and cultural circumstances could now accept religious freedom for all.[19] In my judgment the application of historical consciousness to explain this change too easily slid over the problem of the discontinuity between the earlier and the later teaching and the fact that there was error in the earlier teaching. But there can be no doubt that the methodology of the Declaration on Religious Freedom clearly illustrated historical consciousness at work.

In fact, Catholic social teaching in general had changed and developed with changing historical circumstances, as pointed out in the preceding chapters. In the nineteenth century the Catholic Church opposed liberalistic individualism with its emphasis on freedom, equality, and human rights. But as the twentieth century developed, the church turned its attention to the danger of totalitarianism, especially in the form of communism. Little by little official Catholic social teaching began to defend human freedom, equality, and human rights.[20] The Declaration on Religious Freedom well illustrated this change.

The obvious question arose: What effect would a more historically conscious methodology have in the area of Catholic sexual and medical ethics? I began to reexamine Catholic sexual and medical teaching in the light of this newer methodological approach.

A Personalist Approach

Second, Vatican II called for a more personalist approach. The Pastoral Constitution on the Church in the Modern World (para. 51) proposes as the criterion for the harmonizing of conjugal love and the responsible transmission of life "the nature of the human person and his acts."[21] The emphasis on the person was both new and important.

---

[19] Emile-Joseph de Smedt, "Religious Freedom," in *Council Speeches of Vatican II*, ed. Yves Congar, Hans Küng, and Daniel O'Hanlon (London: Sheed and Ward, 1964), 161–68.

[20] John Courtney Murray, *The Problem of Religious Freedom* (Westminster, MD: Newman, 1965), 47–84.

[21] Pastoral Constitution on the Church in the Modern World, para. 51, in *The Documents of Vatican II*, ed. Walter M. Abbott (New York: Guild, 1966), 256.

The Declaration on Religious Freedom (para. 1) begins by recognizing that "a sense of the dignity of the human person has been imposing itself more and more deeply on the consciousness of contemporary man." Later the declaration (para. 2) affirms "that the right to religious freedom has its foundation in the very dignity of the human person."[22]

How would the criterion of the person affect Catholic sexual and medical ethics? Catholic moral theology had often insisted on the teleology of the God-given human faculties. The malice of lying well illustrates such an approach. The purpose of the faculty of speech is to put on my lips what is in my mind. In lying the individual goes against the God-given purpose of the faculty of speech. Lying is defined as speaking something contrary to what is in the mind.[23] Catholic sexual ethics applied the same criterion of the teleology of the faculty to questions of sexuality. In this light every act of the sexual faculty has to be both open to procreation and to love union since these are the two God-given purposes of the sexual faculty.[24]

Some Catholic theologians even early in the twentieth century had abandoned the older faculty teleology approach to lying for a more personalist and relational criterion. The ultimate malice of lying does not consist in going against the God-given teleology of the faculty of speech but rather in the violation of the neighbor's right to truth. If the neighbor does not have the right to truth, then what one says may be false speech but this does not entail the moral malice of lying.[25] It was only natural that in the light of the criterion of the person that Catholic moral theologians would also call into question the criterion of the teleology of the sexual faculty for determining what is morally right or wrong.[26]

---

[22] Abbott, *Documents of Vatican II*, 675, 679.

[23] Marcellinus Zalba, *Teologia Moralis Summa*, vol. 3 (Madrid: Biblioteca de autores cristianos, 1952), 102–13.

[24] Ibid., 324–26.

[25] Julius A. Dorszynski, *Catholic Teaching about the Morality of Falsehood* (Washington, DC: Catholic University of America Press, 1949).

[26] For an early (1928) criticism of the faculty teleology argument in sexuality in the light of the changed approach to lying, see John A. Ryan, "Birth Control: The Perverted Faculty Argument," in the *Historical Development of Fundamental Moral Theology in the United States: Readings in Moral Theology No. 11*, ed. Charles E. Curran and Richard A. McCormick (New York: Paulist Press, 1999), 120–23. But Ryan still held to the condemnation of artificial contraception (ibid., 132–34). In a recent development, Cardinal Joseph Ratzinger promulgated final changes in the *Catechism of the Catholic Church* that "corrected" the previous teaching of the catechism that explicitly saw the malice of lying in light of the violation of the neighbor's right to truth.

Philosophical anthropology, intimately related to historical consciousness and personalism, came to the fore in the 1960s debate over artificial contraception. Those who disagreed with the official hierarchical teaching often criticized the official anthropology as suffering from physicalism. Physicalism identifies the human moral act with the physical aspect or structure of the act. Yes, the physical aspect is important, but it is only one aspect of the human and at times might be sacrificed for the good of the total human. I also challenged other areas of Catholic moral theology in which the physical was identified with the moral, such as in the third principle of the double effect that calls for the good effect not to be caused by means of the evil effect and the beginning of human life from the very moment of conception.[27] Chapter 9 will discuss the problem of physicalism in greater detail.

An adequate anthropology thus recognizes that the human is the ultimate aspect that brings together all the partial aspects such as the physical, the psychological, the sociological, the medical, the eugenic, the hygienic, and so on. Such an anthropology recognizes the scientific and technological aspects as just one part of the human. The technological or scientific is basically good but limited. Hence, the fully human at times must say no to the technological. One thus cannot simply identify technological progress with human progress. At times the human should and must say no to the absolutization of the technological, which is not bad but is a limited good that must be relativized in the light of the fully human.

Other Vatican II Aspects

Third, Vatican II, especially in its Decree on Ecumenism, recognized the importance of dialogue with other Christian churches. In the pre–Vatican II period, hostility rather than dialogue characterized the Catholic approach to other religions, even other Christian religions. The presence of Protestant observers at the Second Vatican Council and the role they played in the council illustrated the importance of ecumenical dialogue in the renewal of the life of the Catholic Church.

Cardinal Joseph Ratzinger, "Vatican List of Catechism Changes," *Origins* 27 (1997): 262. Apparently, Ratzinger feared that the same relational criterion might be applied to sexual issues.

[27] Charles E. Curran, "Natural Law and Contemporary Moral Theology," in *Contraception: Authority and Dissent*, ed. Charles E. Curran (New York: Herder and Herder, 1969), 159–67.

Catholic theology before the Second Vatican Council had practically no dialogue whatsoever with Protestant thought but tended to treat Protestants as adversaries who had to be refuted. In 1972 at the Kennedy Institute, I decided to write a monograph on the political and medical ethics of Paul Ramsey, the leading Protestant ethicist in the United States at that time. Ramsey, in the late 1960s, had entered wholeheartedly into the area of medical ethics and bioethics with in-depth discussions on various aspects including genetics.[28] Without doubt, many Catholic theologians, including myself, learned much from Ramsey, but, at the same time, I pointed out significant methodological differences between Ramsey's approach and my own approach out of the Catholic tradition. In some ways this was a pioneering work in the early 1970s, but later on all Catholic moral theology became ecumenical so that one could no longer do Catholic moral theology without bringing in the ecumenical dimension.

Fourth, Vatican Council II, especially in its Decree on Priestly Formation (para. 16) called for the renewal of moral theology with a greater emphasis on its scriptural and theological aspects. Pre–Vatican II moral theology was based almost exclusively on human nature and human reason. The realm of the supernatural rested on top of the natural but did not directly affect it. The emphasis of Vatican II and my work on Ramsey helped me focus more on the theological aspects of the discipline of moral theology. Eschatology sees the world in relationship to the fullness of the reign of God. Ramsey's apocalyptic eschatology is one-sided. An apocalyptic eschatology sees an oppositional, or at best, paradoxical relationship between the divine and the human. God's power is made known in human weakness; joy in sorrow, death in life. A more balanced eschatology, in my judgment, should recognize some continuity between the now and the then. God's love is also present in human love and God's beauty in created beauty. The traditional Roman Catholic emphasis on mediation has always seen the divine as also working in and through the human.[29]

Eschatology obviously relates to theological anthropology. In any approach to bioethics, much depends on whether one is optimistic or pessimistic about the human project. Ramsey, in my judgment, is too pessimistic.

---

[28] Paul Ramsey's books on bioethics include *The Patient as Person: Explorations in Medical Ethics* (New Haven, CT: Yale University Press, 1970); *Fabricated Man: The Ethics of Genetic Control* (New Haven, CT: Yale University Press, 1970); *The Ethics of Fetal Research* (New Haven, CT: Yale University Press, 1975); *Ethics at the Edges of Life* (New Haven, CT: Yale University Press, 1978).

[29] Curran, *Politics, Medicine, and Christian Ethics*, 200–205.

I developed what I call the stance of moral theology—the perspective from which the discipline looks at the world. The Christian looks at the world on the basis of the fivefold stance of creation, sin, incarnation, redemption, and resurrection destiny. Creation recognizes the goodness of all that God has made; sin affects creation but does not totally destroy it and is not the last word; incarnation recognizes the basic goodness of the human since God became human; redemption grounds the existence of God's grace already present and working in the world, but resurrection destiny as the future of the reign of God recognizes that the fullness of God's grace and reign will come only at the end of time. Such a stance by definition opposes a one-sided theological anthropology that overemphasizes either pessimism or optimism.[30]

Fifth, in the post–Vatican II Catholic Church, the 1968 encyclical *Humanae Vitae*, reiterating the condemnation of artificial contraception, raised the question about the legitimacy of dissent both in theory and in practice from authoritative noninfallible hierarchical teaching. For many reasons I recognize the possibility and need for such dissent. Chapter 9 will discuss dissent in greater depth. The earlier insistence on a more inductive methodology also argues against the absolute certitude that had too often been connected with conclusions in Catholic moral theology before Vatican II.[31]

The Catholic tradition has long recognized the difficulty in claiming absolute certitude as one moves from the general to the particular and the specific precisely because more circumstances are involved on the specific level. Without doubt a serious tension exists between the two most significant sources of specific Catholic moral teaching—human reason and the authoritative teaching office of the church. The authoritative teaching office always claimed that its teachings were based on human reason but that, in the process of formulating the teaching, the hierarchical teaching office had the assistance of the Holy Spirit. I emphasize, however, that the assistance of the Holy Spirit does not do away with the need for all the human processes of trying to arrive at moral wisdom and truth but helps in this process. The traditional Thomistic teaching long ago raised the question: Is something good because it is commanded or is it commanded because it is good? The response of Thomas Aquinas clearly insisted on an intrinsic morality that something is commanded because it is good. Not all Catholic

---

[30] Charles E. Curran, "The Stance or Horizon of Moral Theology," in *The Pilgrim People: A Vision of Hope*, ed. Joseph Papin (Villanova, PA: Villanova University Press, 1970), 85–110.

[31] Charles E. Curran, *Faithful Dissent* (Kansas City, MO: Sheed and Ward, 1986).

moral theologians agree with the possibility and need for such dissent, and to this day the hierarchical magisterium has taken disciplinary action against some who dissent and has never positively affirmed the legitimacy of such dissent. Thus, this tension between authoritative teaching and human reason continues to exist in Roman Catholicism.

Significant continuity, however, exists between pre–Vatican II and post–Vatican II moral theology. The Catholic tradition insists on being catholic, universal, and inclusive. "Both-and" rather than "either-or" approaches tend to characterize Catholic positions, as illustrated in the understandings of eschatology and anthropology mentioned above. Catholic theology has always seen the divine as mediated in and through the human. The human and human reason are consequently good but limited and subject to sin. Post–Vatican II moral theology continues to give a prominent role to human reason and, in the light of a more inductive approach, human experience. The Catholic tradition of casuistry remains an important but only a partial aspect of moral theology.[32] In my judgment, Richard A. McCormick, the most significant Catholic bioethicist in the latter part of the twentieth century, was primarily a casuist who incorporated Vatican II understandings into his approach. This section thus explains the approach that I took to doing bioethics in the early 1970s.[33]

Looking Backward and Forward from Today

The discipline of bioethics has grown immensely since 1971. Newer questions arise almost every day. The discipline now recognizes many different perspectives—those of the physician, the nurse, the patient, and the health care institution. Bioethics touches on many disciplines—philosophy, theology, law, and political science. The move away from an exclusive quandary ethics has led to a place for virtue ethics and especially considerations of social aspects, such as the distribution of health care. Since Catholic bioethics has also experienced many developments, the following brief observations do not pretend to be comprehensive or exhaustive.

---

[32] Charles E. Curran, *The Catholic Moral Tradition Today: A Synthesis* (Washington, DC: Georgetown University Press, 1999), 1–59.

[33] For an overview and analysis of McCormick's work, see Paulinus Ikechukwu Odozor, *Richard A. McCormick and the Renewal of Moral Theology* (Notre Dame, IN: University of Notre Dame Press, 1995).

A Backward Glance

With regard to Catholic bioethics, the complexity of the issues and the breadth of the discipline mean that one has to specialize in bioethics and cannot be a generalist in moral theology covering all the different areas of the discipline. In the light of this situation, I personally decided in the late 1970s to move out of bioethics and to concentrate more in other areas. Current scholars in Catholic bioethics, with one or two exceptions, tend to specialize primarily in bioethics. The very complexity of the discipline calls for such specialization. With the continuing growth of bioethics specialization will be even more necessary in the future.

The differences within Catholic bioethics have hardened considerably since 1971. On a theoretical plane, three generic approaches exist: the older neoscholastic approach that served as the basis of the hierarchical teaching; a new natural law approach associated with Germain Grisez and John Finnis that strongly supports the positions of the hierarchical magisterium;[34] and a revisionist perspective that disagrees with and dissents from some teachings of the hierarchical magisterium. This revisionist position is not monolithic but includes a variety of positions. The revisionist position today is regularly excluded from Catholic journals and institutes with some connection to the institutional church. The *Linacre Quarterly* is the publication of the Catholic Medical Association. In the 1970s revisionist bioethicists were members of the editorial advisory board and often published in the journal. But from the 1980s Catholic revisionist bioethicists no longer serve on the advisory board and the journal does not publish articles that disagree with the teaching of the hierarchical magisterium.[35] *Health Progress*, formerly called *Hospital Progress*, the official magazine of the Catholic Health Association, published revisionist articles in the 1970s, but lately no article appears that disagrees in any way with official teaching. The Religious and Ethical Directives for Catholic Health Care Services, the official code for Catholic health care institutions, have been even more restrictive lately in their interpretation of hierarchical teaching.[36] The National Catholic Bioethics

---

[34] Nigel Biggar and Rufus Black, eds., *The Renewal of Natural Law: Philosophical, Theological, and Ethical Responses to the Finnis-Grisez School* (Burlington, VT: Ashgate, 2000).

[35] A Catholic ethicist identified more with a revisionist approach published an article in the *Linacre Quarterly*, but the article itself did not disagree with any hierarchical teachings; see James J. Walter, "Human Gene Transfer: Some Theological Contributions to the Ethical Debate," *Linacre Quarterly* (2001): 319–34.

[36] "Religious and Ethical Directives for Catholic Health Care Services," at www. nccbuscc.org.

Center, that began in 1972 as the Pope John XXIII Medico-Moral Research and Education Center, in its publications and workshops, has no place today for positions disagreeing with any existing hierarchical teaching.[37] Thus, no dialogue takes place today in these journals and publications.

At the present time Catholic hospitals in accord with the ethical directives cannot do or cooperate in any way with sterilizations. This position has also hardened since the 1970s and shows no immediate sign of changing.

A Forward Glance

For the immediate future the primary tension within Catholic bioethics over the issue of dissent from hierarchical teaching will continue. The only way for the tension to go away is for one of the two sides to change. Many of us hope that in the future official Catholic teaching will change on a number of these issues. The conclusion to this volume will discuss such change in light of the papacy of Pope Francis. Likewise, the differences and disagreements among Catholic bioethicists themselves will also not go away. However, divisions and differences among Catholic bioethicists tend to be less in the areas of bioethics that are receiving more attention today—virtue ethics and the social aspect of medicine dealing with the just and proper distribution of health care in society.

Much has been written about the fact that religious ethics today plays a much reduced role in bioethics. One illustration of this is the general understanding of the Catholic tradition with regard to what was called the ordinary and extraordinary means for preserving life, which was mentioned in the first section as going back many centuries. Paul Ramsey referred to this as the "oldest morality there is . . . concerning responsibility toward the dying."[38] He had studied the Catholic tradition in some depth and developed his own approach in the light of it. The cover of the November–December 2001 issue of the *Hastings Center Report* has only the following words on the cover: "End of Life Care: The Forgotten Catholic Tradition."[39]

---

[37] For the description of the National Catholic Bioethics Center, see www.ncbcenter.org.

[38] Paul Ramsey, "The Indignity of 'Death with Dignity,'" in *On Moral Medicine: Theological Perspectives in Medical Ethics,* 2nd ed., ed. Stephen E. Lammers and Allen Verhey (Grand Rapids, MI: William B. Eerdmans, 1998), 224.

[39] Michael Panicola, "Catholic Teaching on Prolonging Life: Setting the Record Straight," *Hastings Center Report* 31, no. 6 (November–December 2001): 14–25.

This is not the place to review and evaluate the literature that exists on the marginalization of religious bioethics and what might and should be done about it, but one comment is in order. Within Christian bioethics today, two different approaches exist. Some claim that Christian bioethics should directly address only the Christian community and not the broader human community or the aspects of law and public policy.[40] A second position maintains that Christian ethics addresses two different audiences—the church and the broader human community. Again, a full discussion of these two positions lies beyond the parameters of this chapter, but one point deserves mentioning. The Catholic tradition with its emphasis on mediation, the human, inclusiveness, and universality has always had a concern for what takes place in the world and has tried to address such issues. Recall the two pastoral letters on peace and the economy written by the US Catholic bishops in the 1980s and addressed to both the church and the broader human society. The problems connected with this approach from Constantinianism to the present are well known, but for the Catholic tradition to be true to itself it must continue to address both the church and the world.[41]

In the future the official Catholic approach to law and public policy must become more conscious of the difference between law or public policy and morality as the difference was developed in the Declaration on Religious Freedom of Vatican II. Too often official Catholic statements move from morality immediately to legality or policy. But the Declaration on Religious Freedom proposed a more nuanced approach to the relationship between law or public policy and morality.

The declaration (para. 7) accepted the fundamental principle of a free society—as much freedom as possible and as little restraint as necessary. The document proposes public order as the criterion to justify and require the intervention of the state. According to Vatican II, public order embraces the goods of justice, public peace, and public morality.

In the light of this approach, the following three principles govern the justification of the coercive use of law in a pluralistic society. (1) As much freedom as possible and as little restraint as necessary. (2) Law can and should intervene to preserve and promote justice, public peace, and public morality. (3) There is a pragmatic aspect to all laws. Is the law feasible? Can it be passed? Can it be enforced? Often legislators will be forced to

---

[40] See, for example, Stanley Hauerwas, *Naming the Silences: God, Medicine, and the Problem of Suffering* (Grand Rapids, MI: William B. Eerdmans, 1990).

[41] Curran, *Catholic Moral Tradition Today*, 1–29.

compromise in order to get a law passed that in their judgment is somewhat imperfect but better than nothing. This understanding of law recognizes some pragmatic aspects but, at the same time, also does not reduce law only to the pragmatic as illustrated in the second principle calling for law to protect and promote justice, public peace, and public morality.

In the United States in the last thirty years the Roman Catholic Church has strenuously attempted to support laws prohibiting abortion.[42] How does the foregoing approach to civil law relate to the question of whether or not there should be a law against abortion? In this analysis I will presume the official Catholic teaching that direct abortion is morally wrong. One could justify supporting abortion legislation on the basis of the principles described above by invoking especially the second principle, that law should intervene to protect justice. If one believes that the fetus is a truly human person, then justice demands there be a law to protect the life of the fetus.

On the other hand, one could use the first and third principles in the approach mentioned above to come to the conclusion that there should be no law against abortion in our pluralistic society today. On the basis of the first principle of as much freedom as possible and as little restraint as necessary, one can argue that the present divisions and impasse in this country over abortion mean that the freedom of people who believe in the possibility of abortion should be respected. When the civil society is heavily divided, the presumption is in favor of freedom. Likewise the pragmatic aspects of the above theory of law could argue against an abortion law. Many have pointed out (but not without rebuttal) that laws condemning abortion would ultimately be unenforceable. Above all, pragmatic aspects of feasibility come to the fore. There does not seem to be the possibility of passing such laws at the present time.

In the light of the Vatican II approach, the primary way for the church to affect society is not through the coercive force of law but by freely entering the public dialogue and trying to convince others by the church's own elaboration of and witness to the truth.[43] In my judgment, the pastoral letters of the US bishops on peace and the economy followed this approach

---

[42] Timothy A. Byrnes and Mary C. Segers, eds., *The Catholic Church and the Politics of Abortion: A View from the States* (Boulder, CO: Westview, 1992).

[43] Hermíno Rico, *John Paul II and the Legacy of Dignitatis Humanae* (Washington, DC: Georgetown University Press, 2002), 147–243. Rico here distinguishes this approach, which he sees as grounded in Vatican II, from the approach taken by Pope John Paul II.

and as a result played a very significant role in the public debate over these issues in the United States.

In the future, there is no doubt that there will continue to be acrimonious debates in our society about public policy and laws dealing with questions of bioethics. From the viewpoint of theology, I believe Christian churches, including the Catholic Church, have a right to speak up on these issues and to work for appropriate public policy. However, in so doing, I think the Catholic Church must become much more conscious of the approach to law and morality that was proposed at the Second Vatican Council but often has not been mentioned in the discussion about law and public policy in the United States in the last thirty years.[44] At the very minimum, this approach does not rely only or primarily on law, is more complex, and recognizes more ambiguity about the role of law than official Catholic statements recognize.

In this chapter I have tried to show how I approach bioethics in the light of the Catholic tradition while recognizing that there are other different approaches within the same Catholic tradition. No one can accurately predict what developments will occur as the Catholic moral tradition addresses bioethics in the future.

---

[44] For essays from various positions on the role of the US Catholic bishops in law and public policy, see Charles E. Curran and Leslie Griffin, eds., *The Catholic Church, Morality, and Politics: Readings in Moral Theology No. 12* (New York: Paulist Press, 2001), 141–247, 291–310. For one bishop who employed the criterion about the relationship between morality and law as developed in the Declaration on Religious Freedom, see in the above volume, Joseph L. Bernardin, "Consistent Ethic of Life," 160–69.

Chapter 8

AN APPRAISAL OF POPE JOHN PAUL II'S TEACHING ON SEXUALITY AND MARRIAGE*

Pope John Paul II in his long papacy (1978–2005) wrote extensively on sexuality and marriage. The encyclical *Veritatis Splendor* (1993) covers the whole field of moral theology and occasionally mentions sexuality and marriage in the process.[1] The Apostolic Exhortation *Familiaris Consortio* (1981) considers sexuality and marriage in the context of the family.[2]

The most extensive discussion of sexuality and marriage comes from the talks the pope gave at his first general audiences held weekly from September 1979 to November 1984. Ordinarily a discussion of papal teaching does not focus on the short talks given at the pope's weekly audiences. Often these talks are merely salutatory or homiletical. Popes usually have not used this vehicle as a teaching source for the whole church. Popes, including John Paul II, cannot personally draft and write all the minor talks they give. But in this case, no one doubts that John Paul II is the primary author of these short talks. John Paul II obviously had these talks prepared before he became pope and used them at the beginning of his pontificate. The content of these short talks seems quite inappropriate for a general papal audience. They are too intellectual, too theological, and can only be totally understood as parts of a whole. Most participants in the general audience probably could not—and

---

* Originally published as Charles E. Curran, "Pope John Paul II's Teaching on Sexuality and Marriage: An Appraisal," *University of St. Thomas Law Journal* 1 (Fall 2003): 610–31. Used with permission.

[1] For a helpful collection of the encyclicals of John Paul II, see J. Michael Miller, ed., *The Encyclicals of John Paul II* (Huntington, IN: Our Sunday Visitor, 2001). *Veritatis Splendor* is found on pages 584–661. Subsequent references in the text to *Veritatis Splendor* will be to *VS* followed by the paragraph number. N.B.: The translations of papal texts use exclusive language. I do not note this in every particular case, but it is necessary to call attention to it here.

[2] "*Familiaris Consortio*," in *The Post-Synodal Apostolic Exhortations of John Paul II*, ed. J. Michael Miller (Huntington, IN: Our Sunday Visitor, 1998), 148–233. Subsequent references in the text will be to *FC* followed by the paragraph number.

did not—follow what the pope was trying to communicate. But the talks constitute a real source for understanding John Paul II's approach to sexuality and marriage. These talks have been published in English in one large volume, *The Theology of the Body: Human Love in the Divine Plan*.[3]

This chapter will analyze and criticize the teaching of Pope John Paul II on the theology of the body and human sexuality, the sacramentality of marriage, and the specific norms of the indissolubility of marriage and the condemnation of artificial contraception. The final section contrasts the historically conscious approach of John T. Noonan Jr., who has written extensively on the development of Catholic teaching in the area of marriage and sexuality, with the lack of historical consciousness in the teaching of John Paul II and his failure to recognize significant historical developments in many of these issues.

Theology and Meaning of the Body and Human Sexuality

Karol Wojtyla's training and profession was as an ethicist. His writings before becoming pope dealt primarily with issues of meaning and not primarily with casuistry. As pope, he had to address many casuistic issues dealing with the moral norms of Catholic hierarchical teaching, but he still continued to probe the deeper question of meaning. His long series of general audience talks at the beginning of his pontificate well illustrates such an approach.

John Paul II develops the meaning and theology of the body and human sexuality in the light of his theological anthropology involving creation, the fall, and redemption of the body (*TB* 25–90).

In the garden, in the state of original innocence before the fall ("In the beginning"), the human person experiences three aspects of humanity—original solitude, original unity or communion of persons, and original nakedness. Thanks to the gift of creation, in the very experience of his body, Adam perceives himself as different from all other creation including the animals because he has a unique relationship with God. The pope often refers to this as the first covenant. Through this covenant given by God, Adam experiences his power of self-determination and self-choice in which

---

[3] John Paul II, *The Theology of the Body: Human Love in the Divine Plan* (Boston: Pauline Books, 1997). Subsequent references in the text will be to *TB* followed by the page number.

he recognizes himself as an image of God. But Adam also experiences that he is alone—he is missing someone to share love and life with him (*TB* 35–42).

The second aspect of creation is the original unity or the communion of persons in and through the body (*TB* 42–57). God made woman—the equal and the partner of man. Human beings now appear as masculine and feminine. This sexual difference makes possible the communion of persons in and through their bodies, which reflects God's own Trinitarian life. This "nuptial meaning" of the body is shown in the sincere gift of one to the other. In this context, John Paul II often cites *Gaudium et Spes* 24—"Man can fully discover his true self only in a sincere giving of himself" (*TB* 60–66). Here, the human person finds oneself an even more significant image of the triune God.

The third aspect of original nakedness also contributes to the nuptial meaning of the body. This original nakedness signifies the absence of shame or interior division that allows Adam and Eve to give themselves totally and completely to one another in the sincere gift of love. There is no holding back and no temptation to treat the other as an object (*TB* 57–60).

The fall brought about a threefold break with regard to the human person—a break in the relationship of loving dependence on God, which John Paul II refers to as a breaking of the covenant, the break in the relationship between man and woman, and a break or disunion in the human person brought about by concupiscence. In keeping with the Catholic understanding of the role of sin, the fall does not completely destroy what was present from the beginning but obscures or diminishes the image and likeness of God in the human being.[4]

The theology of the body puts special emphasis on the concupiscence and lust that causes the division within the human person (spirit and body) and thereby affects the community of persons in their one-flesh unity. In this context, Genesis 3:7 is the primary text—"Then the eyes of both were open, and they knew that they were naked, and they sewed fig leafs together and made themselves aprons." Genesis 3:10 adds another element. In response to the call of God after the fall in the garden, Adam replied, "I heard the sound of you in the garden, and I was afraid because I was naked, and I hid myself." Thus, the "man of original innocence" becomes the "man of lust." Lust manifests itself above all in the shame that human beings now experience after the

---

[4] Pope John Paul II, "Apostolic Letter: *Mulieris Dignitatem*," para. 9, in *Theology of the Body*, 454–55. Subsequent references in the text will be to *MD* followed by the paragraph number.

fall. A disquiet exists within human beings. This is the second discovery of sex (*TB* 114–25).

Although John Paul II recognizes that original sin also affects the heart and the spirit (*TB* 122), the emphasis here is on the fact that the body is no longer subject to the spirit. Lust thus affects the relationship of man and woman and the nuptial meaning of the body. Gone is the joyous, spontaneous self-gift of one to the other. The pope mentions at various times three different but interconnected effects of the lust, concupiscence, and shame that affect the nuptial relationship of man and woman. First, the very fact that Adam and Eve hid themselves from one another behind their aprons shows a lack of trust. Notice how this hiding relates to the fact that they hid themselves from God previously because they knew they were naked (*TB* 121). Second, the husband "will rule over you" (Genesis 3:16). The domination of one over the other thus destroys the original equality (*TB* 122–24). Third, the heart is now a battlefield between love and lust. Concupiscence works against the self-control and interior freedom of the original communion of persons. Now the other is no longer a person but is reduced to an object of sexual gratification (*TB* 125–30). Such are the effects of sin on the nuptial meaning of the body and the sexual union of man and woman.

The pope bases the effect of redemption on the nuptial meaning of the body on a number of different scriptural texts, in contradistinction to his emphasis on just Genesis 2 and 3 in describing original innocence and the fall. One series of thirteen talks bears the title: "St. Paul's Teaching on the Human Body" (*TB* 191–232). Here the pope refers to many different Pauline epistles. The human body is the temple of the Holy Spirit and member of Christ (1 Cor. 6:15–20). 1 Thessalonians 4:4 calls for controlling the body in holiness and honor. Paul in Romans 8:23 refers explicitly to the redemption of the body. This redemption by God's grace overcomes the effect of the fall and makes possible once again the nuptial meaning of the body found in original innocence (*TB* 32–34).

The pope puts heavy emphasis on Matthew 5:27–28—if a man looks at a woman lustfully, he has already committed adultery in his heart. The meaning of adultery is transferred from the body to the heart (*TB* 142–44). Redemption thus overcomes the power of concupiscence and lust that sees the other merely as an object of sexual gratification. Concupiscence and lust depersonalize. Male and female, through the redemption of the body, now regain the nuptial meaning of the body because of which they can freely give themselves totally in the self-gift of one to the other. The Sermon on the Mount calls us not to go back to original innocence but to rediscover, on the foundations of the perennial and indestructible meaning of what is human, the living form of redeemed humankind (*TB* 175). Through self-control, continence, and temperance, man and woman can now live out the nuptial meaning of the body. The power of redemption thus completes the power of creation (*TB* 147–80).

Sacramentality of Marriage

John Paul II devoted a series of his general audience talks from July 28, 1982, to July 4, 1984, with some interruptions to the sacramentality of marriage (*TB* 304–80). In keeping with his methodology in these talks, he bases his approach on scripture and in particular on Ephesians 5:21–32. The very first talk begins with the citation of this long passage. This passage in general calls on spouses to love one another as Christ has loved the church. Because of this, a man leaves his mother and father to become one flesh with his wife. This is a great mystery in reference to Christ and the church. Note that the English word "mystery" here is a translation of the Latin word *sacramentum*. Thus, the passage lends itself to be understood in a sacramental way. But, of course, to see any nature of sacramentality in this passage, one has to read quite a bit into the biblical passage itself—which John Paul II is very willing to do.

The passage also appeals to the pope for a number of other reasons. Ephesians here cites Genesis about a man leaving father and mother and becoming one flesh with his wife. Thus the passage refers back to the "beginning" to which the pope has paid so much attention in his previous talks. The passage puts heavy emphasis on the body in keeping with the pope's emphasis on the theology of the body. But, in addition to referring to the human body in its masculinity and femininity, Ephesians speaks of the body in a metaphorical sense—the body of the church—and thus provides a basis for the sacramental understanding of the spousal relationship of husband and wife in light of the relationship of Christ to the church. In addition, the liturgy of the church sees this text in its relationship to the sacrament of marriage. Here, the prayer of the church tells us something about the faith of the church (*TB* 304–6).

Many contemporaries have problems with this text, especially with its understanding of the relationship of husband and wife. Wives are to be subject to their husbands. Despite the obvious literal meaning of the text, John Paul II claims there is no subordination of the wife to the husband in this text. The pope points out that the passage from Ephesians is part of the teaching on the moral obligations within the family—the so-called *Haustaflen* or household codes (*TB* 308). Pope John Paul II explicitly recognizes that our understanding today of the social position of women is quite different from that of the times in which Ephesians was written. However, he insists that "the fundamental moral principle which we find in Ephesians remains the same and produces the same results. The mutual subjection 'out of reverence for Christ' . . . always produces that profound and solid structure of the community of the spouses in which the true 'communion' of the person is constituted" (*TB* 311).

The mutual relations of husband and wife flow from their common relationship with Christ. They are to be subject to one another out of reverence for Christ. There is a mutual subjection of the spouses, one to the other, based on their relationship to Christ. Husbands are then told to love their wives, which "removes any fear that might have arisen (given the modern sensitivity) from the previous phrase: 'wives be subject to your husbands'" (*TB* 310). Love excludes any subjection whereby the wife is a servant, slave, or object of domination by the husband. The communion of husband and wife is based on mutual love and mutual subjection (*TB* 310).

In addition, the pope does not deal with the analogy of Christ to the husband and the church to the wife. Christ is obviously the head of his body, the church. For many Christians, even some today, this means that the husband is the head of the wife and of the family. But the pope's own position is clear—there is a reciprocal and equal love relationship of husband and wife with no one-sided domination by the husband.

In his discussion of marriage as a sacrament, John Paul II uses the term "sacrament" in both a broader and a narrower or more technical sense of a sacrament of the church. In the broader sense, a sacrament is a sign that effectively transmits in the visible world the invisible mystery hidden from eternity in God (*TB* 333, 341). In this sense, creation and redemption are both sacraments. But marriage is the primordial sacrament, signifying the loving relationship of God to his people and of Christ to the church. Marriage is the "primordial sacrament instituted from the beginning and linked with the sacrament of creation in its globality" (*TB* 339). Ephesians 1:3–4 tells us of the mystery hidden in God from all eternity. God chose us in Christ before the foundation of the world that we should be holy and blameless before him. "The reality of man's creation was already imbued by the perennial election of man in Christ" (*TB* 334). The procreative powers of the first couple also continue the work of creation. Thus, marriage is the primordial sacrament of creation itself (*TB* 333–36).

But marriage is also the primordial sacrament of redemption. Although grace was lost after the fall, marriage never ceased to be in some sense a figure of the great mystery or sacrament of God's covenant love for his people. There is a continuity between creation and redemption. The sacrament of creation, as the original gift of grace, constituted human beings in the state of original innocence and justice. "The new gracing of man in the sacrament of redemption instead gives him above all the remission of sins" (*TB* 337). Grace abounds even more. Christ's redemptive love, according to Ephesians, is his special love for the church of which marriage is the primordial sacrament (*TB* 337).

The sacrament of marriage in the narrower and stricter sense of one of the seven sacraments of the church, based on Ephesians, understands the relationship between husband and wife in the light of the relationship between Christ and the church. This analogy operates in two directions. The relationship of Christ to the church tells us something about Christian marriage, whereas the spousal relationship tells us something about Christ's love for the church (*TB* 312–14). The Hebrew Bible prefigured this analogy, as found in the prophets such as Isaiah who rebukes Israel as an unfaithful spouse (*TB* 327–30). John Paul II also appeals to the Song of Songs: "found in the wake of that sacrament in which, through the language of the body, the visible sign of man and woman's participation in the covenant of grace and love offered by God to man is constituted" (*TB* 368). The Book of Tobit also tells us about the truth and power of marital love (*TB* 375–77). The gift of Christ to the church is "a total and irrevocable gift of self on the part of God to man in Christ" (*TB* 338). So too, the total and irrevocable gift of husband and wife to one another takes place in Christian marriage (*TB* 330–32). This total and irrevocable gift is the basis for the unity and indissolubility of marriage.

The matrimonial consent of husband and wife shares in, signifies, and also tells something about the covenant of Christ with the church and of God with his people. "The analogy of spousal love indicates the radical character of grace" (*TB* 330). "The analogy of spousal love seems to emphasize especially the aspect of the gift of self on the part of God to man. . . . It is a total (or rather radical) and irrevocable gift" (*TB* 33).

The pope in these many talks only alludes to the matrimonial vow or consent of the couple, whom he recognizes are themselves the ministers of the sacrament of marriage. One would expect a full-length discussion of this covenant promise of marriage—for better, for worse; for richer, for poorer; in good times and in bad, until death do us part. Perhaps a heavy emphasis on the scriptural basis for the teaching means that the liturgical expression of the meaning of marriage is not developed in these talks. But the marriage vow itself well illustrates the type of love that the pope has been describing and shows the full meaning of the total and irrevocable gift of one to the other (*TB* 360–62).

John Paul II consistently develops his understanding of marriage and sexuality in all three settings—the beginning, the fall, and redemption—with regard to both the metaphysical or objective aspect of human existence and the subjective or psychological aspect of anthropology. The objective aspect especially involves the body, which is the primary topic of all these talks, although, the body is always understood in personalistic terms and not in naturalistic terms. The beginning of creation tells the mystical meaning of the body. Nakedness after the fall involves how sin has affected the nuptial meaning of the body through concupiscence and lust. But redemption renews the possibility of the nuptial meaning of the body with the marital self-gift of husband and wife.

The subjective aspect begins with Adam's experience of loneliness and solitude which gives way then, after the creation of Eve, to the communion of persons and bodies. But the fall brings about the shame that now affects human intentionality as well as the body. Redemption renews the human person who, through God's grace, now experiences purity in heart. Thus the pope develops his understanding of marriage in the light of an anthropology embracing both the objective and subjective aspects of human existence.

Critical Appraisal

The pope has developed his understanding of marriage and sexuality primarily through the long series of general audience talks at the beginning of his pontificate. One cannot easily describe the genre of these talks. Although they have a homiletical tone at times, they are not homilies. Without doubt the talks belong to the genre of teaching. Here, the pope is proposing to the world his understanding of marriage, of its meaning, and of spirituality for Christians today. The talks occasionally cite philosophers and other secular thinkers; the talks also come complete with footnotes. But a theology of the body is not developed in a systematic and complete way. The very nature of short talks presented every week to a different audience militates against an in-depth and totally systematic approach. Since the talks are not a complete and systematic presentation of the pope's teaching on marriage, many aspects remain somewhat unclear and certainly less developed than they would in a truly systematic presentation. I consider three issues—the spirit-body relationship, the meaning of love, and the role of sexual pleasure.

The Spirit-Body Relationship

There is no Manichaean dualism in John Paul II's anthropology of human sexuality. The body and sexuality are not bad (*TB* 165–67). The very title of the book in English, *The Theology of the Body*, argues against any kind of total dualism between the spirit and body or matter. Yet in the world of human existence after sin, the pope frequently refers to lust and its effects on the human person in terms of the body.

In discussing lust these talks frequently cite 1 John 2:15–16, which mentions the threefold aspect of lust—lust of the flesh, of the eyes, and of the pride of life (e.g., *TB* 116, 127, 165, 203). So lust also involves the spirit and not just the body. But there can be no doubt that John Paul II emphasizes the lust of the flesh. The phrase from the Sermon on the Mount (looking lustfully at a woman), which he so often cites, does not condemn the body or sexuality but "contains a call to overcome the three forms of lust, especially the lust of the flesh" (*TB* 165). In another context the talks comment on 1 Corinthians 12:18–25 in which St. Paul refers to the less honorable parts or the unpresentable parts of the body. For John Paul II, St. Paul here calls for respect for the whole human body with no Manichaean contempt for the body. But St. Paul is conscious of historical humankind after sin and in using these terms for the sexual parts of the body testifies to the shame that has been present in human experience ever since the sin of Adam and Eve. This shame is the fruit of the three forms of lust, with particular reference to the lust of the flesh (*TB* 202–3). As a result of such an understanding, these texts frequently refer to "The Opposition in the Human Heart between the Spirit and the Body," which is the title of the July 30, 1980, address (*TB* 128). The problem with "the man of lust" after original sin is that "the body is not subordinated to the spirit as in the state of original innocence. It bears within it a constant center of resistance to the spirit" (*TB* 115).

In the light of such an understanding of the effect of lust and concupiscence for redeemed people, "the body is given as a task to the human spirit" (*TB* 215). This is the spirituality of the body. For the redeemed person, the emphasis is on self-control. "It is precisely at the price of self-control that man reaches that deeper and more mature spontaneity with which his heart, mastering his instincts, rediscovers the spiritual beauty of the sign constituted by the human body in its masculinity and femininity" (*TB* 173). However, John Paul II is not entirely negative about passion. Without doubt, carnal concupiscence and passion suffocate the voice of conscience.

Passion tends to satisfy the senses and the body, but such satisfaction brings no true peace or lasting satisfaction. However, through the radical transformation of grace, passion can become a creative force (*TB* 145–46).

No one can deny the role of concupiscence and lust in human sexuality. Self-control and discipline are absolutely necessary. But John Paul II's incomplete discussion of concupiscence, lust, and self-control seems too one-sided. Yes, sin affects the body, but it also affects the spirit. Sin does not bring about an opposition between spirit and body or between the higher and the lower parts of the human person, as so often seems to be the case in the words used by John Paul II. The senses and passions are not simply forces that must be controlled and directed by reason. The senses and the passions, despite the influence of sin, still can point to and indicate the true and the good. Reason and spirit are not the only realities that can help us discern the true and the good. And, like the senses and passions, they too can become disturbed by sin. Yes, there is need for self-control with regard to sexual passion, but sexual passion is basically a good that is often disturbed by sin. Its basic goodness should not be denied or forgotten. These talks give the impression that passion and sexual pleasure are totally suspect and in need of control. The pope does not seem to acknowledge a fundamental goodness about sexuality despite the ever-present danger of lust and concupiscence. There is just an occasional remark along more positive lines, but the heavy emphasis of the talks remains on the negative reality of sexual passion and the need for spirit and reason to control it.

Meaning of Love

The lack of a systematic and complete theology of the body in these talks also comes through in the sketchy understanding of human love. The subtitle of the English collection of these talks is "Human Love in the Divine Plan," but there is no in-depth or systematic discussion of human love. The general approach is quite clear, but it usually presents just two extremes. Love involves a sincere gift of self to the other—"the personal and total self-giving" (*FC* 20.3). The opposite of love is treating the other as an object or as a means of self-sexual gratification. The contrast is between disinterested giving and selfish enjoyment (*TB* 130). The primary understanding of marriage as a sign of the covenant love of God for human beings, of Yahweh for the people of the covenant, and of Christ for the church makes the love of giving self to the other the basic meaning of marital love. The divine analogue for this love is the love of Jesus who became human and died for us on the Cross in a total gift of self. Theological literature refers to this love as agape—the total giving of self.

Although John Paul II gives primacy to love or the gift of self modeled on God's love, especially as seen in the Incarnation and death of Jesus, the other aspects of love as reciprocity or mutual communion and also self-fulfillment are mentioned occasionally in the talks.

Love as personal communion comes through especially in the loving union of Adam and Eve overcoming the problem of solitude. Here, Pope John Paul II uses the analogy of the love of the three divine persons in the Trinity. The body shares fully in the personal communion of love between husband and wife. Such a love makes Adam and Eve, as husband and wife, images of the love of the Trinity (*TB* 45–48).

In common language today, the erotic signifies what comes from desire and serves to satisfy the lust of the flesh. This is precisely what Matthew 5:27–28 condemns and what the talks emphasize. But eros in the Platonic sense has a positive role to play. Here, eros is the interior force that attracts human beings to what is true, good, and beautiful. In the description of original innocence in the garden, the talks recognize that Adam longed for someone to share love and life with him. The attraction, and even the sexual attraction between man and woman, has a very positive aspect about it. The Song of Songs presents eros as the form of human love in which the energies of desire are at work. Agape love, as described by St. Paul in 1 Corinthians 13:4–8 (love is patient, kind, not jealous), purifies this eros love of the Song of Songs and brings it to completion (*TB* 168–71). Thus, in the talks, there are some indications that eros is not completely negative and even has a positive role to play.

At the very minimum, the full meaning of Christian love with all its dimensions is not developed in a systematic way in these talks. The emphasis is on agape love understood as self-gift. Love as communion is considered but never integrated with love as self-gift. John Paul II does not discuss at length the concept of proper love of self and pays too little attention to this concept in his talks. The focus is on love as self-gift without developing the point that true self-fulfillment and happiness are achieved in and through this self-gift.

Sexual Pleasure

The Theology of the Body, for all practical purposes, ignores the reality of sexual pleasure. All recognize that the drive for sexual pleasure often distorts what the pope calls "the nuptial meaning of the body." But sexual

discussed by celibates

pleasure itself is something that is a good that can be, and often is, abused. One would expect that talks dealing precisely with the body would recognize the role of sexual pleasure in marriage and insist that such pleasure is good. This failure to mention the role and goodness of sexual pleasure is somewhat connected with the previous discussions of lust and love. Lust affects primarily the flesh. The failure to develop the proper role of sexual pleasure seems to be associated with a fear of such pleasure and a tendency to see it primarily in a negative way. The emphasis is on self-control and on the evil of concupiscence. If the talks gave more importance to a proper self-love and true fulfillment, they would also have furnished a proper context for the discussion of sexual pleasure.

Specific Norms

John Paul II, as is obvious, strongly supports and defends the existing hierarchical Catholic teachings on specific moral norms dealing with sexuality. With regard to marriage and sexuality, the two most significant and controversial norms are the prohibitions of divorce and of artificial contraception.

Indissolubility of Marriage

Nowhere in his major papal writings does John Paul II develop the Catholic prohibition of divorce in a systematic and in-depth manner. Throughout his writings, however, he proposes four basic reasons for the indissolubility of Christian marriage and the prohibition of divorce.

The scriptural argument is primary and comes from Matthew 19:3–9. The very first audience talk on marriage in 1979 insists on the unity and indissolubility of marriage in the light of Matthew 19. Jesus claims that Moses allowed divorce because of the hardness of men's hearts, but from the beginning it was not so (*TB* 25–27). This scripture text reminds us of "God's original plan for mankind, a plan which man after sin has no longer been able to live up to" (*VS* 22.2). "Christ renews the first plan that the Creator inscribed in the hearts of man and woman" (*FC* 20).

The sacramental argument sees the marriage covenant as a sign or sacrament of the covenant love of God for the people in the Hebrew Bible and of Jesus for the church. But such covenant love of God and of Christ is an absolutely faithful love. "Just as the Lord Jesus is . . . the supreme realization of the unconditional faithfulness with which God loves his people, so Christian couples are called to participate truly in the irrevocable indissolubility that binds Christ to the Church, his Bride, loved by him to the end" (*FC* 20.4).

The theological argument for indissolubility insists on the role of the grace of God. "To imitate and live out the love of Christ is not possible for man by his own strength alone. *He becomes capable of this love only by virtue of a gift received*" (*VS* 22.3). Jesus freely communicates to his disciples the grace he has received from his Father (*VS* 22.3).

A theological ethical argument also grounds the prohibition of divorce. Christian marriage involves the commitment of the spouses to each other—"a total and irrevocable gift of self" (*TB* 330). Indissolubility is "rooted in the personal and total self-giving of the couple" (*FC* 20). Marital love, as the total gift of self, grounds the indissolubility of marriage.

Artificial Contraception

Pope John Paul II devoted a series of sixteen audience talks in the second half of 1984 to reflections on Pope Paul VI's 1968 encyclical *Humanae Vitae* in which he staunchly defends the condemnation of artificial contraception for spouses. This section of the chapter will very briefly summarize the arguments proposed by the pope.

In keeping with his general approach to marriage and sexuality, John Paul II, in condemning artificial contraception, gives primary significance to truth and to the plan of God. In discussing the meaning of the marital act, "we are dealing with nothing other than reading the language of the body in truth as has been said many times in our previous biblical analyses" (*TB* 388). The pope insists "that the principle of conjugal morality taught by the Church (Second Vatican Council, Paul VI), is the criterion of faithfulness to the divine plan" (*TB* 395).

The pope directly appeals to the authoritative teaching of past popes and especially to Pope Paul VI's 1968 encyclical *Humanae Vitae*. He sees his own exposition of *Humanae Vitae* in terms of trying "to elaborate more completely the biblical and personalistic aspects of the doctrine contained in *Humanae Vitae*" (*TB* 421). (The next chapter will consider the teaching of *Humanae Vitae*.) The questions raised by *Humanae Vitae* "belong to that sphere of anthropology and theology that we have called the theology of the body" (*TB* 421).

Pope John Paul II insists with Pope Paul VI on the "inseparable connection, established by God, which man on his own initiative may not break, between the unitive significance and the procreative significance which are both inherent to the marriage act" (*TB* 386). John Paul II accepts the criterion proposed in Vatican II that sexual morality is "based on the nature of the human person and his or her acts." But here he develops especially his language of the body. The marriage act, in the light of the theology of the body, shows the "value of 'total' self-giving" (*FC* 32.4). "Thus the innate language that expresses the total reciprocal self-giving of husband and wife is overlaid, through contraception, by an objectively contradictory language, namely, that of not giving oneself totally to the other. This leads . . . to a falsification of the inner truth of conjugal love which is called upon to give itself in personal totality" (*FC* 32.4). The papal talks also insist that the church's teaching on the transmission of life calls for the development of discipline, continence, and self-control, which ennoble human marital love (*TB* 399–415).

The many debates within Catholicism on the subject of divorce and artificial contraception lie beyond the boundaries of this chapter. This section has merely tried to briefly describe John Paul II's approach to these issues in light of his understanding of marriage and sexuality, developed earlier. But two comments are in order.

With regard to the indissolubility of marriage, John Paul II stresses the total, radical, and irrevocable self-gift of the spouses to each other. But as pointed out earlier, he fails to give enough importance to love as communion or to the mutuality and reciprocity aspects of love. Likewise, he does not develop the proper love of self. An understanding of love that recognizes the three aspects of self-gift, communion and mutuality, and a proper self-love supports the conclusion that unfortunately, at times, marriages may break down.

With regard to artificial contraception, the analysis of the marital sexual act based on the language of the body puts too much emphasis on the meaning of each and every single sexual act. No one act can ever perfectly express the total commitment of the spouses to each other. The pope's analysis demands too much meaning and symbolism from each and every single act. In addition, there are many sexual acts, such as embraces and kisses, that, by the pope's understanding, do not express total self-giving. The totality of the acts of the spouses in all their different dimensions shows their commitment to each other. But no one single act can always be said to require showing forth the symbolism of total gift. Notice here again the understanding of love as total self-giving.

Further Methodological Assessment

From a positive perspective, the moral teaching of John Paul II on marriage and sexuality avoids the danger often found in past hierarchical moral teaching and in much of academic moral theology of dealing simply with specific issues, norms, and quandaries. The pope here is primarily interested in the meaning and understanding of marriage and sexuality. These talks also bring together moral theology and spiritual theology. Too often, in the past, even in the moral theology of the academy, the disciplinary boundaries of moral and spiritual theology have kept the two aspects separated in practice. The heavy emphasis on scripture brings in this important dimension, which in the past has often not been sufficiently used in Catholic moral teaching. In using scripture, the pope shows an awareness of contemporary critical biblical scholarship. He distinguishes the two different creation accounts in Genesis in accord with the multiple source theory of the first five books of the bible (*TB* 27–32). He begins his long discussion of sacramentality of marriage based on Ephesians 5:21–32 by recognizing the problems scholars discuss about the authorship, date of composition, and intended audience of the letter (*TB* 306). But critical questions of method arise especially in two areas—the use of scripture together with the failure to use other significant sources accepted in Catholic moral theology and the lack of historical consciousness.

Like all interpretations of scripture, the writings of John Paul II show the presuppositions that the person brings to an interpretation of scripture. There is no such thing as the neutral, value-free interpreter of scripture. Without doubt, the pope is always going to see and interpret scripture as supporting existing Catholic teachings. Thus, for example, he uses many scriptural quotes to argue for the unity and indissolubility of marriage. In addition, John Paul II as an academic taught philosophical ethics and metaphysics. He obviously interprets scripture in the light of his own academic interests. John Paul II sees in the first account of creation "a powerful metaphysical content" (*TB* 28). The human being is defined here in a metaphysical way, in terms of being and existence. He sees the good or value in light of this metaphysical approach. The first chapter of Genesis provides "a solid basis for a metaphysic and also for an anthropology and an ethic according to which *ens et bonum convertuntur* [being and the good are convertible]" (*TB* 28). Most biblical commentators would not see such a metaphysics in the first chapter of Genesis. We all must be careful about the presuppositions we bring to our understanding of scripture, but it is evident how the pope's background influences his approach to scriptural interpretation. Recall also his denial of the subordination of wives to husbands in Ephesians 5.

John Paul II gives a long and detailed analysis of Matthew 19 at the very beginning of these talks and frequently cites it elsewhere but never explains the famous exception clause (except for the case of *porneia*) with regard to divorce and the indissolubility of marriage. Especially since he is defending the condemnation of divorce in all circumstances, one would have expected him to deal with this issue. 1 Corinthians 7:10–16 condemns divorce based on the teaching of the Lord, but then St. Paul, in his own name, teaches that a person who becomes a baptized Christian is free to remarry if the previous non-Christian spouse refuses to peacefully live together. Again, the pope never discusses the exception to indissolubility in this text that the Catholic Church today calls the Pauline Privilege.

The papal teaching here explicitly gives great attention to scripture and also to hierarchical teaching, but fails to employ other sources of moral wisdom and knowledge that have consistently characterized the Catholic theological tradition. Tradition itself, in the strict sense of the term, has played a significant role in Catholic theology. Roman Catholic theology has insisted on the need for both scripture and tradition. In fact, in the past, Catholic theology gave the impression of seeing them as two totally separate realities. But the insistence on scripture and tradition today recognizes that the scriptures themselves are historically and culturally conditioned and thus differ somewhat from present-day circumstances. The task of tradition is to understand, appropriate, and live the word and work of Jesus in the light of the present conditions of time and place.[5] One coming out of the Catholic tradition is also surprised by the lack of explicit development of natural law in the general understanding of marriage and sexuality, since natural law continues to be the basis for John Paul II's position on norms governing sexuality. Likewise, the talks give no role to contemporary experience. Contemporary Catholic moral theology recognizes a significant role for experience in moral theology, but such experience cannot be reduced merely to public opinion polls or to what the majority of people think or do. The emphasis on experience in Catholic tradition is not something that has arisen only recently. The *sensus fidelium* (the sense of the faithful) has consistently been recognized as a possible source of truth and wisdom.[6]

---

[5] Harold C. Skillrud, J. Francis Stafford, and Daniel F. Martensen, eds., *Scripture and Tradition: Lutherans and Catholics in Dialogue IX* (Minneapolis: Augsburg, 1995).

[6] Richard R. Gaillardetz, *Teaching with Authority: A Theology of the Magisterium in the Church* (Collegeville, MN: Liturgical Press, 1997), 230–35.

The heavy and almost exclusive emphasis on scripture in these talks thus goes against the traditionally accepted Catholic understanding of the sources for moral wisdom and knowledge. But the somewhat homiletical nature of the talks might furnish a partial explanation of the heavy emphasis on scripture and the failure to develop other traditional Catholic sources of moral wisdom and knowledge.

Historical Consciousness

A significant methodological shortcoming involves the lack of historical consciousness in these talks. The pope employs a static and classicist methodology. The meaning of marriage is the same at all times and all places. At the very beginning of these talks, John Paul II sees in the two accounts of creation a metaphysical and a psychological definition of the human being. These definitions are true for all human beings. The "Elohist" or first account of creation that comes from a later period than the second account of creation in Genesis gives a metaphysical definition of the human being in terms of being and existence. The "Yahwist" or second account of creation gives the subjective definition of the human being. This psychological and subjective understanding of the human being emphasizes self-knowledge. But this subjectivity corresponds to the objective reality of the human being created in the image of God (*TB* 29–31). The papal talks frequently refer to the divine plan or the plan of God for sexuality and marriage that was first revealed in the creation stories of Genesis. The subtitle of the book containing the papal talks on the theology of the body is "Human Love in the Divine Plan."

The pope somewhat frequently refers to historical human beings in these talks, but his historical perspective is theological—human beings before the fall, after the fall, and fallen and redeemed. He even explicitly recognizes his use of historical in this theological sense (*TB* 131, 132; see also 106, 119). The pope very occasionally recognizes historical and cultural conditioning but insists that the words of Christ, "in their essential content, refer to the man of every time and place" (*TB* 212). The pope does recognize changes that occurred in the Old Testament with regard to divorce and polygamy, but these changes are due to the theological reason of the fall. Redemption in Jesus has now restored the original meaning of marriage and its fullness and holds for all Christians down through the ages (*TB* 133–38). Thus, there is no recognition of historical development with regard to the meaning of marriage, nor is the subjectivity of persons different in different historical and cultural circumstances.

As a result of the methodological approach, the pope recognizes no development or change within marriage based on changing historical and cultural circumstances. But historical studies have indicated very great changes and developments in the church's understanding of marriage. For example, for over half of its existence the Catholic Church did not officially accept marriage as one of the seven sacraments. Marriage has been seen both as a contract and a covenant. Some in the early church refused remarriage to widows. The roles of love, procreation, and sexual pleasure have changed greatly in the course of the Catholic understanding of marriage.[7]

It is helpful to contrast the approach of John Paul II with that of John T. Noonan Jr., who has written more than any other scholar on the historical development of Catholic moral teachings. Four aspects in Noonan's writings stand out—moral teachings develop in changing historical contexts; change has occurred in many moral teachings; *sensus fidelium* has played a significant role in development of teaching; and moral norms exist in order to protect and promote values.

Development in Historical Contexts

Contemporary papal teachings, such as the condemnation of artificial contraception for spouses, developed within a complex historical context. Many factors influenced this teaching. General biblical values, especially the sanctity of marriage and the condemnation of unnatural sexual acts, were prominent. In the development of the church, it was necessary to find rational purpose and limits to sexuality. Societal factors, many of which have changed dramatically, such as the role of women, underpopulation or overpopulation, shorter or longer life-spans, agrarian or industrial society, also had a part to play. The teaching itself was formulated and defended against various opponents. Thus, in the beginning, the teaching was aimed at Gnostics, Manichees, and later the Cathars, who were hostile to all procreation. Then, in the nineteenth and twentieth centuries, the teaching was defended against those who advocated artificial contraception, especially the Anglican Church in 1930. Within this context, the teaching on marriage itself changed and developed radically with a much greater emphasis today on the role of love in marriage.[8]

---

[7] Theodore Mackin, *The Marital Sacrament* (New York: Paulist Press, 1989).

[8] John T. Noonan Jr., *Contraception: A History of Its Treatment by the Catholic Theologians and Canonists*, enlarged ed. (Cambridge, MA: Belknap Press of Harvard University Press, 1986).

Changes Have Occurred in History

History shows that great development and change have occurred within Catholic teaching about marital intercourse. Catholic theologians once held as common positions that intercourse during menstruation is a mortal sin, that intercourse in pregnancy is forbidden, and that there exists a natural position for intercourse. Great changes occurred with regard to the role of procreation in marriage. In the early church, the intention of procreation was necessary to justify marital intercourse. Later, the couple did not have to intend procreation. Sterile spouses could have marital intercourse. In the twentieth century, with the acceptance of rhythm and natural family planning, not only did the couple not have to intend procreation, but they could use the infertile periods in a woman's cycle in order to consciously avoid procreation.[9]

Noonan points out, with regard to indissolubility, that by the second part of the twentieth century there were six different classes of marriage in Catholic canon law. The only class that is indissoluble by any authority is a consummated marriage of two baptized persons properly entered into. The other five categories of dissoluble marriages that developed in different times and places are: (1) A marriage that is virginal by vow, agreement or intent, and contracted by two baptized persons, is dissoluble by religious profession or papal dispensation. (2) A marriage that is sexual in intent, contracted by two baptized persons and unconsummated by sexual intercourse, is dissoluble by religious profession or papal dispensation. (3) A consummated marriage of two baptized persons, but limited or negative in procreative intent can be declared invalid at the option of the courts. (4) A marriage impermanent by intention, custom, or assumption, even though contracted by two baptized persons, and consummated by sexual intercourse, can be declared invalid at the option of the courts. (5) A marriage that is sexual in intent, contracted by at least one baptized person, and consummated by sexual intercourse can be dissolved by the conversion and remarriage of the unbaptized partner in certain cases or by papal dispensation in all cases.[10]

Noonan succinctly tries to give some explanation for these changes. St. Paul made an exception in absolute indissolubility with what is today called the Pauline Privilege—if one of two married unbelievers converts and the

---

[9] Ibid., 532.

[10] John T. Noonan Jr., *Power to Dissolve: Lawyers and Marriages in the Courts of the Roman Curia* (Cambridge, MA: Belknap Press of Harvard University Press, 1972), 403.

other party does not but deserts the convert, the convert is free to remarry (1 Cor. 7:10–16). This rule was then expanded under the extreme conditions of African slavery in South America. And the change that occurred then was further developed in modern religiously mixed societies when it became common for nonbaptized persons and Catholics to fall in love and want to be married. Noonan sees historical experience, canonical ingenuity, and the exaltation of papal power as playing dominant roles in these changes.[11] On the basis of this historical evidence, the Catholic Church cannot say that from the very beginning of creation God intended all marriages to be indissoluble.

Noonan summarizes the changes on the issues of usury, indissolubility, slavery, and the persecution of heretics in this fashion: "What was forbidden became lawful (the cases of usury and marriage); what was permissible became unlawful (the case of slavery); and what was required became forbidden (the persecution of heretics)."[12]

Yes, John Noonan has shown in many areas the change that has occurred in Catholic teaching—usury, marriage, slavery, and religious freedom. But Noonan is no historical relativist. He insists, for example, that the Catholic condemnation of abortion has been an almost absolute value throughout history.[13] Noonan tries to shed more light on how legitimate development does occur and how one can distinguish legitimate development from illegitimate development in history.[14]

Sensus Fidelium

From a theological perspective, historical consciousness gives a significant role to the *sensus fidelium* (sense of the faithful). John Paul II seldom appeals to the *sensus fidelium* because of his insistence on the plan of God from the very beginning. Noonan points out in the area of usury that the experience and judgment of the laity had a value for moral teaching. In this context, he

---

[11] John T. Noonan Jr., "Development in Moral Doctrine," *Theological Studies* 54 (1993): 675.

[12] Ibid., 669.

[13] John T. Noonan Jr., "An Almost Absolute Value in History," in *The Morality of Abortion: Legal and Historical Perspectives*, ed. John T. Noonan Jr. (Cambridge, MA: Harvard University Press, 1970), 1–59.

[14] Noonan, "Development in Moral Doctrine," 662–67; for Noonan's description of the theory of development implicitly found in Vatican Council II, see John T. Noonan Jr., *The Lustre of Our Country: The American Experience of Religious Freedom* (Berkeley: University of California Press, 1998), 352–53.

refers to the sixteenth-century theologian Navarrus (Martin Aspilcueta, d. 1586) pointing out the infinite number of decent Christians taking interest on loans. Navarrus could not accept an analysis that would damn the whole world.[15] All should recognize that the *sensus fidelium* is a complex reality that cannot be reduced to majority vote or public opinion polls. But it has been an important factor in developing Catholic moral teaching.

Values and Laws

As a distinguished jurist as well as an eminent historian, Noonan is most interested in the role of law and how laws are formed. He frequently points out that laws exist to protect and promote values. But as other values enter into the picture, or as the priority of values shifts, then new laws develop. Thus, he sees the condemnation of artificial contraception for spouses as defending and promoting five significant values—procreation, education, life, personality, and love. The condemnation serves as a wall to protect these values, but "the wall could be removed when it became a prison rather than a bulwark."[16]

Specific norms thus have a lesser certitude than values because they exist to protect and promote the different values involved. With a classicist and somewhat deductive approach, John Paul II gives too great a certitude to specific moral norms. Once again historical consciousness and historical analysis remind us that specific moral norms cannot have the degree of certitude that exists in more general value statements. This chapter has analyzed and criticized the teaching of John Paul II on sexuality and marriage in regard to both the substance of the teaching and the moral methodology employed. The final part of the chapter has given special attention, in light of John T. Noonan's work, to the lack of historical consciousness in the teaching of John Paul II.

---

[15] John T. Noonan Jr., "The Amendment of Papal Teaching by Theologians," in *Contraception: Authority and Dissent,* ed. Charles E. Curran (New York: Herder and Herder, 1969), 74; for his original historical work on usury, see John T. Noonan Jr., *The Scholastic Analysis of Usury* (Cambridge, MA: Harvard University Press, 1957).

[16] Noonan, *Contraception*, 533.

Chapter 9

THE LONG SHADOW OF *HUMANAE VITAE* ON THE TRADITION*

Pope Paul VI's July 1968 encyclical *Humanae Vitae* has cast a long and broad shadow over Catholic moral theology and the life of the Catholic Church for almost half a century. This moral theology discussion has centered on three issues—the morality of contraception in particular and other sexual issues, natural law theory, and dissent and the role of hierarchical magisterial teaching in the church.

Criterion of Sexual Morality

Humanae Vitae states, "The Church calling men back to the observance of the norms of natural law . . . teaches that each and every marriage act must remain open to the transmission of life" (no. 12). This criterion serves as a basis for the hierarchical approach to many issues of sexuality. For example, masturbation and homosexual acts are gravely morally wrong because they go against this criterion.

This criterion for sexual morality is based on the nature and purpose of the sexual faculty or power (no. 13). The sexual faculty or power has a twofold purpose—love union and procreation—and every marital sexual act must be open to both procreation and expressive of love union.

The vast majority, but not all, of Catholic moral theologians, disagree with the criterion of sexual morality based on the nature and purpose of the sexual faculty and act. As chapter 7 explained, the sexual act exists in relationship to the person and the person's relationship to others. Thus, for the good of the person, or for the good of the marital relationship, one can and should interfere with the sexual act. Some Catholic moral theologians have used the same basic approach to justify homosexual genital acts within a committed homosexual relationship.

---

* Originally published as Charles E. Curran, "Dangers of Certitude," *Tablet* 262 (July 26, 2008): 23–24. Used with permission. Please visit www.thetablet.co.uk.

Natural Law

Humanae Vitae appealed to the natural law basis for its condemnation of artificial contraception for spouses. Natural law is a complex term. In the history of Christian ethics natural law was the Catholic answer to the question of whether Christians share moral wisdom and knowledge with all other human beings. The Catholic tradition, in my judgment to its great credit, insisted that both faith and reason are important sources of moral wisdom. The natural law claims that human reason reflecting on human nature and God's creation can arrive at moral truth. This is the theological aspect of the natural law question and well illustrates the universality or catholicity of the Catholic moral tradition.

The other aspect of the natural law question is the philosophical—what does one mean by human reason and human nature? Here theologians dissenting from the encyclical have described the problem with the natural law approach of the encyclical as "physicalism." Physicalism, as mentioned in chapter 7, identifies the moral aspect of the act with its physical structure or aspect. According to this way of thinking, the physical act of depositing male semen in the vagina of the wife must always be present and can never be interfered with. Some people have maintained that the problem with the Catholic hierarchical teaching is that it is pronatalist at any cost. But such is not the case. The teaching found in *Humanae Vitae* also opposes artificial insemination even with the husband's seed. This indicates the primary problem here is physicalism. The physical marital act must always be present and cannot be interfered with either to prevent procreation or even to help procreation. Artificial insemination goes against the fact that every sexual act must be expressive of love union.

In other areas the Catholic teaching does not identify the human moral act with the physical aspect of the act. For example, not every killing is murder. In another example, the tradition has maintained that in extreme circumstances all created realities are held in common so that someone taking from another what is necessary for life is not guilty of theft.

Most of the specific, disputed absolute norms in Catholic moral theology and life today reflect the problem of physicalism or an analogous reality. Physicalism affects the papal teaching on absolute moral norms in many aspects of sexuality—the absolute condemnations of masturbation, sterilization, all homosexual genital acts, premarital sexual acts, artificial insemination, in vitro fertilization. Present hierarchical teaching condemns all divorce and remarriage for the baptized on the basis of the metaphysical marriage bond that comes into existence after the spouses have exchanged their vows. Proponents of admitting some divorce and remarriage maintain that the metaphysical marriage bond cannot be absolutized apart from the real relationship between the two parties and their children. Obviously this short chapter cannot prove all these positions mentioned here, but the point is that the problem areas in Catholic moral theology and in Catholic life today center on absolute moral norms where the moral aspect of the act is described in physical or analogous terms.

In addition, the basic presupposition of the present teaching is that once you claim something is based on natural law this is true for all times and places. But there are serious problems with this claim. Throughout the centuries there has never been a monolithic philosophical theory of natural law with an agreed-upon body of specific teachings existing either in ethics in general or in Catholic ethics. Many have used the term "natural law," but they have often meant something different by the term. Isidore of Seville (d. 636) affirmed that the common possession of all things is required by natural law, but most Catholics recognize private property as based on natural law. Gratian, the most significant historical figure in Catholic canon law, in his *Decretum* in the twelfth century described natural law as "that which is contained in the law and the Gospel." For Gratian, natural law is found in the Old and New Testaments, but Catholic scholars generally have understood the natural law as based solely on human reason. In discussing natural law, medieval canonists and theologians explicitly dealt with the apparent exceptions to natural law found in scripture such as God's commands to Abraham to kill his son, to the Hebrews to steal from the Egyptians, and to Hosea to marry a harlot.

In the last fifty years, corresponding to the Catholic debate over contraception, the natural law theory used by the papal magisterium has been challenged within the church. Many revisionist Catholic moral theologians have pointed out significant differences between the natural law theory used in papal social teaching and the theory employed in papal sexual teaching. The "new natural law theory" proposed by Germain Grisez and John Finnis firmly supports the particular sexual teachings proposed by the papal magisterium, but strongly disagrees with the theory of natural law used in papal sexual teaching.

Magisterium and Dissent

The role of the papal teaching office is even a more important factor as the basis for Catholic sexual teaching. Pope Paul VI recognized the fundamental importance of the authoritative papal teaching office in his 1968 encyclical *Humanae Vitae*. He could not accept the conclusions of the papal commission appointed to study this issue, "above all because certain criteria of solutions had emerged which departed from the moral teaching on marriage proposed with constant firmness by the teaching authority of the church" (para. 6).

The role of papal teaching authority on moral issues in the church has changed dramatically over time. For all practical purposes, it was nonexistent in the first millennium. Only gradually did it increase in the second millennium. The term "magisterium" as referring to church teaching authority came into existence only in the eighteenth and nineteenth centuries. Historians point out how popes played an ever increasing role in church governing and teaching in these two centuries. A 1962 book (John P. Kenny, *Principles of Medical Ethics*) reports that Pope Pius XII in his role as authoritative teacher gave seventy-five allocutions in the area of medical ethics alone.

Developments in transportation and communication greatly enhanced the authoritative papal role. John W. O'Malley, the distinguished Jesuit historian, points out that the greatest change in Catholicism in its second millennium was the papalization of the church. Today one can rightly refer to the papalization of moral teaching in the church. Catholic theology, however, has recognized that through baptism all the faithful share in the teaching office of Jesus. Likewise, there is a prophetic role in the church. The *sensus fidelium* is an important source of moral wisdom and knowledge for the church. But none of these appear in *Humanae Vitae*.

The absolute moral norms on contraception and sexuality mentioned above rely heavily on natural law and human reason, not on faith. These issues are not core to Catholic faith but are somewhat peripheral. They fall under the category of noninfallible (read: fallible) teaching. Dissent in theory and in practice can be legitimate on such questions when there are sufficient reasons to support it. These teachings cannot claim absolute certitude.

Sociological studies show that many Catholics in the United States disagree with the hierarchical teachings on birth control, divorce, homosexual relationships, and to some extent on abortion and premarital sexuality. However, many Catholics who dissent about absolute norms in the area of sexuality strongly receive and accept the hierarchical teaching on social matters. Note that the problem of physicalism does not exist in the area of social ethics. In one sense, such dissent shows a mature faith, but this dissent creates a problem for the credibility of the hierarchical teaching office in the area of sexuality and also can readily extend to other areas as well.

There is even a more serious problem for the Catholic Church in this area. Recent studies in the United States indicate that one out of three persons who were raised Catholic no longer consider themselves Catholic. Disagreement with some of these absolute moral norms and other issues not belonging to the core of faith constitute a significant part of their problem.

History reminds us that the hierarchical teaching in the past has been wrong on a good number of particular moral teachings—usury, the right of the defendant to keep silent, religious freedom, the ends of marriage, the best form of government. The most glaring error which touched many people was the failure to condemn slavery.

In closing, it is important to recognize significant differences in the response by Catholic theologians and commentators to the use of natural law and the papal teaching as found in the social tradition and in the sexual tradition. As pointed out in part I, there has been little or no disagreement in the contemporary Catholic social tradition about the use of natural law in Catholic social teaching, but there has been much disagreement by Catholic commentators and theologians about the use of natural law in the papal sexual teaching. The reason for this difference comes from the fact that the problem of physicalism, which involves the identification of the human moral act with the physical aspect of the act, does not occur in the social teaching but it is a very salient aspect of the sexual teaching. Likewise, despite the pluralism of different approaches within the Catholic social tradition, there has been practically no dissent from papal teaching in this area, whereas dissent has been a very significant topic in the discussion of the papal teaching in the sexual area. The difference comes from the fact that in the social area the papal teaching is limited to principles and does not involve specific strategies or acts. In the sexual teaching, however, the teaching involves very specific acts that are determined to be always wrong. There have been significant changes in Catholic social teaching over the years and the recognition of the role of historical consciousness, but these factors have not played a significant role in papal sexual teaching. The reforming papacy of Pope Francis has raised the question if this pope will change any of these teachings. The concluding chapter of this volume will address the issue.

PART III

REFORM AT VATICAN II
AND AFTERWARD

Introduction

Vatican II is synonymous with reform in the Catholic Church. The twofold criterion for reform at the council called for the need to go back to the sources of scripture and tradition and to bring the church up to date. The council accepted the understanding that the pilgrim church is always in need of reform (*ecclesia semper reformanda*). True reform involves both continuities and discontinuities. Vatican II did not change any dogmas of the Catholic Church, but it profoundly influenced the understanding and life of the contemporary church.

Chapter 10, "Pope John XXIII and the Reform of Vatican II," takes a deeper look at the pope who called Vatican II and defends the thesis that John XXIII even at the time he called for the council did not have a clear idea of the reform envisioned for the church. The greatness of John was his openness to the call of the Spirit and to listening to other voices calling for change.

Chapter 11, "How Vatican II Brought Spirituality and Moral Theology Together," considers the primary way in which Vatican II brought about the reform of moral theology. The manuals of moral theology, the textbooks of the discipline before Vatican II, focused on preparing future confessors to know what acts were sinful and the degree of sinfulness. Vatican II changed the entire focus of moral theology to deal with the fullness of the Christian life by recognizing that all Christians are called to holiness in their daily lives in the world.

Chapter 12, "The Reform of Moral Theology at Vatican II and After: Through the Lens of Enda McDonagh," discusses the more specific aspects of the reform of moral theology at Vatican II with the emphasis on the theological, the personalist, the spiritual, the liturgical, and the ecumenical dimensions. But significant developments have occurred after Vatican II with greater attention to the other, the marginalized, the local church, and the recognition of the danger of a too optimistic approach. The chapter uses the writings of the prominent Irish theologian Enda McDonagh to develop these ideas.

Chapter 13, "The Need for Reform of the Sacrament of Reconciliation," focuses on the sacrament popularly known in the past as confession, which no longer has a central place in the lives of most Catholics as it did in the pre–Vatican II church. However, God's mercy and forgiveness, as well as our change of heart and growth in the love of God and neighbor, remain central aspects in the Christian moral life. We need a new sacramental liturgy that celebrates these realities in a prayerful, celebratory, and meaningful way.

Chapter 14, "Bernard Häring: A Model for Church Reformers," considers the work of Bernard Häring, the German Redemptorist theologian, who spearheaded the renewal of moral theology even in the pre–Vatican II church and continued after Vatican II to work for church reform in many different aspects. At times Häring the reformer had to raise a prophetic voice about what was happening or not happening in the church, but his approach also recognizes that the reformer must avoid all types of self-righteousness.

Chapter 15, "A Theology and Spirituality for Church Reformers," recognizes that we are pilgrim people in a pilgrim church. Just as in our individual lives we need reform and growth, so too in the life of the church. But neither in our personal lives nor in the life of the church will the fullness of reform ever be achieved. As pilgrim people in a pilgrim church, we need to continue to work for growth and development in our own personal lives and in the life of the church. Reformers need to learn the lesson that the fullness of reform will never be here until the eschaton, and the struggle for reform will always be a part of the life of the church.

Chapter 10

POPE JOHN XXIII AND THE
REFORM OF VATICAN II*

1958

As a newly ordained student priest, I was in St. Peter's Square on the late afternoon of Tuesday, October 28, 1958, the third day of the conclave to elect a new pope. This was the fifth time that crowds came to the square to see if the white smoke from the chimney of the Sistine Chapel would signal that a new pope had been elected. In the previous four times it was at first difficult to discern what was the color of the smoke. Even that late afternoon it was hard to determine whether the smoke was white or black, but the fact that other lights went on immediately after the smoke indicated that we had a new pope. It was early evening before the announcement was made from the balcony of St. Peter's overlooking the huge square that we have a new pope—Angelo Giuseppe Roncalli who will be called John XXIII. The new pope came out to bless the crowd. To be honest, I was disappointed. Pius XII was a thin, ascetic figure with a noble Roman nose who piously made the threefold sign of the cross over the crowd lifting his eyes to heaven. John XXIII was a roly-poly man who before he even finished the blessing started waving to the crowd.

Those more knowledgeable than I pointed out that this would be an interim and caretaker papacy. John was seventy-six years old. His papacy would be short and quite conventional. Yes, his papacy was short—he died less than five years later on June 3, 1963. But how wrong we all were. John XXIII was not a caretaker pope. He gave us Vatican II, which has had such a tremendous influence on the life of the Catholic Church. Vatican II, which began in 1962 and lasted for four sessions ending in 1965, constitutes a most significant legacy of reform.

Many people today think of John XXIII as having from the very beginning a clear understanding of exactly what he wanted the council to do and

* Originally published as Charles E. Curran, "Pope John XXIII," the Bishop John McCarthy Lecture, published by St. Edward's University, Austin, TX. Used with permission.

to achieve. I disagree. I do not think that John had a well-developed concept of what the council should be when he called it. He did not have all the answers. John's ultimate greatness was the fact that he grew. He was open, he listened, and he learned. And it is precisely in this growth that he is truly a model for all of us Catholic Christians today.

Rouquette's Article

Here I have to make a few scholarly disclaimers. I am not a historian. Others have studied Vatican II and the life of John XXIII in great depth and in a very scholarly manner. My approach is somewhat influenced by my own personal experience and the writings of others, especially a fascinating article by the French Jesuit theologian Robert Rouquette, which appeared in the July–August 1963 issue of *Études*, the French Jesuit monthly publication of culture, art, and theology.[1]

Roncalli had been the papal nuncio in Paris from 1944 to 1953. Rouquette, as a well-known theologian and commentator on the French church, was well acquainted with Roncalli and his work in France. Rouquette also later covered the Vatican Council for *Études* and was a strong supporter of the changes brought about by Vatican II.

Rouquette's 1963 article appeared just after the death of John XXIII in June 1963. Rouquette in this article worries about a cult of personality about John XXIII. There is the danger of making him a saint of heroic perfection and genius. John XXIII like all of us was a human being with all our human frailties and problems. He was not an angel. Yes, he was a holy and intelligent man and made an unparalleled contribution to the life of the Catholic Church, but he was not perfect.

Rouquette's article is titled, "Le mystère Roncalli." The basic thesis of the article is there was nothing in what Rouquette saw in France in those nine years that indicated that Roncalli was anything more than a conventional and conservative Catholic churchman. Rouquette reports that before the 1958 papal election he heard one French cardinal say that one thing for sure was that it will not be Roncalli. One of the best French bishops, remarkable for his intelligence and character, who unfortunately died too young, cried when he heard that Roncalli was elected pope. This background explains why Rouquette was happily surprised by what Roncalli did as pope, especially with regard to Vatican II.

---

[1] Robert Rouquette, "Le mystère Roncalli," *Études* 318 (July–August, 1963): 4–18.

Roncalli's Early Life

A brief overview of Roncalli's life also shows few signs of what he would do during the short five years of his papacy.[2] He was born on November 25, 1881, in Sotto il Monte, Bergamo, Italy, the third of thirteen children of pious Catholic parents. He studied for the priesthood, served in the army, earned a doctorate in theology, and was ordained a priest in 1904 for the diocese of Bergamo. He served as secretary to the bishop of Bergamo, taught in the seminary, published a few historical monographs as well as a laudatory biography of his bishop, began editing thirty-nine volumes of St. Charles Borromeo, and worked with youth. In 1921, Pope Benedict XV named him director of the Society for the Propagation of the Faith in Italy. In 1925, he was appointed apostolic visitor to Bulgaria and made an archbishop. Only 40,000 Latin Rite Catholics and 4,000 Eastern Rite Catholics lived in Bulgaria. Peter Hebblethwaite, in his biography of John XXIII, titles this particular chapter "Ten Hard Years in Bulgaria."[3] Roncalli was blamed for handling poorly the marriage of the Orthodox King Boris of Bulgaria to the daughter of King Victor Emmanuel III of Italy. Boris, an Orthodox Christian, agreed with Roncalli to marry her in a Catholic ceremony in Italy but then broke his promise and had a large public Orthodox wedding back in Bulgaria.

In 1934, Roncalli became the apostolic delegate to Turkey and Greece. Both of these countries had very few Catholics. In terms of the Vatican diplomatic corps this assignment was on the bottom rung, but Roncalli did make contacts with Muslim culture and also some relationships with the Orthodox Church. Since he had never attended the Ecclesiastic Academy where the top Vatican diplomats had been trained, Roncalli realized in his own words that he was a donkey and not a horse.[4] But in 1944, Pope Pius XII appointed Roncalli the apostolic nuncio to Paris, the most prestigious Vatican diplomatic post. But herein lies a story.

Pius XII wanted to send Archbishop Valerio Valeri as nuncio to Paris. But Valeri had been the nuncio to the Vichy regime of Marshall Philippe Petain, and Charles de Gaulle refused to accept him as the Vatican nuncio to the new French government because he had been nuncio to

---

[2] For bibliographical information, I am following the well-received work of Peter Hebblethwaite, *John XXIII: Pope of the Century*, rev. ed. Margaret Hebblethwaite (New York: Continuum, 2000).

[3] Ibid., 55–69.

[4] Ibid., 97.

the collaborationist regime in Vichy. For months the impasse continued and neither De Gaulle nor Pius XII budged. On January 1, according to protocol, the papal nuncio, as the dean of the French diplomatic corps, was to present New Year's greetings to the French head of state. If there were no Vatican nuncio, the next diplomat in line was the Russian ambassador, which from the perspective of Pius XII would have been a disaster. So Pius XII blinked! On December 5 Roncalli received a telegram from the Vatican appointing him nuncio to Paris. Yes, Pius XII had lost his battle with De Gaulle, but he would snub De Gaulle by sending him one of the lowest ranking Vatican diplomats.

Roncalli in Paris

Peter Hebblethwaite, the pope's sympathetic biographer, titles the chapter on Roncalli's time in Paris, "Difficult Mission to France."[5] Roncalli proved himself quite adroit in his dealings with the French government, but he was less successful with regard to the French church, as already indicated by Rouquette's comments. Roncalli's time in France corresponded with a rise of intellectual, theological, and pastoral renewal of the French church. Cardinal Emmanuel Suhard of Paris and others recognized that the French working class was estranged from the church. France, which used to send missionaries all over the world, now was itself a mission country. The church needed to evangelize the de-Christianized segment of the populace and overcome the wall separating the church from the modern world. Suhard's writings attracted worldwide attention with the English translation of *Growth or Decline? The Church Today* going through five editions from Fides Publishers in the United States.[6] The priest worker movement grew out of this approach as priests moved out of rectories and worked side by side with other workers in an attempt to evangelize the working class. On the theological front, Jesuits, especially in Lyons, and Dominicans, especially at the faculty of Le Saulchoir, were adopting more historically conscious theological methodologies and moving away from the pre–Vatican II neoscholasticism.

The reaction of the Vatican to these developments was quite negative, and Roncalli as nuncio was seen as the eyes and ears of the Vatican.

---

[5] Ibid., 96–116.

[6] Emmanuel C. Suhard, *The Church Today: Growth or Decline?* trans. James A. Corbett, foreword by John Courtney Murray (South Bend, IN: Fides, 1950).

Pope Pius XII was upset with the leading role played by Suhard in trying to shape the mission of the church throughout the world. Suhard himself never really trusted Roncalli. The strongest and most public Vatican action came with the 1950 encyclical, *Humani Generis,* which condemned the "*nouvelle theologie*" that had been developing in France. No names were mentioned in the encyclical, but Jesuit theologians such as Henri de Lubac, Henri Rondet, and Henri Bouillard lost their teaching positions as did the Dominicans Marie-Dominique Chenu and Yves Congar. In 1953, Pope Pius XII summarily removed the provincials of the three French Dominican provinces. In 1953–54, the Vatican intervened to stop the experiment of the worker priests.

One can well understand why the progressive French bishops and theologians were not happy with the papal election of Roncalli a few years later. Perhaps he did learn something from the French experience, but he was very identified with the opposition to everything that was taking place in France.

In January 1953, Pius XII made Roncalli a cardinal and appointed him archbishop of Venice. Again there was nothing in Venice that indicated what later occurred at Vatican II. Roncalli held a diocesan synod in November 1957, but there was no debate or democratic process but only the acceptance of previously written documents that did not bring about any real change.

The Antecedents and Preparation of Vatican II

After his election as pope, John surprised practically everyone by announcing on January 25, 1959, three major undertakings for the life of the church—a diocesan synod for Rome, an ecumenical council for the universal church, and the revision of the Code of Canon Law. I was doing my doctoral studies in Rome at that time and like everyone else was looking for clues about what John had in mind.

The Roman Synod was held in January 1960. In my view it was a disaster and merely confirmed existing understandings and practices. The only function of the members of the synod (the priests of Rome) was to applaud and approve the prepackaged 755 articles that were read to them. The synod's detailed provisions did not suggest the wind of a new Pentecost.

John XXIII had made his alma mater the Lateran University a full-fledged pontifical university. Its leadership and faculty were quite conservative, clearly associated with the Roman curia, and determined to play a leading role in Catholic theology. In late 1960, Msgr. Antonio Romeo of the Lateran, in its publication *Divinitas,* launched a strong and intemperate attack on the Jesuit professors at the Pontifical Biblical Institute. (Hebblethwaite reports that the pope did not approve of these actions, but that was not known by the general public.)[7] Before I left Rome in June 1961 to begin teaching at St. Bernard's Seminary in Rochester, New York, my teacher and friend, Fr. Francis X. Murphy took me out to lunch. Here he regaled me with stories about the shenanigans of the Roman curia and their attempt to make sure the council did nothing new. Many of these stories appeared in the famous "Letter from Vatican City" published in the *New Yorker* in the fall of 1962 at the beginning of the council. The article was signed by Xavier Rynne (Murphy's mother's maiden name), but years later he admitted he was the true author.

I was not in Rome after June of 1961, but what I heard and read while teaching at St. Bernard's was not encouraging for the future council. In February 1962, John issued the apostolic constitution *Veterum Sapientia,* praising Latin as the official language of the church and calling for all semi-nary professors throughout the world to teach philosophy and theology in Latin. The document also urged all bishops throughout the world to see that none of their subjects "eager for novelties" write against the use of Latin either in teaching the sacred disciplines or in the liturgy. This was certainly a blow for those of us who hoped there might be the use of some vernacular in the liturgy coming from the forthcoming council.

Later in 1962, two of the Jesuit professors at the Biblical Institute, Stan-islas Lyonnet and Maximilian Zerwick, who had been attacked earlier by Rome, were suspended from their teaching. I also found out that my teacher of moral theology at the Gregorian, Josef Fuchs, was not allowed to teach seminarians. In August 1962, the Holy Office under Cardinal Alfredo Otta-viani issued a *monitum* (warning) about the writings of Pierre Teilhard de Chardin, SJ. The signs coming from Rome were ominous. The council was apparently not going to be a vehicle for reform or change in the church.

Meanwhile, the actual work of preparing for the council began. Pope John himself made the decision that the Central Theological Commission and the ten subcommissions that would write the preparatory documents would be presided over by the curial cardinal who headed the corresponding congregation in the curia. Thus, Cardinal Ottaviani, the head of the Holy Office, presided over the Central Theological Commission. The preparation of the documents for the council was firmly in the hands of the Roman curia, which was known for its conservative views. According to Hebblethwaite,

---

[7] Hebblethwaite, *John XXIII,* 211.

the pope worked closely with the curia in preparing for the council. He read all the proposed documents, annotated them, and commented on them. He publicly and lavishly praised the proposed texts as the work of magnificent, edifying, and most devoted hard work. At the end of the fifth session of the Central Commission in April 1962, Pope John maintained that the consent of the bishops would not be difficult to attain for these documents and their approval would be unanimous.[8] The general feeling was that the work of the council would be finished in one session.

The reality turned out completely different. The bishops of the world and the council rejected all the preparatory texts except for the one on the liturgy. The liturgical subcommission had a much broader membership, including most of the outstanding European liturgical scholars. Only in the first session of the council did it become clear that the majority of the council fathers would reject the preparatory documents. As a result, the council ultimately needed four sessions to rewrite and approve its own documents.

A "progressive myth" developed that in having the curia prepare the documents for the council, and even in his own seemingly enthusiastic support of these documents, Pope John was using his peasant shrewdness to outmaneuver the curia. Hebblethwaite rightly rejects this thesis.[9] John was convinced that the curia people had produced good working documents that would be ultimately approved by the upcoming council.

What I have just presented is by definition a one-sided picture of Angelo Roncalli. My purpose was to prove the thesis that Roncalli, when he called the council and even at its very beginning, had no clear idea of the changes that Vatican II ultimately brought about. In a sense the results of the council were truly a surprise even for Roncalli. In the end, I think this fact points to his greatness and his being a role model for all of us. He was open to the call of the Spirit and, as a true pilgrim Christian, recognized the need for change. But this understanding raises the further question. Why did he change? What was it about him that disposed him to be open to change and development?

Why Did John XXIII Change?

As Christians we strongly believe in the grace and gift of the Holy Spirit. All of us are called to be sensitive to the Spirit and to try to discern what the Spirit is calling us to do. However, the role of the Spirit and the personal

---

[8] Ibid., 207–12.

[9] Ibid.

discernment of the Spirit are not always easy to fathom. Also, there were other people at the council and in the work preparing for it who did not grow and change in the same way as John XXIII. But there is no doubt that John himself clearly understood his call for the council as an inspiration of the Holy Spirit. When John mentioned the council to his secretary, Msgr. Loris Capovilla, the pope noticed the worried expression on his face. John said to him that you are fearful that the pope is too old for this venture, but you are far too cautious. "When we believe that an inspiration comes to us from the Holy Spirit, we must follow it: What happens after that is not our responsibility."[10] The Catholic tradition also recognizes that the divine works in and through the human. What was there about John XXIII that made him open to appreciate the need for reform in the church as ultimately found in Vatican II? Four factors come to mind.

First is his own personality. He was a warm person who was open to others and consequently learned from them. He was unpretentious and therefore willing to listen to what others had to say and offer. He was basically optimistic, based on an optimism both of nature and of grace, so that he was not fearful of change. He was open in the best sense of the term.

Second, as mentioned earlier, he had an interest in history and wrote and edited some historical works. Historical study reminds us that things have changed over time. A historical perspective helps open one's mind to recognize the need for ongoing development. In his talk at the opening of the council (even then I do not think he had a clear idea of the reforms that Vatican II actually brought about), he insisted that history is the teacher of life, but some people believe as if they have learned nothing from history.[11]

Third, John had always understood the council to be a pastoral council and not a dogmatic council. By definition the concept of pastoral is more flexible than a dogmatic approach. John saw himself primarily as a pastor and not as a theologian or intellectual. Consequently, he was very open to what would make faith deeper and more penetrating in the daily life of the Christian community and of all believers.

Fourth, John learned much from the advice and participation of a number of influential cardinals and bishops who were upset with the preparatory documents proposed by the curia-dominated commissions. Among these people were Cardinal Bea, whom John appointed as president of the

---

[10] Leon Joseph Cardinal Suenens, *Memories and Hopes* (Dublin: Veritatis, 1992), 65.

[11] Pope John XXIII, "Opening Speech to the Council," in *Documents of Vatican II*, ed. Walter M. Abbott (New York: Guild, 1966), 712.

Secretariat for Christian Unity, and Cardinals Suenens (Belgium), Frings and Döpfner (Germany), Liénart (France), Alfrink (Holland), and Léger (Canada). Suenens had sent to the pope his own proposal for what he thought the council should do and found that the pope was quite receptive to these ideas.[12]

Suenens recalled the first meeting that the steering committee for the council had with the pope. The meeting was quite informal, and during it Suenens asked the pope, Why did you appoint the prefects of the Roman congregations to head the preparatory commissions? The pope laughed and said, "You're quite right, but I didn't have the courage."[13] Obviously, there were many other voices inside and outside the preparatory and actual work of the council who were also calling for more substantial reform. Pope John changed on the basis of what he learned from others.

In conclusion, there is no doubt that Vatican II stands as the legacy of reform of Pope John XXIII for the Catholic Church. But an equally important legacy and the reason why he is a role model for all of us comes from the fact that he was a pilgrim Christian who was always open to the Spirit and grew in wisdom, age, and grace before God and people.

---

[12] Hebblethwaite, *John XXIII*, 210.
[13] Suenens, *Memories and Hopes*, 71.

Chapter 11

How Vatican II Brought Spirituality and Moral Theology Together*

The Second Vatican Council (1962–65) brought about many significant changes in Catholic life and understanding, but clearly its teaching on spirituality should be one of the most significant contributions for the daily life of the people of God. Vatican II's teaching on spirituality has two fundamental assertions—the call of all Christians to holiness and perfection and the fact that the answer to this call to holiness comes in and through our life in the world.

Universal Call to Holiness

Chapter 5 of the Constitution on the Church is titled "The Universal Call to Holiness." The document clearly asserts that all Christians in whatsoever state or way of life are called to the fullness of the Christian life and to the perfection of charity. The holiness of the people of God clearly shows forth in the lives of so many saints in the church. This chapter cites a number of scriptural passages that make this point. Matthew 5:48 concludes the fifth chapter of his gospel with the admonition that all are to be perfect even as the heavenly Father is perfect. This chapter of the Constitution on the Church appeals to many other scriptural quotations to make the same point. Our sanctification is the will of God (1 Thess. 4:3, Eph. 1:4). We are to live as becomes saints (Eph. 5:3); to live as God's chosen ones holy and beloved (Col. 3:12); to possess the fruits of the Holy Spirit unto holiness (Gal. 5:22, Rom. 6:22).

Unfortunately this strong teaching of Vatican II has not become widely accepted and lived within contemporary Catholicism. Three concepts carried over from a pre–Vatican II approach have influenced the general

  * Originally published as Charles E. Curran, "How Vatican II Brought Spirituality and Moral Theology Together," in *Ethics and Spirituality: Readings in Moral Theology no. 17*, ed. Charles E. Curran and Lisa A. Fullam (Mahwah, NJ: Paulist Press, 2014), 80–88. Used with permission.

failure to recognize the call of all Christians to holiness—a poor notion of the saints, an older understanding of Christian perfection limited to those who leave the world to follow the gospel, and a concept of priesthood as mediator between God and the laity in the church.

The Saints

The word saints in the New Testament has different uses—it variously refers to angels, pious Jews who have already left this world, or Christians who died in the midst of persecution. However, the primary usage of "the saints" found over sixty times in the New Testament refers to the members of the Christian community—the community of the disciples of Jesus. The letters of Paul well illustrate such an approach, especially in their opening greetings and often in their conclusions. The First Letter of Peter is addressed to those who are to be made holy by the Spirit (1:2). The letter goes on to cite two famous passages from the Hebrew Bible dealing with holiness: Be holy for I am holy (e.g., Lev. 19:2), and you are a chosen race, a royal priesthood, a consecrated nation (Isa. 43:20–21).

However, today the average Catholic would be quick to deny that he or she is a saint. When Robert Livingston, a Louisiana congressperson, was running for Speaker of the House some time ago, he recognized some personal failings but explained that he was running for the speakership of the House of Representatives and not for sainthood. When I read that in the press, I knew that Robert Livingston was a Roman Catholic. What he said there has become a commonplace among Catholics. I am not a saint. Behind such a remark lies the honest recognition of our own limitations and sinfulness. But still the question naturally arises: Why do Catholics even today deny that they are called to be saints despite the teachings of Vatican II and of the New Testament?

Elizabeth A. Johnson, in her justly acclaimed book *Friends of God and Prophets: A Feminist Theological Reading of the Communion of Saints* (1998), explains why Catholics have lost the New Testament understanding of the saints as the members of the community of the disciples of Jesus. For most Catholics, saints refer to people who have gone before us in a spirit of great sanctity and now act as intermediaries between God and us. As saints they are now close to God, and there they can intercede with God on our behalf. The understanding of the saints as very holy people, much different from ourselves, who have gone before us and intercede for us before the throne of God plays a prominent role in Catholic self-understanding and in the piety of many people. The process of the canonization of saints and the veneration of saints in the Roman Catholic tradition strengthens such an understanding of the meaning and role of saints.

But what happened? How and why did the church forget or lose the New Testament understanding of saints as the people of God, the members of the church? Elizabeth Johnson points out how the original understanding of the saints as the people of God in this world expanded to include also those who had gone before us in death. However, in the beginning those who had gone before us were understood on the basis of a companionship model as an inspiration and encouragement to us but basically equal with us. However, in the early centuries a hierarchical and patriarchal model developed and became predominant. The saints in heaven went from being primarily in communion with us as witnesses in a partnership of hope to become intercessors on our behalf in a patriarchal structure of power and mediation. As a result, the church lost the idea that all of us are saints who are called to holiness. In the light of the limited but very popular under-standing of holiness as associated with the canonized saints who intercede for us before the throne of God, many Catholics today fail to realize that all the baptized are saints who are called to holiness.

Holiness Associated with Leaving the World

Just as a pre–Vatican II theology understood the saints as outside and above the people of God, the same theology identified the holy people as those who left the world and went into religious life. Religious heard the call of Christ to be perfect, left the world, and took the three vows of poverty, chastity, and obedience. Catholics who continued to live in the world thought of themselves as second-class citizens who did not receive a call to holiness but tried to live in accord with the ten commandments and not the evangelical councils. Leaving the world and taking the three religious vows made one holy.

However, even Thomas Aquinas had trouble with this understanding of the vows. For Aquinas all Christians have the same end or goal for their spiritual life—charity that involves loving union with God and neighbor. The three evangelical vows do not change or affect the basic end of charity that is the same for all Christians. The vows concern only the means to the end, and these three religious vows aim at overcoming obstacles that might prevent our growth in the love of God and neighbor. Poverty deals with the obstacle coming from an inordinate love of material goods; chastity with an inordinate love of bodily pleasures; obedience with an inordinate love of the spiritual self. The vows thus deal only with the means to the end and have only the negative function of removing possible obstacles in the way of charity. Unfortunately, both theoretically and practically the vows became ends in themselves rather than means to serve the love of God and neighbor. Thus people who took these vows were better than those who did not take them.

But many theologians today have a different understanding. Vatican II calls for scripture to play a central role in Catholic spirituality, liturgy, theology, and life. The Gospel call to conversion and change of heart challenges all believers. All are called to be perfect, as our gracious God is perfect. The challenge of the Gospel addresses all Christians.

Many contemporary theologians now recognize the primacy of the baptismal commitment. The baptismal commitment to discipleship and following Jesus involves a call to holiness for all Christians and striving for an ever-greater love of God and love of neighbor. All other vows do not add anything to this fundamental vow but specify how the individual Christian lives out the baptismal vow. Thus the marriage vows or the religious vows add nothing to the baptismal vow, which is the same for all, but merely specify how the individual Christian lives out the baptismal commitment. This baptismal commitment involves the call to holiness.

Priests as Mediators between God and God's People

Even today most Catholics look on the priest as called to a greater holiness than laypeople. Such a perspective comes from seeing the priest not as a member of the community of the people of God but rather as the mediator between God and the people. The priest stands outside and above the community of the people of God.

The French school of spirituality in the seventeenth century provided the basis for such an understanding of the priest as a mediator between God and the people. The priest was "another Christ" called to bring God to people and people to God. I learned this concept of priesthood in the pre–Vatican II seminary. Unfortunately such an understanding still predominates for most Catholics today.

However, a Vatican II theology again puts primary emphasis on the community of the disciples of Jesus, the people of God. The priest is not outside and above the community but performs a function within the community. The Constitution of the Church of Vatican II recognizes the primacy of the church as the people of God with the hierarchical and priestly offices exercising functions within the community.

The pre–Vatican II theory and practice of the Eucharist well illustrate the role of the priest as the mediator between God and the community. The priest turned his back to the people, prayed silently in Latin, and consecrated the body and blood of Jesus so that the people in the pews could adore Jesus and then receive communion from the priest. Recall how people knelt at the communion rail to receive communion on their tongue. At the conclusion of the mass the people knelt again to receive the priest's blessing.

Changes in the theology of the Eucharist in the post–Vatican II church illustrate the centrality of the community of the people of God with the priest exercising a special function within the community. The older approach called the priest the celebrant because he alone brought Christ to others. Now the priest is the presider of the assembly, and the whole community celebrates. The role of the people of God in the liturgy involves active participation and celebration, not just passive acceptance of what the priest provides for them.

Again, the postures associated with the Eucharist well illustrate the newer approach. The priest presides as a part of the community and facing it. The presider prays in the name of the community and out loud. At communion people stand, receive communion in the hand, and communicate themselves. The community no longer kneels for the final blessing. Many newer churches put primary emphasis both on the altar table and the community, and some in accordance with the best of the theological tradition have no kneelers. The community stands for the Eucharistic prayer.

The primary purpose of the Eucharist is not the transformation of the bread and wine into the body and blood of Christ but rather through this important change the transformation of the community, the mystical body of Christ. Through Christ, with Christ, and in Christ in the unity of the Holy Spirit, the total community gives praise and thanks to God, the gracious parent for their many gifts and receives the transforming love of God so that their lives might be changed as they go forth from the Eucharist.

Vatican II clearly taught the universal call of all Christians to holiness and sanctity. But this teaching has not taken hold in the Catholic community because of poor understandings of sanctity, holiness, and the role of priests in the community.

Holiness in the World

The second assertion in the teaching of Vatican II about spirituality emphasizes that the call to holiness is lived out in the midst of our daily life in this world. The Pastoral Constitution on the Church in the Modern World develops this idea. According to this document one of the great errors of our time is the dichotomy between the faith that many profess and the practice of their daily lives (no. 43).

The pre–Vatican II approach recognized significant distinctions or dualities—supernatural-natural, gospel-natural law, religious-lay, and divinization-humanization. In fairness these distinctions or dualities did not constitute total dichotomies but existed in a hierarchical ordering with the first element in the duality being more important than the second.

The supernatural-natural duality constitutes the most basic reality that helps explain the others. The natural order involves our temporal existence and life in the world. The supernatural involves our spiritual life—our relationship with God through grace. The natural law governs life in the natural or temporal sphere of this world. The natural law maintains that human reason reflecting on what God has made can determine how God wants us to act in this world. The gospel, or grace, does not directly affect life in the world. Those who want to be perfect leave the world to follow the evangelical counsels. The church has two missions—divinization and humanization. On the supernatural level the church offers God's gracious love and life in word and sacrament to God's people—the mission of divinization. On the natural level or the temporal sphere of this world, the church and its members work with all others for a greater humanization of life in temporal society. The humanizing mission of the church is important for two reasons. First, conditions in the temporal or natural order have some influence on the supernatural order. Second, God has a plan for human existence in this world that all should follow.

The Vatican II approach did away with these dualities. Jesus, faith, and the gospel must affect who we are and what we do in all aspects of our life. The supernatural-natural distinction should not exist. There is no aspect of human existence that is not affected by faith and the gospel. Grace touches the family, the neighborhood, the workplace, recreation, politics, and all aspects of human existence. There is no such thing as the merely natural order.

Justice in the World, the document coming from the 1971 Synod of Bishops, makes the point very clearly: "Action on behalf of justice and participation in the transformation of the world fully appear to us as a constitutive dimension of the preaching of the gospel, or, in other words, of the church's mission for the redemption of the human race and its liberation from every oppressive situation." Thus, the gospel affects daily life, and there is only one mission of the church that involves the preaching of the gospel and the church's mission for the redemption of the human race. Christians living in the world are called to holiness.

William H. Shannon's Contribution

In *Silence on Fire* (1991; rev. ed. 2000), William H. Shannon makes two important contributions to this Vatican II spirituality. First, he insists on the call to holiness in the midst of our daily life in this world. Our author coins a marvelous metaphor to describe the older approach—spiritual apartheid. Spiritual apartheid separates our spiritual life from our life with family, friends, work, play, and the broader social and political life of the world. In developing a spirituality for holiness in the world, the book follows the approach of Thomas Merton, the well-known Trappist monk. However, Merton was not a monk who left the world behind in order to find God only in the monastery. Merton continued to have an important interest in and great concern for what happened in the world and in daily life precisely because he believed that the living God is truly present in the world.

Shannon's book clearly and lucidly explains the basis for a spirituality of holiness in the world. The living God is already present in all things. Too often we think of God as an object. There are many objects in our world, but for believers God is the biggest and the most important object of them all. However, God as object is different from and apart from all the other objects in our lives. But God is not an object. God is a subject—the ground of being who is present in all reality. We cannot separate God from all that is because the gracious God has already chosen to be present there. This understanding of God's presence in all reality stands behind the beautiful opening prayer of the Twentieth Sunday in Ordinary Time (B): "Oh God . . . may we love you in all things and above all things." Such is the prayer of the Christian striving for holiness in the world.

Shannon's second and even more important contribution involves the practical order. Once Catholics learn and accept the Vatican II approach that the call to holiness is addressed to all Christians in our daily lives, an even greater problem arises. Vatican II itself gives us no help in answering the most important and existential question of how we live out this spirituality. *Silence on Fire* puts flesh and blood on the bare bones of the Vatican II skeleton. The prayer of awareness serves as the basis for such a spirituality. This joyful awareness of God by its very nature also involves an awareness of all other people and things precisely because the living God has chosen to be present there. Shannon here develops an approach to prayer that is quite different from the popular notion of prayer as our talking with God through our words. The prayer of awareness is primarily wordless prayer.

But the problem here is obvious. How do you use words to explain wordless prayer? Here Shannon the teacher takes over. The author was a college teacher of theology for forty years. William Shannon is not only a wonderful guide for the spiritual life but also an excellent pedagogue. The book deftly explains the theory and practice of the prayer of awareness that serves as the basis for a life of Christian holiness in the world.

Vatican II by its insistence that all of the baptized are called to holiness lived out in daily life in the world has thus insisted on the close relationship between moral theology and spirituality. In this perspective prayer is not a withdrawal from the world to be alone with God. William H. Shannon in *Silence on Fire* develops in detail the prayer of awareness based on God's presence in all reality.

Chapter 12

THE REFORM OF MORAL THEOLOGY
AT VATICAN II AND AFTER*

Through the Lens of Enda McDonagh

The most significant influence on Catholic life and theology in general and moral theology in particular in the last fifty years was the Second Vatican Council. Since Vatican II, the living tradition of Catholic moral theology has changed and developed. This chapter will consider the reform of moral theology at Vatican II and the developments that have occurred since that have gone beyond what Vatican II did. The chapter will consider these two aspects through the writings of Enda McDonagh. McDonagh is the leading moral theologian in Ireland. He has also taught and lectured frequently in the United States, and his books, mostly collections of essays, have been widely read in this country.

Enda McDonagh, like other Catholic moral theologians, found himself in dialogue with the work of Vatican II in light of his own understanding of what transpired there and the developing life of the church and theology after Vatican II.

Vatican II's Major Contribution to Moral Theology

How, in reality, did Vatican II affect moral theology? The major influence of Vatican II was to make moral theology more theological. Three of the documents of Vatican II illustrate the need for moral theology to become more theological. The Decree on Priestly Formation specifically addresses the renewal of moral theology. "Other theological disciplines should also be renewed by livelier contact with the mystery of Christ and the history of

* Originally published as Charles E. Curran, "Enda McDonagh's Dialogue with Vatican II," in *Beauty, Truth, and Love: Essays in Honor of Enda McDonagh,* ed. Patrick Hannon and Eugene Duffy (Dublin: Columba Press, 2009), 62–86. Used with permission.

salvation. Special attention needs to be given to the development of moral theology. Its scientific exposition should be more thoroughly nourished by scriptural teaching. It should show the nobility of the Christian vocation of the faithful, and their obligation to bring forth fruit in charity for the life of the world."[1]

Chapter 5 of the Constitution on the Church insists on the call of the whole church to holiness. "All the faithful of Christ of whatever rank or status are called to the fullness of the Christian life and to the perfection of charity."[2] "All of Christ's faithful, therefore, whatever be the conditions, duties and circumstances of their lives, will grow in holiness day by day through these very situations, if they accept all of them with faith from the hand of their heavenly Father, and if they cooperate with the divine will by showing every man through their earthly activities the love with which God has loved the world."[3]

As the last chapter pointed out, the pre–Vatican II church maintained that those who are called to perfection and holiness should leave the world and go off to religious life, but that is now changed. Married couples and Christian parents through faithful love should follow their own proper path to holiness, sustaining one another in grace throughout their lives. In a different way, widows and single people are called to their own holiness. Laborers in the midst of their work, which is often tedious, strive for their own perfection, aid their fellow citizens, and raise all of society, even creation itself, to a better mode of existence. Those who are oppressed by infirmity, sickness, and various other hardships in a special way are united with the suffering Christ for the salvation of the world.[4]

The Pastoral Constitution on the Church in the Modern World declares, "This split between the faith which many profess and their daily lives deserves to be counted among the more serious errors of our age. Long since, the prophets of the Old Testament fought vehemently against this scandal and even more so did Jesus Christ himself in the New Testament threaten it with grave punishments."[5]

---

[1] Decree on Priestly Formation, no. 16, in *Documents of Vatican II*, ed. Walter M. Abbott (New York: Guild Press, 1966), 452.

2 Constitution on the Church, no. 40, in Abbott, *Documents of Vatican II*, 67.

[3] Constitution on the Church, no. 41, in Abbott, *Documents of Vatican II*, 70.

[4] Constitution on the Church, no. 41, in Abbott, *Documents of Vatican II,* 69–70.

[5] The Pastoral Constitution on the Church in the Modern World, no. 43, in Abbott, *Documents of Vatican II*, 243.

The first part of the Pastoral Constitution on the Church in the Modern World devotes three chapters to the human person, human community, and human activity. In each of these considerations the document insists there must also be a Christological understanding of these realities. For example, while the communitarian dimensions of human existence are grounded in creation, "this communitarian character is developed and consummated in the work of Jesus Christ."[6] The second part of the Pastoral Constitution aims to discuss five particular issues facing human life and society "in the light of the Gospel and of human experience."[7]

Development of Vatican II Themes

McDonagh rejoiced in the work of Vatican II that called for a new approach to moral theology away from the older manuals. He describes the stony atmosphere of Maynooth in the 1940s and '50s when he was a student there in this premier Irish seminary. "The fortress church with its stone ramparts of precise teaching and Latin liturgy, and with its granite doctors of divinity, enjoyed (if that be the word) its most powerful period from the 1860s to the 1960s."[8] McDonagh in his writings developed four significant Vatican II themes—(1) the demise of the manuals of moral theology; (2) the theological dimension; (3) the connection of morality with spirituality and liturgy; (4) the ecumenical dimension.

Demise of the Manuals

The manuals of moral theology, the textbooks of the discipline of moral theology in the pre–Vatican II church, came into existence in the post-Tridentine church to train confessors for their role as judges in the sacrament of penance. These texts dealt primarily with Christian misconduct (not its conduct) following the approach of the Ten Commandments. Natural law obligations were primary and increasingly supplemented if not altogether overshadowed by the provisions of canon law. The approach of the manuals was act-centered, legalistic, minimalistic, and casuistic. There were no attempts to connect these many laws describing what is sinful and

---

[6] The Pastoral Constitution on the Church in the Modern World, no. 32, in Abbott, *Documents of Vatican II*, 230.

[7] The Pastoral Constitution on the Church in the Modern World, no. 46, in Abbott, *Documents of Vatican II*, 248.

[8] Enda McDonagh, *Faith in Fragments* (Dublin: Columba Press, 1995), 36.

the degrees of sinfulness with the primary biblical injunction to love God with your whole being and your neighbor as yourself.[9] This theology tended to indoctrinate rather than inspire.[10] Moral theology, supposedly the most practical of theological disciplines, was interested primarily in categorizing personal sins for confessional practice. Personal moral development and social justice issues were not even discussed.[11] Looking back thirty years later, McDonagh admits it is difficult to recall and relive the excitement of Vatican II's convening and concluding. The stones were rolled back. The petrified church became flesh and blood once more. A new approach of a life-centered moral theology replaced the narrow and limited scope of the manuals.[12]

In his latter writings reflecting on the change of moral theology, McDonagh points out that the work of renewal had begun before Vatican II. Fritz Tillmann, the Bonn scripture scholar in the 1930s, called for a more theological and scriptural approach to moral theology. Bernard Häring's *Law of Christ* attempted a new moral manual with the broader purpose of elucidating the moral life of the Christian called by God in baptism to be a follower of Jesus. The call for renewal in moral theology even before Vatican II came in the context of other renewal movements then going on in the church. The biblical renewal developed the biblical basis for the Christian moral life in the work of scholars such as Rudolf Schnackenburg and Ceslaus Spicq. The theology of the church with the emphasis not on the juridical structures of the hierarchical church but on the church as the body of Christ and the people of God called for a different approach to moral theology as reflecting on the life of discipleship in the body of Christ. The liturgical renewal called for the active worshiping community of all the baptized who were called to live out a Christian life of service within the church and world. The ecumenical movement made Catholics more aware of the narrow legal focus of their moral theology and the need for more biblical, Christ-centered, and charity-inspired developments of the Christian moral life.[13]

---

[9] Enda McDonagh, *The Making of Disciples: Tasks of Moral Theology* (Wilmington, DE: Michael Glazier, 1982), 22–24; Enda McDonagh, *Invitation and Response: Essays in Christian Moral Theology* (New York: Sheed & Ward, 1972), 16–19.

[10] McDonagh, *Faith in Fragments*, 34.

[11] Enda McDonagh, *Vulnerable to the Holy in Faith, Morality, and Art* (Dublin: Columba Press, 2004), 35.

[12] McDonagh, *Faith in Fragments*, 36.

[13] McDonagh, *Invitation and Response*, 18–21; McDonagh, *Making of Disciples*, 22–24.

Even before Vatican II, McDonagh himself was aware of the need for a new approach to a life-centered moral theology away from the narrow scope of the manuals. Even in the 1950s, he was apparently discontent with the existing manuals of moral theology and in his readings and interests strayed beyond the confines of "pure" theology. Moral theology, as mentioned, was closely associated with canon law. In keeping with that understanding, McDonagh in the late 1950s was sent to the University of Munich to get a second doctoral degree in canon law. But rather than work on a canonical and casuistic topic, his 1960 dissertation discussed church/state relations.[14] McDonagh's creative and imaginative intelligence, even in the pre–Vatican II days, anticipated the need for change in the focus of moral theology that Vatican II ultimately proposed for the whole church.

Emphasis on the Theological Dimension

McDonagh, in keeping with this important Vatican II emphasis, has insisted on the theological aspect of his understanding of morality and social ethics. No Catholic moral theologian of this period has emphasized the theological aspect as much as McDonagh. Even immediately after Vatican II, he believed the various divisions of theology (e.g., dogmatic, moral, and scriptural) had not been helpful in practice to provide an integrated theology that brings Christian theory and practice together. The end of all Christian theologizing is the making of disciples. For this reason he does not even want to call himself a moral theologian. The end of moral theology, accompanied by the end of the self-enclosed dogmatic theology, could prepare the way for a rebirth of an integrated theology. The end of moral theology (also including the notion of purpose) is the making of disciples and the remaking of theology itself.[15]

The essays collected in *Between Chaos and the New Creation* (1986) and the *Gracing of Society* (1989) continue the emphasis on a more integrated theology centered on the community of the disciples of Jesus announcing, discerning, promoting, and bearing witness to the reign of God, which is the new social existence of human beings. The earlier volume deals with the deep dialectic of Christian existence struggling between chaos and new creation.[16] The gracing of theology or a theology of society follows

---

[14] McDonagh, *Vulnerable to the Holy*, 36.

[15] McDonagh, *Making of Disciples*, 2–8.

[16] Enda McDonagh, *Between Chaos and New Creation: Doing Theology at the Fringe* (Dublin: Columba Press, 1986), 9.

the method of faith-hope-love seeking understanding.[17] McDonagh in the 1980s was teaching more in the area of social ethics but he titled his course "A Theology of Society" for two reasons. First is his continuing interest in developing an integrating moral theology into the one science of theology. Second, he wanted to underscore the social nature of God, grace, salvation, and humanity itself.[18]

His last collection of essays (2004) uses the metaphor of *Vulnerable to the Holy* to bring together faith and daily life. Here it seems to me that McDonagh is employing what is perhaps the most distinctive characteristic of the Catholic theological tradition—the concept of mediation, which understands the divine as being mediated in and through the human. Thus, all the essays in this collection maintain that in the central areas of Christian living discussed in the volume, from the very personal areas of friendship, sexuality, and marriage to the great contemporary social issues of HIV/AIDS and peace and war, openness and vulnerability to others is crucial, cruciform, and Christian.[19]

Spirituality, Liturgy, and Morality

Vatican II insisted that spirituality and morality cannot be separated. McDonagh throughout his search for an integrated theology has tried to bring together the aspects that have too often been separated—theory and praxis, faith and life, spirituality and morality, holiness and the apparently secular. Again, *Vulnerable to the Holy* connects morality and spirituality especially in the form of prayer. McDonagh insists on a deep relationship between prayer and poetry. Prayer is awareness of and response to God, the ultimate reality. Poetry is the human expression of reality often in its tragic mode. Prayer and poetry deal with mystery, inspiration, and the search for adequate and beautiful form. Not only in poetry and in literature, but also in other art forms such as painting and sculpture, one becomes vulnerable to a deeper beauty and otherness.[20] Yes, art work has to be appreciated for what it is in itself, but the believer sees in the work of art the creator and redeemer God.[21]

---

[17] Enda McDonagh, *The Gracing of Society* (Dublin: Gill and Macmillan, 1989), 1–7.

[18] Ibid., 48–80.

[19] McDonagh, *Vulnerable to the Holy*, 9.

[20] Ibid., 137–90.

[21] Ibid., 9.

Probably many believers see some connection between art and prayer, but McDonagh also insists on a connection between politics and prayer. Again, most Christians would probably recognize that prayer should lead to political involvement in working for a more just human society. But for McDonagh the relationship between prayer and politics is a two-way street. Objections to this understanding easily come to mind. For many politicians there is absolutely no connection between political involvement and prayer. Even for most believers political involvement does not lead to prayer. But McDonagh insists on the movement from politics to prayer. In political involvement we open ourselves to the transforming mystery of the other with attitudes of wonder, awe, thanksgiving, humility, and forgiveness. These are the same basic characteristics of prayer. The openness to the other in politics by its inherent dynamism leads to openness to the transcendent God as the one who is mediated in and through the political involvement with the other and especially the other in need. Social and political activity for the Christian should lead to prayer.[22]

In his striving for a more integrated theology, McDonagh brings together morality and liturgy. Liturgy and Christian life go together. In so doing, he goes beyond Vatican II. Vatican II, with its call for a renewed moral theology, failed to explicitly recognize the important relationship between liturgy and moral theology. According to the Constitution on the Liturgy, liturgy should be a major course in the seminary. Professors of dogmatic, spiritual, and pastoral theology as well as of sacred scripture, should bring out the connection between their subjects and the liturgy.[23] No mention is made of moral theology—a fact that illustrates the hold of the manualistic approach to moral theology even on the participants of Vatican II. But from his earliest writings McDonagh recognized the close relationship between liturgy and moral theology. An early essay shows how both liturgy and Christian life have Trinitarian, covenantal, and community aspects.[24] A later essay on society and the sacraments tries to bring together the first document of Vatican II on the liturgy with the last document on the church in the modern world. Too often the emphasis on sacraments and liturgy has been too personal and has failed to recognize the important relationship to the community and the broader society. This

---

[22] McDonagh, *Making of Disciples*, 99–111.

[23] Constitution on the Liturgy, no. 16, in Abbott, *Documents of Vatican II*, 144–45.

[24] McDonagh, *Invitation and Response*, 96–108.

particular essay brings together political and liberation theology with liturgical and sacramental theology.[25]

In light of his previous publications, one can readily understand why
Enda McDonagh was invited to write the article on liturgy and Christian
life for the *New Dictionary of Sacramental Worship* published in 1990.[26] A
large part of this article probes the connection of the liturgy and the sacraments with the kingdom values or virtues. The primary kingdom values or
virtues, as mentioned above, are faith-hope-love, which bring about our
entry into the reign of God and support our continuing involvement in
the reign of God. The essay then considers four more particular kingdom
values—truth, liberation and freedom, justice and equality, and solidarity
and peace. With his emphasis on the community, McDonagh relates all of

these to the community of the church and the community's role in making
the reign of God more present in our world. Liberation calls us to renounce
the demons of sin, oppression, and exploitation in the Christian community
and in the world in which we live. Justice and equality in the reign of God
give special place to the poor, the marginalized, and the needy. Solidarity
and peace call for reconciliation and a flourishing in community.

The liturgical and sacramental symbol and reality of communion
confront the sacramental community with the problem of consumption
and consumerism in our world. The rich consume the poor, the powerful
consume the powerless, we consume our environment. Jesus was consumed
by the political and religious leaders of his time—*consummatum est*. In
contrast the communion of the sacraments in general and of the Eucharist
in particular as a sharing in the bread of eternal life and the cup of salvation brings about a sharing in the love and the life of the triune God. The
symbol and reality of the communion celebrated in the sacraments radically
confront the consumption so prevalent in our society.[27]

Ecumenical Dimension

Vatican II with its Decree on Ecumenism brought the Roman Catholic
Church into ecumenical dialogue with other Christians and into interfaith
dialogue with other religions. McDonagh's life and work have had a strong
ecumenical dimension. In his writings he has been in dialogue with many

---

[25] McDonagh, *Between Chaos and New Creation*, 76–88.

[26] Enda McDonagh, "Liturgy and Christian Life," in *New Dictionary of Sacramental Worship*, ed. Peter E. Fink (Collegeville, MN: Liturgical Press, 1990), 742–53.

[27] McDonagh, *Faith in Fragments*, 104–7.

Protestant moral theologians throughout the world. In more practical activities, McDonagh has worked ecumenically in Ireland in dealing with the issues arising in Northern Ireland and also with regard to the social issues and church issues facing the Republic.

In his writings he has made some creative suggestions for how the ecumenical dimension might be more present in the life of the Catholic Church, but unfortunately his suggestions have not been accepted by church authorities. One of the positive results of ecumenical dialogue is the full restoration of the mutual acceptance of baptism done in other churches and communions. By their baptism all different Christians are called to work for the unity of the church and for a greater presence of the reign of God in our world. In certain societies where Christianity is a source of division, as in Bosnia and Northern Ireland, interchurch celebration of baptism creatively demonstrates the unity of all the baptized and challenges the destructive divisions that religion has brought about. In such situations, the joint celebration of the entry rite into the body of Christ would put flesh and blood on the ecumenical understandings we accept in theory. Ecumenical dialogue has also made great progress in that Orthodox, Roman Catholic, and many Reformed churches agree on both the memorial and sacrificial aspects of the Eucharist. In light of this, McDonagh sees the possibility and even the need for some intercommunion after due preparation. One suggestion calls for the Church Unity Octave Week to be a week of penitential preparation for a shared Eucharist on the final Sunday.[28]

Developments after Vatican II

McDonagh's theology developed in the years since Vatican II, and in five areas in particular his later approach differed from the Vatican II approach—(1) a more theological approach especially to social morality; (2) the need for a local theology; (3) a challenge to the more optimistic view of historical progress found in Vatican II; (4) an emphasis in anthropology not primarily on the person as in Vatican II but on the other; (5) the doing of theology from the fringe and not from the center as in Vatican II.

A More Theological Approach to Social Morality

As mentioned previously, the primary emphasis of Vatican II was to make the discipline of moral theology more theological. Perhaps no Catholic

---

[28] McDonagh, *Vulnerable to the Holy*, 51–59.

theologian has developed the theological aspect of moral theology as much as McDonagh. His primary criticism is that post–Vatican II Catholic social morality does not emphasize enough the theological character of its method and approach.[29]

McDonagh explicitly criticizes *Gaudium et Spes*. As noted earlier, *Gaudium et Spes* certainly calls for a more theological approach, but this emphasis exists especially in the first part of the document dealing with more methodological and generic understandings such as the person, human action, the human community, and the role of the church in the world. The second part deals with five more specific issues: marriage, culture, socio-economic life, political life, and the fostering of peace in the community of nations. There is no doubt that the second part dealing with these five specific issues is much less theological. A primary reason for this comes from the fact that the two parts were drafted as two very different sections. In fact, the original idea was simply to publish the second part only as an appendix because according to some it was not theological enough.[30] Only late in the council deliberations was it decided to publish both parts in the one document, but in a sense the second part was never developed and integrated into the approach of the first part.[31]

As developed in chapter 2, the official hierarchical teaching on social morality or ethics is often called Catholic social teaching and involves the post–Vatican II social encyclicals—Pope Paul VI's *Populorum Progressio* and the three encyclicals of Pope John Paul II—*Laborem Exercens, Sollicitudo Rei Socialis*, and *Centesimus Annus*. All of these documents in keeping with the practice introduced by Pope John XXIII in *Pacem in Terris* in 1963 are also addressed to all people of good will.

By definition, therefore, these documents are not going to emphasize only the distinctive theological aspect of Catholic teaching but rather an approach and proposals that can be accepted by all people of good will. McDonagh criticizes these encyclicals as not being theological enough.[32] But McDonagh has to respond to the question if he also wants to address all people of good will and whether or not his theological approach will

---

[29] McDonagh, *Gracing of Society*, 20–21.

[30] Enda McDonagh, "The Church in the Modern World (*Gaudium et Spes*)," in *Modern Catholicism: Vatican II and After,* ed. Adrian Hastings (New York: Oxford University Press, 1991), 100.

[31] Mark G. McGrath, "Note storiche sulla Costituzione," in *La Chiesa nel Mondo di Oggi,* ed. Guilherme Baraúna (Florence: Vallecchi, 1966), 155–56.

[32] McDonagh, *Gracing of Society*, 21.

be able to accomplish that. A more explicitly theological approach to social morality easily appeals to a less heterogeneous society, but in a more heterogeneous and pluralistic society such an approach will not appeal to all people of good will.

Be that as it may, there is no doubt that McDonagh has attempted to develop a more theological approach to society. The central doctrines of God, church, the Holy Spirit, salvation, grace, and sacraments have not been vital sources for the development of Catholic social morality.[33] One example of the impoverishment of post–Vatican II moral theology in this area is the concept of justice. The Aristotelian and Thomistic notion of justice reigned before Vatican II, and it still continues to heavily influence even post–Vatican II Catholic social morality. Liberation theology has taken a different course. The biblical approach as distinguished from the philosophical approach sees justice as a characteristic of God and his/her dealings with the covenant people of Israel. The primary criterion of biblical justice is the treatment of the poor, the needy, the disabled, the marginalized, the sick, and the stranger. In keeping with the essay genre that he uses to develop his thoughts, the concept of this justice is not fully developed, but he concludes that transformative justice could offer a way into a genuinely theological moral theology.[34]

A rather long essay reflects on his course which is not titled social ethics but rather "Theology of Society."[35] Theology is a multicolored reality— a science, an art, a praxis. Faith-hope-charity (a favorite description of his Christian theological starting point) bespeaks engagement for the Christian in the service of God and neighbor. Society is simultaneously the context, the subject, and the object of theology. Here he stresses the kingdom values of freedom, justice, peace, and truth. (Interestingly enough, Pope John XXIII in *Pacem in Terris,* on the basis of a natural law methodology, insisted on the four virtues or values of love, justice, truth, and freedom as the way to bring about peace.) McDonagh, however, develops these virtues or values from a theological and biblical perspective.[36]

---

[33] Ibid., 34.

[34] Ibid., 27.

[35] Ibid., 48–80.

[36] Pope John XXIII, *Pacem in Terris,* no. 35, in *Catholic Social Thought: The Documentary Heritage,* ed. David J. O'Brien and Thomas A. Shannon (Maryknoll, NY: Orbis Books, 1992), 136.

A Local Theology

Vatican II conceived of Catholic theology as a universal theology for the whole church throughout the world. The universalizing tendencies of Catholic life and thought had become even more pronounced in the nineteenth and twentieth centuries. But as McDonagh points out, the seeds of differentiation were also present even at Vatican II. Shortly afterward, Latin American liberation theology led the way toward more particular theologies, but the particularization of theology soon embraced many different aspects—regions, social differences, culture, race, and gender. Writing in 1986, McDonagh claims that the move to particularity constitutes the greatest single change in theology since Vatican II. The recognition of historical consciousness was behind this move to particular theologies.[37]

McDonagh wants to hold on to both the universal and the particular aspects of Catholic theology. The danger of the claim to universality is that this claim is really a particular theology at work, thus involving in its own way a theological imperialism. There remains, however, a need for the universal. After all, Catholic by definition means universal. We need particular theologies, but theology must communicate across the boundaries of geography, culture, history, social class, race, economic differences, and gender. The many particular Christian communities share considerations of faith, understanding, and practice that are common to all Catholics.[38]

From his earliest writings McDonagh recognized his own social location. The very first collection of his essays refers to the inescapably autobiographical character of theology. One does theology in response to particular situations and demands and in light of one's own concerns, interests, and abilities.[39] His subsequent work described theology as sociobiography in light of recognizing the important social dimensions affecting the world, the church, and the theologian.[40]

In his 1986 collection, *Between Chaos and New Creation*, he brings together six essays under the heading "Constructing a Local Theology." The social context of this consideration is the world in crisis with Ireland sharing in that crisis but in its own ways.[41] The whole world has been aware

---

[37] McDonagh, *Between Chaos and New Creation*, 91–95.

[38] Ibid., 91–122.

[39] McDonagh, *Invitation and Response*, viii.

[40] Enda McDonagh, *Doing the Truth: The Quest for Moral Theology* (Notre Dame, IN: University of Notre Dame Press, 1979), 1–13, 187–207.

[41] McDonagh, *Between Chaos and New Creation*, 3.

of the problems of Northern Ireland and especially the role that religion has played there. But the Republic has faced its own problems. Scandals have wracked the church. The hierarchical leadership has been slow to act and has not responded to the many problems facing the church. There is a growing lack of credibility in the church and a move by many people in Ireland away from the church. Truly the church in Ireland is experiencing its winter. The church itself has not dealt creatively with the problems it is facing internally and with the growing secularization in Ireland. Despite the recent economic success in Ireland that is so often mentioned, the country is faced with continued poverty and a growing gap between the rich and the poor. Individualism seems to have become ever more significant as a cultural phenomenon, and there is much less concern about the community and especially the needs of the poor, the marginalized, and the oppressed.[42] These have been difficult times of crisis, and McDonagh has proposed some creative and imaginative ways of helping the fragmented community of Ireland and the church in Ireland to struggle with these crises.

A Move Away from the Overly Optimistic Approach of Vatican II

McDonagh perceptively points out in an article written twenty-five years later on the Pastoral Constitution on the Church of the Modern World that this document shows an insufficient awareness of the tragic dimension of human existence. The understanding of history and progress is much too optimistic, and the document fails to recognize the eschatological aspects, especially the apocalyptic aspects of eschatology.[43]

McDonagh recognizes that the 1960s were optimistic times.[44] By changing the Catholic Church quite dramatically and calling for reform of the church, which had not been experienced in the Catholic Church in the last four centuries, Vatican II itself thus contributed to the optimism that many Catholics experienced. In my own country, Catholics lionized the work of the two Johns—John XXIII and the Second Vatican Council and John F. Kennedy, who proclaimed that the torch now had been passed to a new generation born in this century. We were overly optimistic and even naively optimistic about both the church and the world.

---

[42] McDonagh, *Faith in Fragments*, 7–89.
[43] McDonagh, "The Church in the Modern World (*Gaudium et Spes*)," 102–3.
[44] Ibid., 102.

McDonagh maintains that the optimistic aspect of *Gaudium et Spes* comes from the failure to recognize enough the presence of sin in the church and the world and the fact that the fullness of the reign of God will come only at the end of time.[45] The theological and historical context of the document helps explain the problem. This document rightly tried to overcome the separation between faith and daily life, the separation between the supernatural and the natural. In a pre–Vatican II theology the world was seen as the realm of the natural governed by reason and natural law. The document emphasized that faith, grace, and Jesus Christ were now present in the world and trying to transform it. Just as there had been a great impetus for reform and change in the church because of Vatican II, many Catholics in the light of Vatican II began to think that progress and development would readily take place once we realized the role of grace and faith in transforming the world. From a theological perspective this approach forgot the presence of sin in our world and the fact that the fullness of the reign of God will come only at the end of time.

In the pre–Vatican II understanding, Catholic theology was often guilty of a natural law optimism that failed to recognize the presence and power of sin in the world. Even a Vatican document issued on the tenth anniversary of *Pacem in Terris* recognized that the famous encyclical of Pope John XXIII needed another chapter titled "Bellum in Terris" in light of the violence and the wars that have marked human history and are still in existence at this time in many parts of our world.[46] The danger of not recognizing enough the presence of sin in the world became even more grievous in light of the attempt to see faith, grace, and the redeeming love of Jesus transforming the world.

McDonagh has pointed out the lack of eschatology in the document. An analysis of the document clearly shows this lack of the eschatological future. The first two chapters of part 1 deal with the human person and the human community. Both chapters neglect the eschatological aspect. The first chapter ends with a section on "Christ as the New Man," while the second chapter ends with a section on "The Incarnate Word and Solidarity."[47] Only

---

45 Ibid., 102–3.

46 Cardinal Maurice Roy, "Reflections on the Occasion of the Tenth Anniversary of the Encyclical *Pacem in Terris* of Pope John XXIII," in *The Gospel of Peace and Justice: Catholic Social Teaching since Pope John*, ed. Joseph Gremillion (Maryknoll, NY: Orbis Books, 1976), 548.

47 Pastoral Constitution on the Church in the Modern World, nos. 22 and 32, in Abbott, *Documents of Vatican II*, 220–22 and 230–31.

the third chapter on human activity brings in the eschatological aspect with a final section "A New Earth and a New Heaven."[48] The theological problem here is a collapsed eschaton that results in a too optimistic approach to history and human progress.

Historical events influenced McDonagh and all of us in the realization that *Gaudium et Spes* was too optimistic in its view of human history and its progress. Experience in the church universal and the local church reminded believers of the sinful nature of the church and the fact that the church is only the sacrament and sign of the reign of God, which will come about fully only at the end of time. We are a pilgrim church always in need of reform.

In the church *Humanae Vitae* provided a great shock. The failure of the institutional church to hear the needs of the divorced and gays and lesbians has disillusioned many. The most alienated people in the church today are women who are denied any true leadership roles in the church. The emphasis on authority and centralization and the lack of creative leadership have frustrated many Catholics. McDonagh points out that the church in Ireland has suffered from these same realities compounded by problems indigenous to the Irish church.[49]

We have also become much more conscious of the problems facing our world. Violence, war, injustice, ecological devastation, and poverty in all its many forms of hunger, homelessness, and illness are all very prevalent on our earth. Instead of overcoming the gap between the rich and the poor, the last few years have seen a growing gap, not only between the various parts of the world, but also in practically all of our countries. In McDonagh's words, there are many crises facing our world and our church today.[50]

The danger of overoptimism shows itself today in a poor understanding of the meaning of the Christian virtue of hope. Very often today I hear the question: Is there any hope for the church? Paul's understanding of hope in the Letter to the Romans reminds us of the true meaning of hope. If you can see the goal, there is no hope. Hope is hoping against hope. Hope sees light in the midst of darkness, joy in the midst of sorrow, and life in the midst of death. One who does not know how to suffer does not know how to hope. Yes, there have to be some positive signs that are present, but hope does not

---

[48]　Pastoral Constitution on the Church in the Modern World, no. 39, in Abbott, *Documents of Vatican II*, 237–38.

[49]　McDonagh, *Vulnerable to the Holy*, 22–83.

[50]　McDonagh's writings from the mid-eighties have pointed out all these problems.

depend on what we can feel, see, or touch. Chapter 15 will develop in more detail a theology and spirituality for church reformers. McDonagh's writings have attempted to provide hope for the church in Ireland in the midst of the many crises it faces.[51]

McDonagh explicitly reflects on the good number of friends and others who have left the church while he and others choose to remain. Unfortunately, now as in the time of Jesus cowardice and power seeking have prevented the church community and its leaders from recognizing their mediating-reconciling role proclaimed by Jesus. Structural change in the church is necessary, but it will never solve all our problems. The community of the church experiences the presence and power of the divine within the created, human, pilgrim, and sinful community of the church. The pilgrim and sinful church lives in the betweenness of Good Friday and Easter, the half-life and half-light between the death of Jesus and the resurrection of Christ. Faith and sacrament only partially remove the darkness and doubt of our mediated access to God's loving presence. Life for all in the church, leaders and members alike, is by turns illuminating and disillusioning, transforming and frustrating. The pilgrim community of the church should be generous in its boundaries and welcoming of the gifts of all the faithful, not just of the "party faithful" but of the partly faithful, which in reality involves all of us, members and leaders, always in need of being sustained, forgiven, and transformed by the inbreaking God. The essay that develops these ideas is titled "A Communal Hope."[52]

Less Emphasis on Person and More on Community and the Other

McDonagh appreciates the renewed anthropology of *Gaudium et Spes* with its attempt to recognize both the personal and the social dimensions of the human person, but in the end this document puts more emphasis on the personal than on the social and the communitarian. The individual person remains dominant while the social aspects seem subordinate. In reality the person is only a person-in-relationship-in-structures, as person-in-community, and is in an immediate dialectic with a community-of-persons.[53]

---

[51] McDonagh, *Faith in Fragments*, 20–89; McDonagh, *Vulnerable to the Holy*, 22–83.

[52] McDonagh, *Vulnerable to the Holy*, 73–83.

[53] McDonagh, "The Church in the Modern World (*Gaudium et Spes*)," 102.

From his earliest writings McDonagh emphasized the importance of community. One becomes a person only in and through community.[54] Just as the community forms the person, so the person forms and changes the various communities of family, school, neighborhood, city, nation, and world. Only such a community can deal with the problems facing our society today—waste, pollution, devastation, injustice, poverty, and war.[55] Community is in many ways the central theme in the essays found in the *Gracing of Society*.

More than any other Catholic moral theologian McDonagh has emphasized "the other." The scriptural connection between otherness and holiness as well as the philosophical work of Emmanuel Levinas has influenced him.[56] His early emphasis on the Christian life as gift and call sees the moral obligation in terms of a call that has an unconditional character about it. The source of the call-obligation is another person or a group of persons. In transcending self to reach out to the call of the other a certain disintegration of the subject occurs, followed by a reintegration of the subject in relationship to others and other communities. But in keeping with his recognition of the sinful and tragic dimensions of human existence, the other constitutes not only a gift but also a threat. The twofold aspect of gift and threat calls the person to conversion, true liberation, and proper relationships.[57]

The emphasis on the other has continued to grow in McDonagh's later writings. An essay in *Faith in Fragments* recognizes that the recovery of the other/stranger "both human and divine" is at the heart of the renewal of ethics and of God's place in it. God is the stranger God, and we who believe the stranger God has come to us must also accept and bring into relationships the human strangers both in the form of individuals and groups. Such an approach challenges the exclusiveness so often present in our world based on economic, cultural, political, and gender factors.[58] This essay became seminal for the development of the theme of the other, ethics, and holiness in *Vulnerable to the Holy* published in 2004.

In this last collection of essays both the attraction and the threat of the other, the beauty and the horrors of every body, every where, and every when render us vulnerable to the Holy. Encounter with the other requires

---

[54] McDonagh, *Invitation and Response*, 6–8.

[55] McDonagh, *Making of Disciples*, 77–79.

[56] McDonagh, *Vulnerable to the Holy*, 8–9.

[57] Enda McDonagh, *Gift and Call: Toward a Christian Theology of Morality* (Dublin: Gill and Macmillan, 1975), 39ff.

[58] McDonagh, *Faith in Fragments*, 137–45.

for us a letting be that has both passive and active aspects. Passive letting be calls for patient and loving acceptance of the different other. The active aspect of letting be means that letting be is not merely a toleration of the other but a loving acceptance and enablement of the other. The same call to let be also serves as the criterion for the proper relationship of human beings with the environment and opposes the utilitarian ethic that sees the environment merely as a means for the satisfaction of human individuals. Letting be in the passive and active senses of accepting and enabling requires for its completion a letting go. This calls for respectful acceptance of the other's privacy and freedom and reaches its height in the willingness to forgive our enemies—the most painful aspect of letting go.[59] In the essays in this book McDonagh develops our relationships to others, to art, to the natural environment, and even to our other self as making us vulnerable to the ultimate other—the Holy.

Theology from the Fringe

The recognition of the tragic dimension of human existence, the emphasis on the other, and the influence of liberation theology brought McDonagh to realize that we live between chaos and new creation, calling for doing theology from the fringe. Vatican II's theology was a universal theology primarily emanating from the center. McDonagh now does theology from the fringe in accord with the liberation emphasis on the privileging of the poor, the oppressed, and the marginalized. Human history shows forth the biblical dialectic between destructive human chaos and new divine creation slipping again into chaos that reached its pinnacle in the Paschal Mystery of Jesus. Human suffering and human destructiveness continue to encounter the co-suffering, inexhaustible, and creative God in life, liturgy, and literature.[60]

In this context McDonagh again acknowledges the positive approaches put into place by *Gaudium et Spes* but also points out the danger of theology that is not done from the fringe. Latin America and the third world face great poverty and privation. The economic form of liberalism with its center and periphery, the powerful and the powerless, and the dominating and the dominated becomes an instrument of oppression for the powerless, the peripheral, and the marginalized. From a theological perspective

---

[59] McDonagh, *Vulnerable to the Holy*, 12–20.
[60] McDonagh, *Between Chaos and New Creation*, 1–9.

the theology of the West, the North, and Europe no longer provides the churches in the third world with the Christian inspiration and theological analysis they need. Despite its many positive contributions even for the deprived, *Gaudium et Spes* must be supplemented and even transformed in these very different worlds.[61] In reading the signs of the times *Gaudium et Spes* gave insufficient attention to the tragic aspects present even in Europe to say nothing of the problems of the two-thirds world. Hope can only be hope by arising in, through, and beyond failure and the tragic.[62]

McDonagh's local Irish theology makes the same point. Ireland has its share of poverty, violence, and even fratricidal killing. The Irish church and people cannot really be people of hope unless they first acknowledge and recognize their participation in the grief and anguish (*luctus et angor*) of the times and their complicity in all of this. Theology at the fringe puts the spotlight on the chronically and terminally ill, gypsies, the homeless, the handicapped, the unemployed, prisoners, gays and lesbians, and all other deprived minorities.[63]

The Maynooth professor uses the same theology from the fringe in dealing with the Irish church. The church is not the reign of God but its herald or servant. The church always stands under the challenge and judgment of the reign of God. The pilgrim church is always a sinful church in need of reform. The leadership of the Irish church has unfortunately held onto a triumphalistic notion of the church with its power in and over society, but all have recognized from verifiable evidence that this approach has not worked. Look at the precipitous decline in the number of religious and priestly vocations and the growing number of people who do not participate in the Eucharist and then the problems created by clergy sex abuse and their cover-up by church leadership. McDonagh in his gentle way has challenged the Irish church in the way it treats gays and lesbians and women. A church that recognizes and confesses its own sinfulness and complicity in the problems could become a source of hope and light for a suffering and tragic world looking for light and hope.[64]

Vatican II is synonymous with reform in the Catholic Church. This chapter has pointed out the reforms in moral theology that took place at

---

[61] Ibid., 191.

[62] Ibid., 192–93.

[63] Ibid., 193–94.

[64] McDonagh, *Faith in Fragments*, 18–39; McDonagh, *Vulnerable to the Holy*, 22–83.

Vatican II. The reform of moral theology, however, has not ended with Vatican II. A living tradition is constantly developing. The second part of the chapter has pointed out significant changes that have occurred after Vatican II. The chapter has used the writings of Enda McDonagh in discussing both aspects.

Chapter 13

THE NEED FOR REFORM OF THE
SACRAMENT OF RECONCILIATION*

Sin, God's merciful forgiveness, and penance have been central realities in the Christian life. So important are these realities that in the Catholic tradition, penance or reconciliation is one of the seven sacraments. The reality of penance involves more than just the sacrament, but the sacrament gives a special importance and significance to the reality of penance. The sacrament of penance, popularly known as confession, played a very prominent role in the pre–Vatican II church in the life of Catholics. Today, however, many Catholics no longer celebrate the sacrament of penance. The reality of sin and of the mercy and forgiveness of God, however, are most important realities in the Christian life. Pope Francis has stressed the importance of mercy. This chapter maintains that people have abandoned the present rite of auricular confession, because it is no longer meaningful in their lives. Reform and change in the sacrament of penance are urgently needed so that the Catholic people become more aware of the mercy and forgiveness of God and the need to change our hearts and grow evermore in our love of God and neighbor.

Historical Development

History reminds us of the developing practice of sacramental penance in the church.[1] The New Testament testifies to the forgiveness of sin and the reconciliation of the sinner with the Christian community, but various forms of such reconciliation have taken place over time. One of the most significant developments in the early history concerns the possibility of receiving reconciliation or penance more than once—a controversy that

---

* Originally published as Charles E. Curran, "Auricular Confession: Some Inadequacies," in *Performing the Word: Festschrift in Honor of Ronan Drury,* ed. Enda McDonagh (Dublin: Columba Press, 2015), 249–56. Used with permission.

[1] James Dallen, *The Reconciling Community: The Rite of Penance* (New York: Pueblo, 1986).

continued until the seventh century. From the fourth to the sixth centuries there emerged what is most properly called "canonical penance," since it was governed by the canons or church laws. Sometimes this has been called public penance, and on the basis of that a few thought it involved the public confession of sins, but such was not the case. The canonical penance took place in three stages—entry into the order of penitents through the hands of the bishop, a long stage of severe expiation, and finally reconciliation with the Christian community through the hands of the bishop. Since this very severe process could not be repeated, it gave way in the seventh and later centuries to what was called tariff penance. The minister was the priest or monk, not the bishop; confession played a larger role; the minister assigned a penance to be done according to what was found in the penitential books; then what was now begun to be called absolution was given. In all these variations of sacramental reconciliation there were questions and even abuses that had to be addressed.

The Fourth Lateran Council in 1215 and especially the Council of Trent in its fourteenth session in 1551 inaugurated what became the format of the sacrament of penance until the present time. Trent called for the confession of all mortal sins to the priest at least once a year according to their number and species. The emphasis was now on confession; satisfaction was reduced to a prayer; and the priest gave absolution after the confession of sins and the assignment of the penance.

As a result of this format the sacrament became known as confession. The Catholic Reformation stressed the role of confession in the life of the faithful. So important was the sacrament of confession that it shaped the course of moral theology in seminaries that existed from the Council of Trent until Vatican II. The courses in moral theology had the purpose of training future confessors in determining what acts were sinful and the degree of sinfulness. By the twentieth century, the confession of devotion, involving just venial sins, became very common. On Saturday afternoons and evenings lines of penitents waiting to go to confession were commonplace in Catholic churches. Religious women and men and priests were expected to go to confession on a weekly basis.[2] Confession played a very important role in the life of all Catholics. Today confession plays a much smaller role. The sharp decline in confession in the period after Vatican II is acknowledged by all.

---

[2] Susso Mayer, "Devotional Confession," *Orate Fratres* 18 (1944): 159–65; Susso Mayer, "Devotional Confession II: Reasons Recommending Its Practice," *Orate Fratres* 18 (1944): 258–64.

The Pre–Vatican II Experience

How does one evaluate the practice of confession that played such a significant role in the pre–Vatican II church? There can be no doubt that for some people the role of penance was truly an experience of the forgiveness and mercy of God, and helped the penitent to transform her or his life. This was especially true of penitents who had experienced special crises or problems in their lives. Also for some the devotional confession was a source of spiritual growth.

However, the Catholic practice of confession in the pre–Vatican II church is associated with some negative aspects. The practice of penance contributed to the phenomenon known as "Catholic guilt." So commonplace is this concept and reality that even Wikipedia has an article on "Catholic Guilt." At the very minimum some of the context surrounding confession, especially the parish mission, contributed to the existence of Catholic guilt. Parish missions were an important part of Catholic devotional life. A number of studies have documented the role of the parish mission in Ireland and the United States in the latter part of the nineteenth century and the early part of the twentieth. These missions were usually held once a year in every parish. The preaching aimed to bring people to confession, and the fear of hell was the primary motivating factor. The emphasis on fire and brimstone brought about guilt, which then brought the person to confession. Parish missions still exist today, but they are no longer that prominent in Catholic life. In addition the newer approach to missions stresses God's love, mercy, and forgiveness.[3]

Closely associated with guilt is fear. Many Catholics approached confession with trepidation and even fear. The surroundings of the stark and dark confessional box greatly contributed to the trepidation of the penitent. Many penitents never experienced the joy of celebrating the mercy of the loving God whom we call Mother and Father. The theological context for confession conceived of the Christian life as a life of duty in obeying the commandments of God and not the loving response to the gift of God's love. The motivation of the fear of hell played a major role in motivating

---

[3] Michael Baily, "The Parish Mission Apostolate of the Redemptorists in Ireland," in *History and Conscience: Studies in Honor of Sean O'Riordan, CSsR*, ed. Raphael Gallagher and Brendan McConvery (Dublin: Gill and Macmillan, 1989), 274–96; Brendan McConvery, "Hell Fire and Poitín Redemptorist Missions in the Irish Free State," at www.historyireland.com; James A. Wallace, "Reconsidering the Parish Mission," *Worship* 67 (1993): 340–51.

Catholics to do their God-given duties. For many the sacrament was not primarily an experience of God's mercy.

Connected with the emphasis on sin and the fear of hell was the phenomenon of scrupulosity. The scrupulous person experiences the fear of sinning in all that one does. Scrupulosity paralyzes the person who always lives in fear of committing sin and going to hell no matter what one does. Scrupulosity affected many Catholics in the area of sexuality, especially because every sexual sin involves a mortal sin that would send one to hell. Another manifestation of scrupulosity, which some older readers might still remember, was the difficulty many priests had in praying or saying the words of consecration. Some priests repeated the words a number of times because they were fearful that if the words were not said correctly there would be no consecration of the bread and wine, and the priest himself would commit a grave sin. No priests were ever scrupulous in making sure they said exactly the opening prayer of the Mass (*Introibo ad altare Dei*) because the validity of the sacrament did not depend on saying these exact words.

Post–Vatican II Practice and Theory

Since Vatican II the role of confession (the name of the sacrament has properly been changed to reconciliation, but the basic ritual remains the same) in the church has changed dramatically. The people of God for the most part no longer see confession as an important part of their lives. This article will now show that there are good theological reasons why the majority of Catholics today do not go to confession. The Christian moral life is no longer understood as the duty of obeying God's law under the fear of eternal damnation. The Christian life involves, rather, a loving response to the gift of God's love. The primary motivating factor of the Christian life is not fear, but the good news that we have been justified by God through Jesus and the Holy Spirit with the gift of God's love and the call to friendship with God.

The centrality of confession in the present ritual does not recognize in practice the broader dimensions of the reality of penance. From the time of Thomas Aquinas in the thirteenth century, Catholic theology has recognized three fundamental acts of the penitent—contrition, confession, and satisfaction. Even the manuals of moral theology with their narrow focus on training confessors for determining what acts were sinful and the degree of sinfulness continued to recognize the three fundamental acts of the penitent.[4] The

---

4 Bernhard Poschmann, *Penance and the Anointing of the Sick* (New York: Herder

present ritual, however, so stresses confession that contrition as the basic change of heart and satisfaction are for all practical purposes neglected.

There is also a more basic problem with the present ritual—the understanding of sin itself. Sin is seen as an act against the law of God. For many in the pre–Vatican II church, confession involved reciting a laundry list of particular actions. The contemporary understanding of sin has changed. Sin is now seen in relational terms. Contemporary Catholic moral theology in general sees the moral life in relational terms—our multiple relationships with God, neighbor, world, and self. The basic scriptural summary of the Christian life—to love God above all things and to love our neighbor as ourselves—sees the life of the disciple of Jesus in relational terms. Our relationship to God by definition includes all the relationships to others, the world, and self. How can you love the God you do not see if you do not love the neighbor you do see? Christian moral life involves growth in these basic relations. Acts have a meaning and importance only insofar as they manifest and develop these relationships.

Such a relational approach also affects our understanding of sin. Sin is not primarily an act but involves our multiple relationships with God, neighbor, world, and self. Elsewhere I have pointed out in some detail how the first chapter of Genesis well illustrates the relational understanding of sin.[5] The sin of Adam and Eve was not primarily their disobedience of God's command but rather their deeper refusal to accept the relationship of loving dependence on God. This broken relationship is illustrated by the fact that after their sin when God came down in the cool of the evening to walk with them in the garden, they hid themselves. Also in the end they had to leave God's garden because they had broken their relationship with God. But sin also affects our relationship with others. Adam and Eve were to become two in one flesh, totally committed to one another, but when confronted by God about what they had done, Adam put the blame on Eve—She did it, not me. The mythical story of Genesis tells how their son killed his brother as a consequence of sin. Sin affected also their relationships to the world. In accord with the cultural understanding of the time, as a result of sin Adam experienced toil and weariness in his work and Eve brought forth her children in labor and pain. With regard to their relationship to one's self, it was only after sin that they experienced division

---

and Herder, 1964), 168–79.

    [5] Charles E. Curran, *The Catholic Moral Tradition Today: A Synthesis* (Washington, DC: Georgetown University Press, 1999), 73–77.

within themselves as illustrated by the fact that they felt the need to cover their nakedness.

The Catholic understanding today recognizes both mortal sin and venial sin in relational terms. In a relational approach, mortal sin involves the breaking of our multiple relationships while venial sin weakens the multiple relationships. The relationship to God is known and manifested in these other relationships to neighbor, world, and self.

In the light of the relational model of sin the inadequacy of seeing sin as an act against the law of God becomes evident. One cannot determine the state of a relationship based only on observing one act. My being angry with my friend may very well be a sign that the relationship is broken, but it might also indicate only that I had a bad night. Most people would consider it a rash judgment if one judges another person on the basis of one act alone. The inner heart of the person can be understood only in the light of a variety of different individual acts. If mortal sin is understood as a particular act, then obviously there can be many mortal sins. In a relational understanding there is no doubt that mortal sin is a much less frequent occurrence in the Christian life than it was thought to be in the pre–Vatican II church.

A relational understanding of sin goes hand in hand with the relational understanding of growth in the spiritual and moral life. Catholic spirituality has consistently emphasized the need for growth in the spiritual life. The New Testament insists on the importance of growth. Some decades ago George T. Montague published his book, *Maturing in Christ: Saint Paul's Program for Christian Growth.* The Christian through the Spirit is a new creature called to be transformed into the fullness of life.[6]

Throughout the centuries spiritual writers have emphasized this growth in various stages. For some, spiritual growth involves moving from one virtue to another. In the first stage the Christian serves God through fear; in the second stage one serves God through hope and expectation of recompense; in the third stage, the Christian serves God through charity and love. Others such as St. Bernard describe the stages of growth in terms of progress in one virtue, such as progress in love or charity. Many are familiar with the three ways proposed by Ignatius of Loyola in the *Spiritual Exercises.* The purgative stage involves struggle against sin and temptation, insisting on mortification and the reception of the sacraments. The second stage—the illuminative way—concerns growth and progress in the virtues through the imitation of

---

[6] George T. Montague, *Maturing in Christ: Saint Paul's Program for Christian Growth* (Milwaukee: Bruce, 1964).

Christ, who is light and life. The third stage, the unitive way, is identified with the mystical life, involving a deeper level of union with God in prayer and emphasizing the role of the gifts of the Holy Spirit.[7]

As developed in chapter 11, The Constitution on the Church of Vatican II in its fifth chapter emphasized the call of the whole church to holiness. All the faithful of whatever status are called to the fullness of the Christian life and to the perfection of charity.[8] The pre–Vatican II church insisted on the distinction between the laity as those who live in the world and obey the Ten Commandments and the religious who leave the world to follow the evangelical counsels. The gospel after Vatican II was not a counsel for a few, but a call for all the baptized. Moral theology today must recognize and develop the call to holiness of all the baptized.

The relational understanding of the Christian life furnishes a good way of describing the Christian call to holiness and perfection. Just as sin is seen in terms of multiple relationships, so too conversion involves multiple relationships. Even before Vatican II, Bernard Häring insisted on the basic reality of conversion as the fundamental reality of the Christian moral life. The very basic conversion is the change from sin to grace, which is the very opposite of mortal sin as the move from grace to sin. Häring, however, stressed the need for continual conversion in the Christian life after this basic conversion. Continual conversion puts flesh on the bones of the call to holiness.[9] Continual conversion is likewise to be understood today in relational terms—the growth in our relationships with God, neighbor, world, and self. The insistence on the multiple relationships and the interrelatedness of the relationships overcomes the danger in some forms of spirituality mentioned above, which restrict holiness only to our relationship with God. On this basis one can appreciate why the International Synod of Bishops in 1974 insisted that action on behalf of justice and the transformation of the world is a constitutive dimension of the preaching of the gospel.[10] Growth in spirituality must include more than just growth in our direct relationship to God.

---

[7] Gustave Thils, *Christian Holiness: A Precis of Ascetical Theology* (Tielt, Belgium: Lannoo, 1961), 474–77.

[8] Constitution on the Church, nos. 39–42, in *Documents of Vatican II*, ed. Walter M. Abbott (New York: Guild, 1966), 65–72.

[9] Bernard Häring, "La conversion," in *Pastorale du Péché*, ed. Ph. Delhaye et al. (Tournai, Belgium: Desclée, 1961), 65–145.

[10] Synod of Bishops, 1971, *Justice in the World*, in *Catholic Social Thought: The Documentary Heritage*, exp. ed., ed. David J. O'Brien and Thomas A. Shannon (Maryknoll, NY: Orbis Books, 2010), 306.

The sacrament of reconciliation seen in a relational anthropology of sin and conversion thus should contribute greatly to the realization that all the faithful are called to growth in their moral and spiritual lives.

The Sacramental Aspect

As mentioned, the ritual of auricular confession flourished in a context that conceived the moral life primarily as a series of duties based on obedience to God's commands, and not the contemporary context of a loving response to the merciful God who has first loved us. As a result, the contemporary understanding of sacramentality remains very much in the shadows in the celebration of the rite of confession. The sacraments are saving encounters in which the love of God comes to us through Jesus and the Holy Spirit and we change our hearts in response to this love. The sacraments in general are joyful celebrations of God's merciful gift of love to us and our response. The sacrament of penance or reconciliation in particular celebrates the mercy and forgiveness of God, who is willing to embrace us even after we have broken our relationships or fallen short in them. The sacrament of reconciliation therefore should be a joyful celebration of the mercy and forgiveness of God. Our first response is praise and thanksgiving for this totally undeserved gift.

The sacrament of penance, however, is not magic; it also calls for a response on the part of the penitent. To its credit, the Thomistic understanding of auricular confession avoided a one-sided magical understanding of the sacrament. Thomas Aquinas as an anthropological realist recognized that the sinner must always have the change of heart, whether forgiveness occurs inside or outside the sacrament. In fact, Aquinas held that forgiveness often occurs before the sacramental celebration itself. The person's heart is already changed before the sacrament is celebrated. The grace of the sacrament does not supply for any lack or deficiency on the part of the penitent.[11] However, the format of auricular confession fails to recognize the primacy of God's merciful gift and the sinner's first response of praise and thanksgiving.

Sacramental rituals reveal much about our understanding of God. The theological context and the ritual of auricular confession portray God as the sovereign Lord who is to be obeyed. The contemporary sacramental approach emphasizes the primacy of God's love and mercy, recognizes God as the gracious Mother and Father who without any merit on our part

---

[11] Poschmann, *Penance and the Anointing of the Sick*, 178–79.

shares love and life with us and is always willing to show mercy and forgiveness in our sinfulness and shortcomings. In Catholic practice today there is still too much emphasis on God as the one who is to be obeyed rather than the loving parent who makes us adopted children and sisters and brothers of Jesus.

Another aspect of sacramentality that is missing in auricular confession is the reconciliation with the church. The confessor acts as a minister of the church, but the role of the church is really not visible. Sacraments by their very nature are called to make visible and present the realities they celebrate. The older canonical penance gave a very significant role to the ecclesial aspect. The sinner was installed into the order of penitents, and after a long, harsh penance, the sinner was reconciled to the church community through the laying on of hands by the bishop. The role of reconciliation with the church is a difficult one for many people to appreciate today. To make this aspect more present in the sacramental celebration will not be easy, but at least a more community celebration of the sacrament is a good start.

This chapter has emphasized the inadequacy of the present rite of auricular confession in light of Pope Francis's emphasis on the mercy of God and of contemporary understandings of sin, conversion, growth in the Christian life, and sacramentology. The theological positions developed here give some direction toward a renewed ritual for the sacrament of reconciliation, but this chapter does not attempt to develop such a rite. The historical section reminds us of the many changes in the ritual of the sacrament responding to new needs and situations. Now is the time for another significant change.

Chapter 14

Bernard Häring*

A Model for Church Reformers

In 1993 Pope John Paul II issued his encyclical *Veritatis Splendor* on moral theology, which strongly condemned many developments in Catholic moral theology and the crisis that had been brought about by the fact that many Catholic moral theologians disagreed with and dissented from some moral teachings of the hierarchical church teaching office (*magisterium*).

Bernard Häring, the foremost Catholic moral theologian in the second half of the twentieth century in the Catholic Church, reacted to the encyclical with an anguished *cri de coeur*: "Let us ask our pope: are you sure your confidence in your supreme human, professional and religious competence in matters of moral theology and particularly sexual ethics is truly justified? We should let the pope know that we are wounded by the many signs of his rooted distrust and discouraged by the manifest structures of distrust which he has allowed to be established." Häring ended this particular article by insisting on the need to honor God's gracious forgiveness by forgiving each other for the harm we have inflicted on one another and the anger we may have harbored in our hearts.

This stinging criticism reflects Häring's insistence on the need for the virtue of loving criticism within the church. Such an attitude does not entail a loveless or consistently negative criticism. Only those who appreciate and praise what is good in the church can offer a healthy criticism of what is not in keeping with the gospel and the signs of the times. Blind conformity is not a virtue. Without absolute honesty and sincerity Catholic theology will never be credible. Häring has insisted that creative freedom and creative fidelity should characterize both the Christian life and the role of theology reflecting on that life.

---

* Originally published as Charles E. Curran, "Speaking the Truth in Love: Bernard Häring," in *Not Less Than Everything: Catholic Writers on Heroes of Conscience, from Joan of Arc to Oscar Romero,* ed. Catherine Wolff (New York: HarperCollins, 2013), 93–102. Used with permission.

Who was Bernard Häring, and how did he himself strive to live out creative freedom and creative fidelity as a Catholic Christian? The biographical facts of his life furnish the setting within which he made his significant contributions to the church. Häring was born in Böttingen, Germany, the eleventh of twelve children to devout Catholic parents in 1912. He entered the Redemptorist order and was ordained a priest in May 1939. He was drafted into the German army as a medic and served in France, Russia, and Poland. After the war he received his PhD in theology at Tübingen University and taught moral theology at the Redemptorist theologate in Gars-am-Inn in Upper Bavaria. His most important teaching role was at the Alphonsian Academy in Rome for over thirty years before retiring to Gars in 1986. He was a *peritus* (expert) and active participant in the work of the Second Vatican Council (1962–65). He died in Gars on July 3, 1998.

Häring's Reform of Moral Theology

Häring's major gift to the church was his work as a moral theologian reflecting on the Christian life, but he also was a most significant voice for church reform and the development of the spiritual life of Christian people. As a moral theologian, Häring wrote the most significant book in Catholic moral theology in the second part of the twentieth century—*The Law of Christ*, originally published in German in 1954, and translated into fifteen languages. *The Law of Christ* proposed a biblical, liturgical, Christological, and life-centered moral theology. He pioneered a new approach to moral theology that opposed the method of the manuals of moral theology with their concern only for training confessors for the sacrament of penance by learning how to distinguish what is sinful and the degrees of sinfulness.

Häring's moral theology was based on the good news of God's loving gift for us and our grateful response. We are called to be perfect as the gracious God is perfect. Christians have to experience growth and continual conversion in their moral life and in their multiple relationships with God, neighbor, world, and self. Häring staunchly opposed any legalism that made God into a controller rather than a gracious savior.

Almost twenty-five years after having published *The Law of Christ*, Häring published first in English his completely new three-volume synthesis of moral theology—*Free and Faithful in Christ*. He continued to publish many other volumes and articles in the area of moral theology. His 1972 book on medical ethics appeared in six languages and was the occasion of a very painful investigation of Häring by the Congregation for the Doctrine of the Faith. This investigation was going on at the same time that Häring was suffering from throat cancer and at times very close to death.

The fact that Häring taught at the Alphonsian Academy in Rome from 1954 to 1986 gave him both prominence in Rome and the opportunity to teach many students (almost all clerics) from all parts of the world. A significant development over the years in his moral theology was his emphasis on the healing power of nonviolence.

There is some truth in the criticism that Häring's moral theology at times lacked academic rigor and was too homiletical in style. Häring was not an academic writing primarily for fellow academicians but was a church person writing for the church. However, his moral theology came from a deep and creative intelligence and included significant dialogue with philosophy, sociology, psychology, and medicine.

Other Reform Efforts

A second important area of Häring's many writings, courses, and lectures throughout the world was church reform in general. He was a most active participant in Vatican II. Pope John XXIII read his 1963 book[1] on what the council should do and sent him a message expressing his joy in reading the book and his complete agreement with it. Häring worked on the documents on the Church in the Modern World and the Decree on Priestly Formation. Cardinal Fernando Cento, the co-president of the mixed commission working on the document on the Church in the Modern World, publicly called Häring the "quasi-father of *Gaudium et Spes.*"

In addition to his work inside the council, Häring carried on an indefatigable mission outside the council. He frequently addressed various groups of bishops from all over the world. The fact that Häring was fluent in eight different languages made him a much sought after speaker to explain the implications of reform in the church for the bishops at the council. He also frequently commented to press panels in all these different languages and was recognized by all as a very competent and forthright proponent of reform in the church. In many publications and lectures, Häring ceaselessly pointed out the dangers of legalism and pharisaism in the church. He frequently differed, even at times publicly, with some leading figures in the church but always made an effort to avoid making enemies of anyone.

---

[1] Bernard Häring, *The Johannine Council: Witness to Unity,* trans. Edwin G. Kaiser (New York: Herder and Herder, 1963).

Häring was an early advocate for change in the papal teaching condemning artificial contraception for spouses and had a great influence as a member of the commission that was established by the popes to study this issue. When Pope Paul VI issued *Humanae Vitae* in 1968 reaffirming the teaching, Häring forthrightly and publicly disagreed. His differing positions on contraception, sterilization, the pastoral care of divorced people, and some aspects of medical ethics made it inevitable that he would ultimately come under investigation by the Congregation for the Doctrine of the Faith. Until his death, Häring remained an important voice throughout the world for reform in the church. His intense love for the church at times compelled him to be a loving critic.

Bernard Häring also was an intrepid proponent of a renewed spirituality in the church. Anyone who ever met him realized he was a person of prayer. His own spirituality permeated all that he did. His theoretical understanding of moral theology insisted on the intimate connection between the moral life and the spiritual life of the Christian. In 1963 in his first year as pope, Paul VI asked Häring to give the annual Lenten retreat to the pope and the Roman curia.

In his summer vacations and at other times, Häring traveled the world, not only giving lectures in moral theology but also giving retreats to all the people of God as well as clergy and religious. Even in his retreat work, Häring carried out an ecumenical ministry. For example, at the invitation of Dr. Douglas Steere, the Quaker observer at Vatican II, he gave spiritual exercises at the Dayspring Retreat Center outside Washington, DC, every year until his larynx was removed. Häring also encouraged religious orders of women throughout the world to establish houses of prayer.

Häring's Influence on Me

This sketch of Häring's life and work has given a basic understanding of his contributions, but Häring has played a very significant role in my personal life and work. My appreciation for Häring was summed up in the dedication of my 1972 book, *Catholic Moral Theology in Dialogue*—"To Bernard Häring CSsR—teacher, theologian, friend, and priestly minister of the gospel in theory and practice on the occasion of his sixtieth birthday." As a very young priest of the diocese of Rochester, New York, I was doing doctoral work at the Alphonsian Academy in Rome from 1959 to 1961. I was scheduled to teach moral theology at the diocesan seminary in Rochester. After four years of theology at the Gregorian University, I was opening up somewhat from my conservative theological orientation. I did not write my dissertation with Häring, but I was truly thrilled and nourished by his classes (in Latin) in which he developed his approach to moral theology. At my invitation many fellow priests living with me at the American college in Rome came to hear him and were greatly impressed.

In 1961 I started teaching in the seminary in Rochester, trying to emulate the approach of Häring. One year early in my teaching the two-semester course I did not open the required manual until March 1. I first wanted to show the full depth and breadth of the Christian moral life before getting into the manual with its focus on sinful acts. I later read in Häring's autobiography that he had done the same thing when he began teaching moral theology. I was the primary mover in bringing Häring to the United States in 1963 to give lectures and workshops during the summer. In subsequent years Häring came back many times to the United States during the summer, but he also traveled through many parts of Africa, Latin America, and Asia giving lectures and retreats.

On July 29, 1968, Pope Paul VI's encyclical *Humanae Vitae* reiterating the condemnation of artificial contraception for spouses was publicly released. I was the leader and later the spokesperson of what started as a group of ten of us mostly from Catholic University who read the encyclical that night and drafted a response to it. Our short ten-paragraph statement concluded that Catholics could responsibly decide to use birth control if it were for the good of their marriage. After finishing the statement we called a number of other theologians in the country looking for more signatures. I reached Häring in California, read him the statement, and was ecstatic when he agreed to sign. On the morning of July 30 I acted as the spokesperson for the then eighty-six Catholic scholars, including Bernard Häring, who had signed the statement. Ultimately more than six hundred signed. This forthright and early response to the encyclical gained worldwide attention. Häring himself then and later without doubt became the most prominent and public figure in the Catholic world for disagreeing with the conclusion of the encyclical.

In the summer of 1979, I was informed that I was under investigation by the Vatican Congregation for the Doctrine of the Faith for my dissent on a number of moral issues. That fall I went to Rome to consult with Häring and others. Throughout the process I stayed in close touch with Bernard. After much correspondence back and forth it became clear in late 1985 that the Congregation for the Doctrine of the Faith was going to take action against me, which they ultimately did in declaring that I was neither suitable nor eligible to be a Catholic theologian. However, they did agree to have an informal meeting of myself with Cardinal Ratzinger and some officials of the Congregation in March 1986. I was able to bring one adviser. All along Häring had agreed that if there were such a meeting he would accompany me.

Häring's presence was a source of great strength and consolation to me. He began the session by reading a two-page paper titled "The Frequent and Long-Lasting Dissent of the Inquisition/Holy Office/CDF." It was Häring at his forthright best at speaking to power. In the end he strongly urged Cardinal Ratzinger to accept a compromise that I would not teach sexual ethics at Catholic University and there would be no condemnation. The meeting ended without any solution or action.

The next day, the fourth Sunday of Lent, six of us went to Häring's religious house to celebrate a liturgy at which he presided. The gospel was the parable of the prodigal son. Häring in the homily looked at me and said that the church was the prodigal son who had taken all my treasure and my work for moral theology and fed it to the pigs. But the Holy Spirit was calling on me and the others present to take the role of the father and forgive the church. Only with a spirit of forgiveness and hope can we continue to celebrate the Eucharist. He ended the homily by repeating twice that Christians are people who have hope.

In the last few years I have often been encouraged by the witness of Bernard Häring. These have not been not good times for us progressive Catholics who are working for church reform. The Vatican before Pope Francis resolutely opposed any attempts to bring about progressive change in the church. A defensive centralization continues to mark the attitude of the Vatican to any attempts to bring about change. John Paul II recognized there was a crisis in moral theology because many moral theologians dissented from papal teaching. But the Vatican has adamantly fought such change and even taken punitive action against those who have dissented on matters that are not essential to the Catholic faith. Meanwhile, all of us have seen family and friends leave the Catholic Church because of its intransigence. Many people have asked me if I see any signs of hope in the church today. I remind them and myself that hope is not hope if you see it in front of you. St. Paul tells us that hope is hoping against hope. Hope is believing in light in the midst of darkness and life in the midst of death. The next chapter elaborates a spirituality and theology for church reformers.

Bernard Häring was truly a person of hope. He faced death many times in World War II. He almost died in the operations trying to cure his cancer of the throat. The person who spoke in more languages to more people in all parts of the world than any other theologian, preacher, or missionary later had his vocal cords removed and had to learn to speak from the esophagus, which was not easy either for him or for his listeners. In the last years of his life he experienced the return of a centralization and authoritarianism he thought had been vanquished by Vatican II.

Häring's witness of critical love for the church, his forthrightness, and his hope even in the midst of darkness enabled him to continue the struggle for church reform. His witness gives hope and strength to all who work for reform in the church.

Chapter 15

A Theology and Spirituality
for Church Reformers*

The Catholic Church in the beginning of the new millennium and at the end of the long papacy of John Paul II suffers from a strong authoritarianism and centralization that seem to go against the Vatican II understanding. This authoritarian centralization of the church in the Vatican shows itself in many ways in the life of the church today. To be appointed a bishop in the church, a candidate must never have uttered even a word against an existing papal teaching such as the fact that women cannot be ordained in the church or even the condemnation of artificial contraception for spouses. Only very safe men are chosen as bishops. Centralization shows itself in many other different ways such as in the demand of the Vatican to decide the smallest matters of liturgical language and customs for individual language groups and countries. This essay, however, was written before the papacy of Pope Francis. The next chapter, which is the Conclusion, will discuss the role of Francis as a church reformer.

Problems in the Contemporary Catholic Church

Many theologians throughout the world have been condemned in one way or another. No field in theology has felt this chilling wind from the Vatican more than moral and pastoral theology. The list is long and distinguished—Ambrogio Valsecchi, Stephan Pfürtner, Bernard Häring, Anthony Kosnik, John McNeill, André Guindon, René Simon, Marciano Vidal, Sean Fagan, and myself. In addition, there are many other moral theologians who have suffered at the hands of church authority or have been investigated whose cases are not that public.

---

* Originally published as Charles E. Curran, "A Theology and Spirituality for Church Reformers," in *Quench Not the Spirit: Theology and Prophecy for the Church in the Modern World,* ed. Angela Hanley and David Smith (Dublin: Columba Press, 2005), 30–43. Used with permission.

Moral theology has been a neuralgic area precisely because moral theologians deal with the practical issues that people face in their daily life. As we know, most of these contentious issues in Catholicism today center on issues of sexuality—contraception, sterilization, divorce, homosexuality, use of reproductive technologies, and so on. These moral theologians are not challenging the core issues of faith but rather the complex specific moral issues that people face in daily life. On the whole, these moral theologians have been dedicated members of the church, striving to be faithful both to the gospel teaching and to the signs and needs of the times.

The tensions felt by Catholic moral and pastoral theologians are also felt by practically all those who are engaged in full-time ministry in the church. I refer to these people as the level of lower middle management in the church. People ministering in the field in all areas often feel torn between the official teaching of the church and the needs of the people to whom they minister. Many such ministers try to avoid the problems and contentious issues as much as they can, but this is not always possible.

But in my opinion, women in the Catholic Church have experienced more problems and frustrations than any other group. The hierarchical church will not even talk about the ordination of women in the church. Even apart from ordination, women lack any true leadership roles in the church. Most of the women graduate students whom I have had in theology in the last few decades have had a crisis of faith somewhere along the line. What they experience in life is not what they have come to understand about the church. I can readily understand why some Catholic women have left the Roman Catholic Church, but I admire and support as much as I can those who have remained in the church working for change despite all the problems.

The recent pedophilia scandals throughout the world have reminded us that we are a sinful church. The cries of the poor innocent victims can be heard all over the globe. Priests and ministers took advantage of these most innocent and vulnerable people in order to satisfy their own sexual desires. But in the eyes of many, the behavior of some bishops in the church was even more unconscionable. They put institutional survival and "the good name of the church" above the needs of the innocent victims. This issue has made every Catholic mother and father aware of the sinful aspect of the church.

Yes, there are many good things going on in the church today, and all of us can never forget them. But many of us who lived through the changes of Vatican II are quite frustrated today. Very often in the last few years, friends of a similar mentality have often asked me the question: "Is there any hope for the church?"

Hope and Eschatological Tension

To address this question, we must first understand the meaning of hope. In Romans 4–8, Paul reminds us that hope is not hope if you see the goal or the object ahead of you. Hope is only hope in the midst of darkness. Hope is hoping against hope like Abraham and Sarah in the hope that God would give them offspring. Hope is not based on what we see at the present time. Hope believes that God is present and working in our world even when we do not see or feel God's presence. But we also believe we can experience some presence of God in our lives and our world.

Some years ago I published a book analyzing and criticizing the moral theology of Pope John Paul II.[1] One of my negative criticisms maintains that John Paul II has too triumphalistic a view of the church. According to this thinking, the church is holy and without spot, carrying on the mission of the risen Jesus in our world. But the pope fails to recognize that the community of the disciples of Jesus is a pilgrim church, even a sinful church, which, in the thought of Vatican II (*Lumen gentium*, no. 8), is always in need of purification—*ecclesia semper purificanda*.

Ironically, many of us somewhat liberal and somewhat disenchanted Catholics have the same triumphalistic understanding of the church. Maybe this triumphalism comes from our pre–Vatican II genes, but its presence cannot be denied. We too expect the church to be holy and without spot. We are unwilling to live with the tensions and problems in the pilgrim church. The very fact that we raise the question about there being any hope for the church seems to indicate a triumphalistic notion of hope that has to see what it is we are hoping for. We are reminded of the true meaning of hope from the witness of our mothers and fathers in the Jewish religion. They did not lose hope after the destruction by Sennacherib and did not lose hope after the slaughter of six million Jews in the Holocaust. They are witnesses to all of us that hope is hoping against hope.

Without doubt, hope and the Paschal Mystery of Jesus—the dying and the rising of Jesus—are central realities in the Christian life. The Paschal Mystery can be understood in different ways. Lutheran theology and spirituality tend to see the Paschal Mystery in dialectical and paradoxical terms.[2]

---

[1] Charles E. Curran, *The Moral Theology of Pope John Paul II* (Washington, DC: Georgetown University Press, 2005).

[2] For a detailed explanation of the Lutheran paradoxical approach, see H. Richard Niebuhr, *Christ and Culture* (New York: Harper and Row, 1951), 170–85.

There can be no doubt that Luther here is following in the footsteps of the apostle Paul. Paul often appeals to paradox—life in the midst of death, power in the midst of weakness, joy in the midst of sorrow. Catholic theology and spirituality have approached the Paschal Mystery from what might be called a transformationist and not a paradoxical perspective.[3] Catholic theology, in my judgment to its great credit, has insisted that the divine works in and through the human. Thus, the Catholic tradition sees God's truth in human truth, God's beauty in human beauty, and God's life in human life. But the human never fully expresses the divine and is also wounded and deeply affected by sin. Consequently, there are occasions when paradox is true, but the overriding perspective or motif is that of transformation or conversion of evil into good. At times, God's power is known in human weakness and God's joy in the midst of sorrow, but also human power, truth, beauty, justice, and glory point to the greater power, truth, beauty, justice, and glory of God.

The transformationist motif or perspective rests on an eschatology that recognizes that God's creative and redemptive presence is already in our somewhat sinful world but that its fullness will come only at the end of time. The Christian lives out the tension between the "now" and the "not yet." This is the eschatological tension that characterizes the life of the Christian and the life of the church in this world. Thus, we need a theology and spirituality of a pilgrim people and a pilgrim church to live out this inevitable tension. We have hope in the power of God working, but we have to live with the imperfections and even the sinfulness of the present. However, even now there are realities in the life of the church on which we can build to bring about the greater presence of God in our church.

Six Aspects of a Pilgrim Approach

This chapter will now develop six different aspects in the Catholic tradition that help us live out the tension of the now and the not yet with its realization that the fullness of the reign of God will come only at the end of time, but here and now there are signs and realities of God's presence in the church that we can use in our attempt to bring greater reform to the church.

---

[3] Maurice Schepers, "An Integral Spirituality of the Paschal Mystery," *Worship* 75 (March 2001): 98–106.

Mediation

First, the understanding of the church in the Catholic perspective well illustrates the Catholic insistence on mediation—the divine is mediated in and through the human. The church is a visible human community with human officeholders. What I have called the principle of mediation, others call the sacramental principle[4] or the analogical imagination.[5] The divine comes to us in and through the human. The Incarnation well illustrates this reality. God comes to us in and through the humanity of Jesus. In reality, our whole understanding of God manifests the principle of mediation. No one has ever seen God. We take from our human experience the understanding of the best that we know and we apply it to God. Thus, God is known as mother, father, good shepherd, and so on. The whole sacramental system illustrates the principle of mediation. The Eucharist is the primary reality in Christian celebration and life. God, the Father, through Christ, and in the Spirit is present to us in and through the Eucharistic meal. In human affairs, the celebratory meal is the primary way we bring together family and friends to share food and wine, memories and hopes, joys and sorrows. Likewise, the symbols of water, oil, bread, and wine are the signs of God's coming to us. Catholic moral theology insists on mediation in its acceptance of the theological aspect of natural law. How do we know what God wants us to do? Do we go immediately to God and ask God? No. God has given us our human reason by which we can understand how God wants us to use all that God has given us.

In my judgment, the principle of mediation is a glory of the Catholic tradition that thus recognizes the basic goodness and importance of all that God has made. But one also has to accept the limitations of the human and the fact that sin affects the human. In the church, the Holy Spirit works in and through the human. In some Protestant understandings, the church is primarily an invisible society and the individual is related internally and invisibly to God. Here you avoid the problems and limitations of the human, but you also lose the basic understanding of the goodness and significance of the human and God's working in and through the human. To put up with the limitations, imperfections, and sinfulness of the human follows from the importance of the human in the Catholic tradition.

---

[4] Richard P. McBrien, *Catholicism*, rev. ed. (San Francisco: Harper, 1994), 9–12.

[5] Andrew M. Greeley, *The Catholic Myth: The Believers and Beliefs of American Catholics* (New York: Scribner, 1990), 36–64.

Church as God's Way

Second, the church is not a voluntary society but rather is God's way of being present to us through Jesus and in the Spirit. Most groups to which we belong today are voluntary societies. We join to share with other people who have the same goals, ideals, and interests. A good number of Christians today understand the church as a voluntary society, especially in light of our emphasis on the individual and on freedom. We join a church because we like the minister, the people in the church, the music, and even the architecture of the building. But if we find another church that is more appealing, we join that church.

In the United States, Protestants often see the church as a voluntary society, and this comes through in the language they use about the church. In talking about the church, Protestants will often ask: "What church are you a member of?" You become a member of the church by your free choice. Catholics, especially those "of a certain age," normally ask: "What parish do you belong to?" You don't choose the parish; you belong to it!

Here a distinction is necessary. I think there should be some choice about what particular church community you belong to. But the church itself remains the way in which God comes to us and we go to God. We are members of the Christian community because we believe this is God's plan. The practice of infant baptism in most churches reminds us that we do not choose the church as the way to be present to God. We belong to the church in somewhat the same way we belong to human families. Those who share this understanding of the church are much more committed to the church than if the church were just another voluntary association.

Church Universal and Particular

Third, the tension between the church universal and the church particular or between unity and diversity exists in the church. The church catholic by its very language is a universal church—a church that strives to embrace all people of all races and nationalities. Here the church takes seriously the biblical injunction of Jesus to preach the good news to all humankind. The church catholic is not a congregational or national church but a universal church. The danger of a congregational or even national church is identifying God with the goals and understanding of a particular congregation or nation. The church universal must transcend all congregations and all nations in order to be able to criticize them in the name of the gospel. But inevitably great tensions will arise between the church universal and the church national or local. Look at the experience of the worldwide Anglican community today as it deals with the issue of homosexuality. In a sense, it is much easier to have a smaller homogeneous church with like-minded people in it, but this is not the church catholic.

A one-sided commitment to single issues works against the unity of the universal church. If one insists only on a particular single issue (no matter from the left or the right) the danger exists of fracturing the church universal. I can understand how at times individuals might feel the need to abandon the church because of a single issue (ordination of women, homo-sexuality). But as a church universal, we at times need to be willing to put up with sharp disagreements on what we think is an important single issue. Long ago, Paul reminded the early Corinthian Christian community that there was nothing wrong with eating meat sacrificed to idols. But if a sister or brother in the community was scandalized by it, he would not eat the meat (1 Cor. 10:23–33).

Similar to the tension between the church universal and the church particular is the tension between unity and diversity in the church. Without doubt, the Roman Catholic Church has definitely given more importance to the universal church and to unity rather than diversity in the church. But even here the Catholic tradition has recognized the need to distinguish the various levels of church teachings because all are not of the same importance and centrality. Some truths are core and central to our faith, but others are more remote and peripheral. Even pre–Vatican II Catholic theology recognized this reality. Various teachings of the church were given a "theo-logical note" which attempted to distinguish how central and important the teaching was. The highest category was divine and revealed faith and then went down in less importance and centrality to divine faith, proximate to faith, Catholic teaching, common teaching, more probable, less prob-able, and all the way down to the last category of "offensive to pious ears." Thus, even the pre–Vatican II church distinguished what was core from what were remote and peripheral aspects of faith.[6] Ever since the nineteenth century, Catholic theology also sharply distinguished between infallible and noninfallible teachings. The vast majority of church teachings fit into the noninfallible category. Volumes have been written on this subject, but it is sufficient to recall that noninfallible really means fallible.

---

[6] Sixtus Cartechini, *De Valore Notarum Theologicarum et de Criteriis ad eas Digno-scendas* (Rome: Gregorian University Press, 1951).

Thus, the Roman Catholic Church recognizes the distinction between what is core to faith and what is less central and less important. Such a distinction does not entail a cafeteria Catholicism according to which one picks and chooses whatever one likes. To be Catholic, one must recognize and accept the core claims of faith—creation, redemption, sanctification, the Trinity, the sacramental system, and the articles of the Creed. But there are many other areas, especially specific moral issues, that are not that core and central to Catholic faith. Dissenting theologians have insisted that dissent or disagreement can be acceptable when the reasons behind noninfallible moral teachings are not convincing.

There can be no doubt that in the present Roman Catholic Church there continues to be a strong emphasis on the church universal and the unity of the church without giving enough importance to the local church or legitimate diversity in the church.[7] But there are elements in the Catholic tradition that call for a greater emphasis on particularity (e.g., the inculturation of faith, the collegiality of all bishops in the church) and the recognition of legitimate diversity in the church as expressed in the theological justification of some faithful dissent in the church.

The guiding principle in these tensions comes from the old axiom—in necessary things, unity; in doubtful things, freedom; in all things, charity. This axiom has been variously attributed to many including Augustine and Philip Melanchthon, but the real author seems to be Rupert Meldenius, a comparatively unknown seventeenth-century Lutheran theologian.[8]

The Pilgrim Church

Fourth, the pre–Vatican II Catholic Church was too triumphalistic. The church was identified with the kingdom of God and was a perfect society. The church was holy and without spot. Vatican II rightly criticized the triumphalism in the church. The church is not the kingdom of God but only a sign of the kingdom. The kingdom of God will never be fully present in this world. The church is a pilgrim church that, in accord with the well-known Protestant axiom, is a church always in need of reform and

---

[7] For a discussion of these issues by two cardinals, see Kilian McDonnell, "The Ratzinger/Kasper Debate: The Universal Church and Local Churches," *Theological Studies* 63 (2002): 227–50.

[8] Philip Schaff, *History of the Christian Church*, 2nd ed. (New York: Charles Scribner's Sons, 1911), 6:650–53.

change.[9] Here we see the eschatological tension that colors all human existence between the two comings of Jesus. Just as none of us as individual Christians ever lives the fullness of the gospel, so too the pilgrim church by its very nature always falls short and is in a very true sense a sinful church. The church is called to be one, holy, Catholic, and apostolic, but it never fully lives up to this call. Often a poor understanding of mediation has made us forget the pilgrim nature of the church. Yes, the church does mediate the divine to us, but it mediates the divine in and through its human and pilgrim existence so that one cannot fully identify the church with the divine or the fullness of the reign of God.

To his credit, John Paul II apologized more than any other previous pope for the sins of members of the church.[10] But note that his apologies were for the sins of members of the church and not for the sins of the church. He was not able to recognize that the church itself is sinful.[11] But if the church is the pilgrim people of God, then it will always be a sinful church which never fully lives up to its calling. But, as pointed out earlier, many liberals in the church today also have difficulty accepting the pilgrim and sinful nature of the church. The church will never be perfect. We must constantly strive to reform the church as well as ourselves. Such is the nature of life in the church that recognizes the tension between the now and the not yet aspect of the reign of God.

Tradition and Reason

Fifth, the Catholic Church recognizes the role of ongoing tradition as well as an important role for human reason. The Catholic tradition has never accepted the axiom of scripture alone. In keeping with its "both-and" approach, the Catholic tradition has insisted on both scripture and tradition.

---

[9] Gérard Philips, "History of the Constitution," in *Commentary on the Documents of Vatican II*, 5 vols., ed. Herbert Vorgrimler (New York: Herder and Herder, 1967), 1:109.

[10] Pope John Paul II, *Tertio Millennio Adveniente,* nos. 133–36, in *Origins* 24 (1994): 401ff.; *Incarnationis Mysterium,* no. 11, in *Origins* 28 (1998): 450–51; "Jubilee Characteristic: The Purification of Memory," *Origins* 29 (2000): 649–50.

[11] John T. Ford, "Pope John Paul II Asks for Forgiveness," *Ecumenical Trends* 27 (December 1998): 173–75; Francis A. Sullivan, "The Papal Apology," *America* 182, no. 12 (April 8, 2000): 17–22; Aline H. Kalbian, "The Catholic Church's Public Confession: Theological and Ethical Implications," *Annual of the Society of Christian Ethics* 21 (2001): 175–89.

A pre–Vatican II Catholicism put these two together poorly by often understanding scripture and tradition as two quite different sources of revealed truth. Now we see the two as very closely related. The scriptures themselves are historically and culturally conditioned. One cannot go from a particular scripture quote (for example, the role of women in church) to a conclusion that it is necessarily valid today. We believe that the Holy Spirit helps the church understand, live, and appropriate the word and work of Jesus in light of the ongoing circumstances of time and place. Tradition, in the words of Jaroslav Pelikan, is not the dead faith of the living but the living faith of the dead.[12] Especially in the pre–Vatican II church there was a tendency to think that tradition stopped fifty years before we were born.

Ongoing tradition has played a very significant role in the historical development of Roman Catholicism. The Christological and Trinitarian councils of the early church well illustrate this reality. We came to proclaim that there are three persons in one God and two natures in Jesus. But person and nature are technical Greek terms that are not found in scripture. The first disciples of Jesus would not understand what was meant by talking about three persons in God and two natures in Jesus. But the early church found it necessary to use these Greek technical terms to understand more appropriately the biblical message about both God and Jesus. It was not enough simply to repeat what the scripture said. The role of ongoing tradition is even much greater with regard to the sacramental life of the church. For the greater part of its existence, the Catholic Church did not recognize the existence of seven sacraments. Only in the twelfth century did we finally accept marriage as the seventh sacrament.[13] Earlier chapters in this volume have shown that the Catholic moral tradition is a living tradition.

In addition, the Catholic tradition gives a significant role to human reason. Here again, the Catholic "and" insists on both faith and reason.[14] A famous Catholic axiom recognizes that faith and reason can never contradict each other. This does not mean that reason can prove faith, but

---

[12] Jaroslav Pelikan, *The Vindication of Tradition* (New Haven, CT: Yale University Press, 1984), 66. For my development of this point, see Charles E. Curran, *The Living Tradition of Catholic Moral Theology* (Notre Dame, IN: University of Notre Dame Press, 1992).

[13] Theodore Mackin, *The Marital Sacrament* (New York: Paulist Press, 1989), 274–324.

[14] For Pope John Paul II's discussion of faith and reason, see his encyclical *Fides et Ratio*, in *The Encyclicals of Pope John Paul II*, ed. J. Michael Miller (Huntington, IN: Our Sunday Visitor, 2001), 833–913.

Catholicism has consistently emphasized that faith seeks understanding and understanding seeks faith. In fact, this describes very well the role of theology. To its great credit, the Catholic Church was the home of the first universities in the West because of its high regard for human reason. Catholic moral theology has given reason a very important role. By using the human reason God has given us, we can reflect on what God has made and determine what should be done. A church that accepts ongoing tradition and a significant role for human reason has the tools to deal with proper development and change in the church.

Church Structure

A sixth aspect concerns structures and structural change in the church. Catholics recognize there are certain structural elements that belong to the very nature of the church such as the office and role of bishops and of the bishop of Rome. But in the course of history, there have been significant developments and changes of structure within the church. The bishop of Rome has obviously needed assistance and help in carrying out his role. But the institution of the Roman Curia, as we know it today, has changed greatly over time. Only in 1588 did Pope Sixtus V bring about the formal organization of the Roman Curia. Subsequent popes have often changed the structure of the curia with the latest change made by Pope John Paul II in 1988.[15]

The pre–Vatican II church was more authoritative, defensive, and centralized than at any other time in its history. In the role of moral theology, both the pope and the Roman Curia began playing a much greater role in the nineteenth century. The curia often intervened to give solutions to complex issues such as the distinction between direct and indirect abortion.[16] Thomas Bouquillon, the professor of moral theology at the Catholic University of America at the end of the nineteenth century, criticized moral theologians for too quickly looking for answers from the Roman Congregations.[17]

Vatican II changed our theoretical understandings of the church, but the older structures have continued to exist. Vatican II insisted on the church as the people of God, but our structures do not give enough of a role

---

[15] James H. Provost, "*Pastor Bonus:* Reflections on the Reorganization of the Roman Curia," *Jurist* 48 (1988): 499–535.

16 John Connery, *Abortion: The Development of the Roman Catholic Perspective* (Chicago: Loyola University Press, 1977), 223–303.

[17] Thomas Bouquillon, "Moral Theology at the End of the Nineteenth Century," *Catholic University Bulletin* 5 (1899): 267.

to all the people of God. Vatican II emphasized the role of the local church and the collegiality of all bishops with the bishop of Rome, but the present structures still see the church as centralized in the Vatican. A much greater role must be given to the local, national, and regional levels of the church universal.

The tension between some moral theologians and the hierarchical magisterium reminds us of the many changes that must take place in the way in which the hierarchical magisterium functions in the church. Here too the magisterium must recognize the roles of the whole people of God and of the particular and local churches. History shows us that the hierarchical magisterium has had to learn before it can teach. Such a learning process is especially true in the area of moral issues that depend so much on the experience of the whole church. The hierarchical magisterium must recognize that the teaching on specific moral issues belongs to the category of noninfallible teaching—in other words it is fallible. Above all, the hierarchical teaching office must acknowledge that in the past its teachings have been wrong and have changed. Think of all the changes that have occurred in areas such as interest taking, the meaning of marital sexuality, capital punishment, the right of the defendant not to incriminate oneself, religious freedom, democracy, and many other areas.[18] The whole church has learned from the experience of Christian people even though such experience at times has been wrong, as illustrated in the case of slavery.

Yes, we badly need a change of structures in the church today, but structural change will not be a panacea. Think of the problems in the Anglican Church today even though that church has much more participatory structures. We need better structures, but such structures will never solve all our problems and tensions.

We who work for reform in the church will always know the eschatological tension between the now and the fullness of the reign of God. The church, like ourselves as individuals, will always fall short and be a sinful church. As we are called to be more faithful followers of Jesus in our personal lives, so too we are called to be a more faithful community of the disciples of Jesus. Our Catholic tradition provides some ways and directions for working for change in the church. In this process we reformers must also avoid the danger of writing off or putting down those who disagree with us. The pilgrim and sinful church will always know the tensions of trying to do the truth in love.

---

[18] Charles E. Curran, ed., *Change in Official Catholic Moral Teachings: Readings in Moral Theology No. 13* (New York: Paulist Press, 2003).

This chapter brings to a close "Part III: Reform at Vatican II and After-ward." All these chapters in this part and in the first two parts of the volume were originally written before Pope Francis became the bishop of Rome. Catholics and non-Catholics alike recognize that Pope Francis has brought much reform to the Catholic Church. In a concluding chapter, this volume will address the the living tradition of Catholic moral theology and ongoing reform in the church in light of the papacy of Pope Francis.

CONCLUSION

Pope Francis on Reform
and the Catholic Moral Tradition

There is no doubt that Pope Francis is a reformer. This forcibly struck me as I watched his first public appearance on the balcony of St. Peter's after he was elected. Three aspects stood out in those few minutes.

First, the name Francis. No pope had ever taken the name Francis. There was already something new and different—perhaps even startling—about this name. Church historians recognize that Francis was not an establishment figure; in fact, he was often suspect by some in the institutional church. Later the pope explained that he chose the name of St. Francis of Assisi because of his great love for the poor. He wanted a church that is poor and for the poor. Francis also appreciated his great concern for peace and God's creation.

Second, the first words from Francis after he appeared on the balcony in St. Peter's Square were "*buona sera*"—good evening. What was so unusual about that? For one thing, previous popes never began with such a greeting. Why not? Meetings with the pope, even to this day, are called papal audiences. The *Oxford English Dictionary* describes an audience in this sense as a formal interview or hearing, especially granted by a monarch. Monarchs do not greet their subjects with a friendly and informal "*buona sera*." Francis, however, made it clear he was not a monarch speaking to his subjects, but a father greeting his children or a believer greeting fellow believers as one of them.

Third, the first official act of the pope in the appearance just after his election in the balcony of St. Peter's is to give his first blessing to the crowd as the new pope. Francis broke the long-standing tradition by first asking the crowd to pray for him. Then he bowed as they prayed for him before he gave them his papal blessing.

This chapter will consider the reform of Pope Francis under four headings—style, priorities, the church, and moral teaching and life. The first three aspects, however, also have ramifications for his approach to moral teaching and life.

Reform in Style

A simpler style characterizes this pope. Perhaps the best sign of this is when he chose to break the one-hundred-year-old tradition that popes live in the papal apartment in the apostolic palace. Francis, however, chose to live with many others in the Domus Sanctae Marthae, a five-story guest house on the edge of Vatican City. The building has 105 two-room suites and 21 singles. It was built originally to house the cardinals coming for the conclave to elect the pope, but most of the time the building houses priests working in the Vatican and also has a number of guest rooms for visitors. Pope Francis chose room 201. He eats his meals in the common dining room downstairs and usually presides at the seven a.m. Eucharist for Vatican employees in the chapel of the building. The pope himself pointed out that the papal apartments in the apostolic palace are not luxurious but large and tastefully decorated, but he wanted to live a life in community with others. This was a very important personal reality for him. Recall that even as the cardinal archbishop in Argentina he had lived in a small apartment and often traveled in the city by public transport.

Stories and anecdotes abound about the simple lifestyle of the pope. He discarded much of the formal papal garb for a simple white cassock. He has dropped in unannounced to eat in the cafeteria with Vatican workers. Pope Francis was photographed receiving the sacrament of reconciliation (going to confession) in St. Peter's Basilica. Francis has often been quoted as saying that a simple lifestyle is good for us, helping us to better share with those in need. Many people were startled the day after his election when he went back personally to pay what he owed at the guest house where he stayed before the conclave.

In his daily activities he comes across as concerned, caring, and merciful, especially to those in need. His participation in the rite of washing feet on Holy Thursday well illustrates his approach. His recent predecessors had presided at the liturgy in St. Peter's and there washed the feet of twelve priests. In 2013 at a juvenile detention center in Rome, he washed and kissed the feet of twelve people who included two women and two Muslims. In 2014, he washed and kissed the feet of twelve disabled people. On Holy Thursday 2015, the pope visited a prison in Rome and washed the feet of twelve prisoners—six men and six women, plus a very small child of one of the women. These symbolic actions reinforce his understanding of the papal ministry to be one of service to God's people, especially those on the margins.

One endearing story reported in Spanish newspapers tells of his telephone call to a young Spanish man who had been sexually abused by a priest. The man had written the pope a five-page letter about his suffering. The pope called him on the telephone to ask forgiveness for what the church had done to him. The Spanish press even reported the supposed conversation. The pope asked to speak with Daniel (not the real name of the person). Daniel asked who was calling. The pope identified himself as Father Jorge. Daniel responded that the caller must have the wrong number, because he did not know any Father Jorge. Then the voice on the other side said, "I am Pope Francis." Daniel could not speak for a time, because he was so overcome with emotion. The pope then told him how moved he had been in reading Daniel's letter and wanted to call and ask for his forgiveness.

The press continues to report stories about the pope's style. A newspaper, for example, ran the story of 150 homeless people who were invited to see the famous Sistine Chapel. Who was there to greet them? Pope Francis!

The style of Pope Francis is perhaps best described as pastoral. Francis himself follows the advice he has given to bishops, priests, and theologians to be "shepherds living with the smell of sheep." As cardinal archbishop of Buenos Aires, he spelled out some details of that metaphor. A priest who limits himself just to carrying out his administrative duties for a tiny flock is not a true shepherd. He is a hairdresser putting curlers on sheep rather than going out to look for the lost ones. The reality today is the mirror image of the gospel story of the shepherd who left the ninety-nine to go out looking for the one who was lost. Today, there is one in the pen, and we are called to go out looking for the other ninety-nine.

Reform of Priorities

Francis insists on giving priority to what is most important. The most important Christian reality is the good news of the kerygma—the joy of the gospel. He has opposed a pastoral ministry obsessed with the transmission of a disjointed multitude of errors to be opposed or moral obligations that must be obeyed. Pope Francis worries that priorities will be undermined and the beauty of the kerygma will be replaced by a grim sexual morality. When this happens, the moral edifice of the church is likely to fall like a house of cards. We have to put first things first.[1]

---

[1] Pope Francis with Antonio Spadaro, *My Door Is Always Open: A Conversation on Faith, Hope, and the Church in a Time of Change* (London: Bloomsbury, 2014), 78–79.

Pope Francis's first important official document, the apostolic exhortation of November 2013, bears the title *Evangelii Gaudium*—the joy of the good news. The very first paragraph clearly summarizes the point. The joy of the gospel fills the hearts and lives of all who encounter Jesus. Those who accept the offer of salvation are set free from sin, sorrow, inner emptiness, and loneliness. With Christ, joy is constantly born anew. The good news of God's love for us is the basis for the whole of Christian faith and Christian life.[2]

Pope Francis sees the good news of God's love for us primarily in terms of God's mercy. He explicitly recognizes in his own experience the primacy of God's mercy. The motto of his papal coat of arms reads *miserando atque eligendo* (literally: by having mercy and choosing). This shows the importance he gives to God's mercy. The first question raised by Antonio Spadaro in the famous interview with the pope: "Who is Jorge Mario Bergoglio?" The answer was: "I am a sinner whom the Lord has looked upon with mercy." He reacted in a similar way when asked by the cardinals if he accepted his election as bishop of Rome. "I am a sinner, but I trust in the infinite mercy and patience of our Lord Jesus Christ" (18–20).

From a theological perspective, the primacy of mercy emphasizes that the recipient is a sinner as Francis said. But the believer is also the beneficiary of God's good creation and a recipient of God's redeeming love. To see the essence of God's love totally in terms of mercy is somewhat restrictive and leaves out some dimensions of God's loving gifts to us believers. Yes, we are sinners, but we are also part of God's good creation, and above all we are redeemed by God's grace and become friends of God. There is no doubt, however, that Francis definitely sees mercy as the primary manifestation of God's love and logically recognizes himself, then, as a sinner.

Pope Francis, in addition, sees mercy as most important for the church as a whole. On March 13, 2015, he announced that he was convoking a jubilee year to be called the Holy Year of Mercy to make ever more evident the mercy of the church as a witness of God's mercy. The bull spelling out

---

This book is the famous long interview given by Pope Francis to Antonio Spadaro SJ, which was published in different Jesuit periodicals throughout the world. This interview is the most extensive and most theological of the interviews granted by the pope. When references to this particular interview are made, the page number will be noted in the text.

2 Pope Francis, "Apostolic Exhortation: *Evangelii Gaudium*," at http://w2.vatican. va. When the references to this document appear, the paragraph number will be indicated in the text.

the jubilee of mercy begins by recognizing: "Jesus Christ is the face of the Father's mercy. These words might well sum up the mystery of the Christian faith." According to the pope, the motto of this holy year is "merciful like the Father."[3]

His reflection describing the holy year heavily depends on scripture. In this context, he cites Luke 6:37–38 about not judging and not condemning. If anyone wants to avoid God's judgment, the individual should not judge the sister or the brother. Human judgments touch no deeper than the surface, whereas the merciful God looks into the very depths of the soul (14). One recalls in this context the famous remark made by the pope in a press conference on the plane returning to Rome from Brazil when asked about gays—who am I to judge. These statements, however, must be seen in a larger context. The pope in this document directs the invitation to conversion ever more fervently to those whose behavior distances themselves from the grace of God. He refers there to people who belong to criminal organizations and those who perpetuate or participate in corruption (19). These statements exist, thus, in some tension with the judge-not statements. It is also notable that in this context he does not mention sexual sins.

In this document, the pope also discusses the relationship between justice and mercy. For God mere justice is not enough. God goes beyond justice with mercy and forgiveness. But justice still has a place. Anyone who makes a mistake must pay the price, but this is just the beginning of conversion (21).

In a true sense, every pope or Christian leader should always have as the first priority the good news of God's gift of love and life to us. What then is so distinctive about the approach of Pope Francis? First, Francis chooses to describe this priority in terms of mercy. No one virtue or attitude can ever exhaust the total reality of God's gift to us. Any virtue or description of God's gift to us is necessarily limited, precisely because there are so many other virtues that have a different content. Francis chooses to see God's gracious gift in terms of mercy. What explains this choice? As already mentioned, his own personal spiritual experience is an important factor. He experiences himself as a sinner who has received God's gracious mercy. But I think there is another factor. In the present church, Francis does not think the proclamation of the mercy of God comes across to most people. Other aspects in the church's life and circumstances have received more emphasis,

---

[3] Pope Francis, "*Misericordiae Vultus*," at http://w2.vatican.va. When references are made to this document, the paragraph number will be indicated in the text.

so that many today do not experience the primacy of God's mercy in the life, teaching, and proclamation of the church. These two factors help explain why Francis has made mercy, and not love, for example, the distinctive aspect of the good news of the gospel.

A second characteristic aspect of Francis's approach is to emphasize that the primacy of mercy must become visible and present in every aspect of the life of the church. Mercy is not just the primary aspect that is first considered and then one moves on to other realities. All that the church is and does must bear witness to God's mercy. The ministers of the church have the special call to emphasize the priority of God's mercy in their proclamations, their ministry, and their life. The insistence on the need for the church in its life and ministry to bear primary witness to God's mercy again comes from the recognition that the church today is often perceived as a lawgiver or a judge.

Third, in terms of the priorities for the church, it is important to recognize a hierarchical ordering of what the church should do. In the interview with Spadaro, the pope points out that the particular teachings of the church on moral matters, such as abortion, homosexuality, divorce, and contraception are not of the highest priority. These teachings are very well known by all. He is in no way challenging or disagreeing with these teachings, for he is truly a son of the church. The pope acknowledges that others in the church have criticized him for not speaking more about these issues. For Francis, however, it is a matter of priorities. The church and its ministers must above all proclaim, show, and live the mercy of God. The most essential things come first. We have to find a new and better balance. The proclamation of God's mercy comes before moral and religious imperatives. The message of the gospel cannot be reduced to certain aspects that are relevant but do not go to the heart of the message of Jesus. When we do speak of these particular moral issues, we have to talk about them in the context of God's love and mercy (54–59).

The most important social issue that takes priority over all other social issues concerns poverty and the liberation of the poor. *Evangelii Gaudium* discusses the issue in two different places. It is the first challenge of today's world mentioned in chapter 2. We must say no to an economy of exclusion, a new idolatry of money, and a financial system that rules rather than serves. Here he opposes the absolute autonomy of the market and a trickle-down economic theory, which has never really worked in practice and places a crude and naïve trust in the goodness of those wielding economic power (53–58).

The inclusion of the poor in society is the first specific issue mentioned in chapter 4, "The Social Dimension of Evangelization." Here Francis calls for both a change of heart and attitudes as well as a change of structures. The word *solidarity* has become a little worn and at times poorly understood. Solidarity calls for the recognition of the social function of property and the universal destiny of created goods to serve the needs of all. These aspects are more important than private property. Property must serve the common good, which is the basis for the pope's strong assertion that solidarity calls for us to restore to the poor what belongs to them (189). Unfortunately at times, human rights are used as a justification for an inordinate defense of individual rights or the rights of the rich. We must put into practice the option for the poor (186–208). Pope Francis here is following in the footsteps of his predecessors, but he gives priority to this option for the poor.

Reform of the Understanding and Structure of the Church

A third important area of reform concerns the church. This section will consider first the general understanding of the church and then the institutional structure of the church. Pope Francis firmly accepts and follows the teaching often mentioned at Vatican II that the church is always in need of reform. To support his thesis that the church is always in need of reform, Francis cites in *Evangelii Gaudium* his predecessor Paul VI. According to Paul VI, the church must look within itself with penetrating eyes, pondering the mystery of its own being. A vivid and lively self-awareness inevitably leads to a comparison between the ideal image of the church as Christ envisioned it and the actual image that the church presents to the world today. Francis also cites Vatican II that Christ summons the church to a continual reformation in its pilgrim journey to be ever more faithful to its own calling (25–26).

When asked to describe the church by Father Spadaro, Francis answers with the words of the Constitution on the Church of Vatican II. Francis sees the church as the holy faithful people of God. The people of God are on a journey through history with joys and sorrows. He recognizes that all are called to holiness and sees this sanctity in their daily activities in the world. Here he emphasizes holiness and the patience of the people of God. This patience means not only responsibility for the events and circumstances of life but also as a constancy in going forward day by day (49–51).

Pope Francis emphasizes the role of the laity in two areas that previously have not received much attention. The first is the laity's role in evangelization. In the past, the work of proclamation belonged to the clergy and religious in the church, but this is not the approach of Francis. His first section in chapter 3 of *Evangelii Gaudium*, "The Proclamation of the Gospel," insists that the entire people of God proclaim the gospel. In all the baptized, the sanctifying power of the Spirit is at work compelling all to evangelization. The new evangelization calls for personal involvement on the part of all the baptized. Evangelization is not something done by professionals in the church with the rest of the faithful as the passive recipients. The second area concerns the important role of popular piety in the church. All the baptized have an effective co-naturality born of love. In the years after Vatican II, the church has become more conscious of the important role of popular piety. Popular piety, the living of faith and the gospel in a particular time and place, has much to teach the whole church. Expressions of popular piety constitute a *locus theologicus*—the traditional name for a place in which the church learns about theology and faith. Popular piety, the piety of the people, is a form of evangelizing (111–34).

A Missionary and Poor Church

In *Evangelii Gaudium*, the pope proposes the dream he has for the church to be a missionary church that has an impulse capable of transforming everything the church is and does for the evangelization of today's world rather than for its own self-protection and promotion. A missionary and evangelizing community knows that the Lord has taken the initiative and therefore we can move forward, boldly take our initiatives, go out to others, especially those who have fallen away, stand at the crossroads, and welcome the outcast. A missionary and evangelizing community gets involved by word and deed in people's daily lives; it bridges differences; it is willing to abase itself if necessary; and it embraces human life, touching the suffering flesh of Christ in others. The church takes on the smell of the sheep, and the sheep are willing to hear its voice (24–27).

Francis wants a church that is bruised, hurting, and dirty because it has been out on the street rather than a church that is unhealthy because it is centered on and clings to its own security. He does not want a church claiming to be the center of all things, which ends up caught in a web of obsessions and procedures. The church should be moved not by the fear of going astray but by the fear of being shut up within structures that give a false sense of security, within rules that make us harsh judges, within habits that make us feel safe, while at our door people are starving and looking for something to eat (49). This document is truly Francis's "I Have a Dream" document.

In this vision of the church, the two priorities of mercy and the poor come to the fore. In the interview with Father Spadaro, the pope speaks of his vision and his dream of a church that is truly mother and shepherdess. The church's ministers must be merciful, accompanying people like the good Samaritan who comforts, cleanses, and raises up the neighbor in need. The pope clearly sees that what the church needs today is the ability to heal wounds and warm hearts. The church is a field hospital after battle. The first task is to heal the wounds of those who are suffering (54–55). The poor have a very special place in his vision of the church. The church must go out to everyone, but the pope asks to whom should it go first? The gospel gives us a clear indication—not to your friends and wealthy neighbors but above all to the poor and the sick—those who are usually despised and overlooked. The gospel message is clear: the poor are the privileged recipients of the good news. There is an inseparable bond between our faith and the poor. We can never abandon them (48).

In *Evangelii Gaudium,* Francis again insists on a church that is poor and for the poor. It is not just a question of the church helping and ministering to the poor. The poor have much to teach us. Not only do they share with us the *sensus fidei,* but in their difficulties they know the suffering Christ. We need to let ourselves be evangelized by them. The new evangelization is an invitation to acknowledge the saving power at work in the lives of the poor and to put them at the center of the church's pilgrim way. We are called to find Christ in them, to lend our voice to their causes, but also to be their friends, to listen to them, and to embrace the mysterious wisdom that God wishes to share with us through the poor (198).

In addition to his understanding of the church and its role, Francis in *Evangelii Gaudium* has also recognized the need for a change of structures and institutions in the church. In his apostolic exhortation *Evangelii Gaudium,* the renewal of structures comes from the need to make the church more mission oriented, to make pastoral activity on every level more inclusive and more open. The pope points out he himself must think about conversion and finding new ways to exercise his office in the church. The papacy and the central structure of the universal church need to hear the call for change and conversion. Here the pope puts his finger on what advocates of church reform have indicated is the primary problem in church structures and institutions. Excessive centralization, according to the pope, rather than proving helpful complicates the church's life and missionary activity. In this document, the pope briefly insists on the need for collegiality and synodality in the church and fruitful ways to realize these realities. Collegiality, however, has not been fully realized in the church. The juridical status and doctrinal authority of bishops' conferences has not yet been elaborated (32).

In his major interview that appeared in Jesuit publications, Francis mentioned the great number of cases involving a suspicion of orthodoxy that are sent to Rome. He points out these cases should be investigated by the local bishops' conferences that can also rely on the Vatican and should not be sent to the Vatican (61). The pope with some regularity talks about the need for collegiality and synodality in the church.[4] Although Pope Francis has spoken in general about the problem of overcentralization and the need for collegiality and synodality, there has been no real detailed development of the ramifications of these principles.

Particular Structural Changes

This section will now discuss some of the particular structural and institutional aspects that have changed since Francis became the bishop of Rome in 2013. Vatican II called for the role of local, national, and regional bishops' conferences, but later popes have greatly curtailed their role and authority. Francis, as noted above, calls explicitly for more genuine doctrinal authority for these conferences, but this basic principle has not been developed in practice. Francis, however, in practice has taken a very significant step forward. In his first apostolic exhortation, he cites documents from international conferences of bishops about twenty times. This is something entirely new in papal documents. Not only does it recognize some genuine doctrinal authority in these documents, but it also shows that the universal church can and should learn from the local conferences of bishops. Up until this time, papal documents employed a top-down approach. The word went out from the pope to all the churches throughout the world, but now there is a true two-way street working.

In October 2014, an Extraordinary Synod of bishops met to discuss topics related to the family. In October 2015, a larger synod called the Ordinary Synod met to discuss the same topic. Vatican II called for this

---

[4] Drew Christiansen, "Listen for This Word 'Synodality,'" at http://americamagazine. org.

new structure of the international synod of bishops. Later Paul VI accepted the idea and established them but limited their role to giving advice to the pope. They did not have doctrinal authority as such. Many at Vatican II and afterward thought these international synods of bishops should have some doctrinal authority of their own and not just be advisory to the pope. Obviously, the pope himself would be a part of these synods. In reality, the synods were not free to discuss the disputed issues in the church but were carefully controlled by curial authorities. The approach of Francis was completely different. Francis urged all the participants in the synod to speak boldly. Francis did not want anyone to say they feared to speak out for fear of what others might think or say. As a result of this, the first synod involved very open discussion and differences among the participants. For the first time since Vatican II, Catholics in the whole world have heard their bishops publicly discussing and disagreeing about what is good for the church. It remains to be seen exactly what doctrinal authority these international synods of bishops might have.[5]

The curia is the bureaucracy that assists the pope in his role as universal pastor. Here Francis has not only talked about reform but has set up a process to bring it about. One month after his election, the pope appointed a group of cardinals (eventually numbering nine) to advise him in the government of the universal church and to prepare a plan for restructuring the curia. The conclave before the election of Francis had talked about the need for such a reform. The curial reform is twofold. First, the role of the curia is to be of service based on the principle of subsidiarity—that is to be of service to local churches throughout the world rather than to exercise centralized power in the church. The curia has been a primary instrument in bringing about the centralization in the church and control over all churches throughout the world. This is both a theological issue of trying to overcome the overcentralization in the church and a turf battle, because local bishops and cardinals have themselves experienced the tendency of the curia to exercise control over them in their dioceses. Too often the curia forgets that the local bishop has the primary responsibility for the local church. The local bishop is not simply a franchisee of the papal government. The second part of the envisioned reform is to reorganize the many offices in the curia. This group formally called the Council of Cardinals has met quite frequently but has not yet submitted any detailed plan of reform.

---

[5] Thomas Reese, "How the Synod Process Is Different under Pope Francis," at http://ncronline.org.

One very startling related event was the annual Christmas address the pope gave to the curia. This address was far from a stylized Christmas greeting; in Francis's own words it was an examination of conscience in preparation for the feast of Christmas. He identified fifteen curial diseases that can weaken our service to the Lord. Among these diseases are thinking ourselves as immortal or indispensable, spiritual petrification, rivalry and vainglory, gossiping and backbiting, idolizing superiors, worldly profit or self-exhibition.[6] I am sure that none of his hearers expected such a talk. It shows that the pope was very serious about reform of the curia and its members.

Pope Francis has also initiated other instances of institutional and curial reform. The pope has made new appointments and proposed new reforms for the Vatican bank. He also established a Pontifical Commission for the Protection of Minors to advise on child protection policies for the church. The commission comprises seventeen members, one of whom is a survivor of clerical sexual abuse. Again one can only wait for the result of the work of this commission.

On a number of occasions, including the interview with Spadaro, the pope has spoken about the role of women in the church. Women are asking important questions that need to be addressed. The church cannot be itself without women playing their role. The feminine genius is necessary whenever we make important decisions. The challenge is to think about the specific roles of women in the exercise of church authority, but the pope has also maintained that women cannot be ordained priests (62–63).

Some have expressed dissatisfaction with the pope's understanding of women and the role of women. He emphasizes the specific gift and genius of women and seems to maintain a view of the complementarity of male and female characteristics. But such an approach comes across to many as a patriarchal view that still makes women secondary. The best example of this was his reference to more women theologians as "strawberries on the cake."[7]

Francis in his interview with Jesuit publications has also stressed the prophetic role in the church. Vatican II recognized the prophetic role in the church as distinct from the hierarchical role. Francis points out that religious have an important prophetic role to play in the church. He certainly

---

[6] "Pope's Address to Roman Curia," at www.zenit.org.

[7] David Gibson, "Lost in Translation? 7 Reasons Some Women Wince When Pope Francis Starts Talking," at www.cruxnow.com.

would agree with Vatican II that all the baptized share in the prophetic office of Jesus. Francis is realistic about the effects of the prophetic role in the church. Prophets makes noise, an uproar, and some might even say a mess. But prophecy is like yeast in the church (149). This is certainly a change from all teaching and policy coming down in an orderly fashion from the top in a centralized church. The pope thus recognizes that the Spirit speaks in different ways in the church.

Pope Francis solved an institutional problem that seriously riled the Catholic Church in the United States—the investigation of US Catholic nuns. Since 2008, the Vatican initiated two investigations. The first investigation begun in 2008 by the Vatican congregation in charge of religious throughout the world concerned the quality of religious life of nuns in the United States. There was concern mentioned about a certain secular mentality and feminist spirit among the nuns. The long and frequently contentious investigation came to a peaceful end in December 2014 with a generally appreciated report acknowledging the achievements and challenges facing the dwindling number of nuns in this country.[8] The second investigation begun by the Congregation for the Doctrine of the Faith in 2012 involved a committee of three bishops with the mandate of overhauling the Leadership Conference of Women Religious (LCWR) because of concerns the organization strayed from Catholic teaching in its speakers and publications. The Vatican abruptly ended the investigation in April 2015 with the leadership of LCWR meeting with Pope Francis.[9] Both of these investigations evoked strong support for the nuns from many sectors of the US Catholic Church. Press reports indicated that the Vatican definitely wanted to settle these issues before Pope Francis's visit to the United States in the fall of 2015.

Reform of Moral Teaching and Living

There is no doubt that Francis sees himself in general as a reformer, and most people in the church and broader world agree. In this section the direct focus is on reform with regard to the teaching about the moral life and the living of the Christian moral life. Francis himself is not a trained moral theologian, but he obviously sees himself as a pastor intimately concerned with

---

[8] Laurie Goodstein, "Vatican Report Cites Achievements and Challenges of US Nuns," *New York Times*, December 16, 2014.

[9] Laurie Goodstein, "Vatican Ends Battle with Catholic Nuns' Group," *New York Times*, April 16, 2015.

the moral and spiritual life of the Catholic people. This section discusses reform with regard to the teaching about and living of the moral life under three aspects—moral life is much more than just obeying a few absolute moral norms; the relationship between the pastoral and the moral; the possibility for change in the contested moral norms proposed by the hierarchical magisterium, especially in the area of sexuality.

More Than Obedience to Absolute Norms

For Francis, it is obvious that the Christian moral life is much more than the obedience to a few laws. This fits in with his understanding of the priorities as discussed earlier. Too often the Catholic understanding of morality has been seen primarily in terms of obedience to norms. Francis has strongly differed with such an approach. In his homilies, Francis frequently mentions the call to holiness. Do not be afraid of holiness, of aiming too high. Let yourself be loved and purified by God. We should be enfolded by the holiness of God. Francis cites the teaching of Vatican II that all Christians are called to holiness. The pope also cites the well-known statement of the French writer Léon Bloy that the only real sadness in life is not becoming a saint.[10]

In keeping with Vatican II's contribution of bringing spirituality and morality together, Francis consistently talks about the spirituality of Christians living in the world. The question is: Where does the Christian find God? Spadaro's interview has a long discussion on seeking and finding God in all things (95–109). God is present in the past, because we can see there the footsteps of God's presence. God is also present in the future as promise. But for us, God is above all encountered in the world of today. We need a contemplative attitude in order to find God in all things. In this quest for the presence of God in all things, there is always a great area of uncertainty. If one claims to have all the answers, this is proof that God is not with such a person. Abraham, Moses, and all the great people of faith had doubts. We are all searching for God, and the search is never ending. The pope emphasizes here the importance of discernment (a word very much associated with St. Ignatius) in the whole process. There are always thorns and weeds in our lives and in the world around us, but there is still room there for the good seed to grow.

Note how this model of the spiritual and moral life differs from the older understanding of a moral life in terms of obedience to the law of God.

---

[10] This and other similar passages are found in the *Church of Mercy: A Collection of Homilies, Writings, and Speeches of Pope Francis* at www.goodreader.com.

We are seeking for God in all aspects of our life. The primary reality for the Christian is not obedience to God's command but the discernment of God's presence in our daily lives and our response to that presence. Francis, however, still gives the priority not to our efforts to find God but to God's loving gift. When we seek God, we discover God is there to welcome us and to offer God's love. The encounter with God is not something we control. God is the God of surprises. In his addresses and homilies, Francis is not a moral theologian but rather a pastor urging the Christian people to find God in all aspects of life. Pope Francis worries that priorities will be undermined and the beauty of the kerygma will be replaced by a grim sexual morality. When this happens, the moral edifice of the church is likely to fall like a house of cards. We have to put first things first (78–79).

Pastoral Approach and Moral Teaching *what*

The second area concerns the relationship between the pastoral approach and the moral teaching approach. Francis as a good pastor tries to exhort believers to strive for sanctity and the fullness of the Christian life with its continual growth in love of God and neighbor, but as a pastor of mercy he also recognizes the needs of those who find themselves in very difficult situations. God's mercy is present and acting in both these situations—the upper end and the lower end of the Christian moral life.

Evangelii Gaudium addresses this issue. The task of evangelization exists within the limits of languages and circumstances. With mercy and patience a pastor must accompany people through the stages of personal growth as they occur. A small step in the midst of great human limitations can be more pleasing to God than a life that outwardly appears to be orderly. God's mercy spurs us on to do our best (44–45).

In the Spadaro interview, Francis expresses the same reality in different words. It is useless to ask a seriously injured person if she has high cholesterol and the level of her blood sugar. You have to heal starting from their particular situation. It is necessary to accompany them with mercy. When that happens, the Holy Spirit inspires the priest to say the right thing (54–57).

The pope in these contexts is not a casuist proposing what specifically should be done in each case, but nonetheless, more could have been said about exactly what is the right thing that the priest should say in this situation. What does such an approach mean for a married gay couple or for a poor single mother contemplating abortion because she is unable to provide for her existing children? What is to be done in these situations?

The pope himself refers to the stages of personal growth. Moral theologians have talked about gradualness or the law of graduality. The Catholic tradition has always recognized the need for growth in the moral and spiritual life. The principle that you cannot ask people to do more than they are existentially capable of doing makes good sense. Francis seems to be saying that the person in need of healing now cannot be expected to fulfill all the particular moral obligations that are pertinent. Accompanying someone on the journey who is in need of healing does not seem to mean that at this stage the person must fulfill all the relevant moral norms.

In Catholic moral theology Bernard Häring, whose reforming approach was discussed in chapter 14, distinguishes between the role of moral teaching and the role of pastoral counseling. If a woman who conceives after being raped believes in good faith that she has to abort the child, Häring says she does not have to be told that this is wrong, but he would not tell her that it is a good thing to do. In the light of this distinction between moral teaching and pastoral counseling, theologians have talked about the law of gradualism or graduality. Pope John Paul II accepted such a concept provided it did not mean the gradualness of the law. Even here it is not certain exactly what he meant, but he seemed to be putting some restrictions and limits on the law of gradualness. In the light of some comments made by Pope Francis, some members of the synod on the family used the law of gradualness to justify the participation of some divorced and remarried people in the Eucharistic banquet.[11] Both in theory and in practice much work has to be done on the meaning of the law of gradualness.

Pope Francis in the famous interview recognizes another more generally accepted approach in Catholic moral theology—the distinction between objectively wrong and subjectively guilty or responsible. The pope here quotes the *Catechism of the Catholic Church* in support of this important distinction and uses it to defend his comment on the plane returning from his first trip to Brazil. He said then that if a homosexual person is of good will and in search of God, who is he (the pope) to judge such a person. In these instances Francis sees himself primarily as a pastor who is interested in the person. Like God we must accompany people with mercy (56–57).

In concluding this section, two points need to be mentioned. First, it is not totally clear what Francis means in these cases, and there is obviously room for different opinions about what he is saying. Also, Francis is looking

---

[11] John L. Allen, "The Synod's Key Twist: The Sudden Return of Gradualism," at www.cruxnow.com.

at these issues primarily from the perspective of the pastor who is accompanying the person on the journey. But an even more important perspective is that of the conscience of the individual person.

Will Francis Change the Disputed Moral Teachings?

This brings us to the third aspect in this section: Will Francis, who is obviously a reformer, change the teachings in the area of sexuality such as contraception, sterilization, artificial insemination, in vitro fertilization, gay marriage, divorce, and remarriage? As pointed out in chapter 9, the two realities involved here are the natural law theory, which is the basis for the sexual teaching and the authoritative papal teaching on these issues. In reality, the most important aspect is the authoritative papal teaching. In his encyclical *Humanae Vitae* (para. 6) Pope Paul VI recognized the conclusion of the majority of the study commission calling for a change in the teaching on artificial contraception, but he could not accept such a conclusion, because it went against the constant teaching of the church.

Pope Francis has rightly pointed out these are not the primary or more important aspects of the Christian moral life. For the people involved in these issues in their daily life, however, they are very significant. Some have decided in their conscience they can act against these teachings and still fully participate in the Eucharist and church life. Others have left the church because of these teachings. Note the difference with the teaching excluding women from the priesthood. This involves the external forum or the structure of the church and cannot be solved by the conscientious discussions of individuals. The ordination issue is very painful for many women and men as well.

As already pointed out, Francis has declared himself a son of the church who supports the existing teaching on sexual realities. He likewise has said that the issue of ordaining women in the church is not open to discussion. Thus his own words clearly show he is not in favor of changing these existing teachings.

The discussions that have taken place in the synod on the family also indicate there is no support within the hierarchical church for any change. As noted, the pope has encouraged free and unfettered discussion in the synod, but in the discussion on the family in the 2014 synod there was no discussion whatsoever about artificial contraception. The primary practical issues discussed at the synod was the change in pastoral practice allowing some divorced and remarried people to fully participate in the Eucharistic banquet. No one even proposed challenging the teaching on divorce and remarriage. In fact, many who supported the pastoral change made it very clear they were still strongly defending the existing moral teaching. There was also much opposition to changing the pastoral practice precisely because for many it amounted to a change in the teaching itself.[12]

Chapter 9 briefly proposed reasons why the church should change its teaching, but such reasons have obviously not been accepted by the hierarchical magisterium. The question then naturally arises: Why do Pope Francis and other hierarchical teachers in the church oppose changing these teachings? The primary reason stems from the belief that the Holy Spirit assists the hierarchical magisterium in teaching what is true and the will of God on practical moral issues. Would God ever allow the hierarchical magisterium to teach something that is erroneous and not the will of God? The magisterium aims to help people discover and live out God's will in this world, so it is unthinkable that the hierarchical magisterium could be hurting people rather than helping them.

The credibility of the church would suffer if the hierarchical magisterium affirms the teaching had been wrong. Who would ever again believe what the church says on any issue? Those Catholics who, with great personal sacrifice, have lived according to the teaching on contraception, divorce, and gay relationships, would rightly be very upset if these teachings were to change.

The Catholic Church has had great difficulty ever admitting that its teachings had been erroneous or wrong, especially when such teachings affect people in their daily lives. Even Vatican II with its reforming spirit could not admit that church teaching had been wrong on the matter of religious liberty. All recognized that what the church held in the nineteenth century and throughout the first part of the twentieth century was changed at Vatican II. The primary issue in the debate on religious freedom of Vatican II was the issue of how the magisterium could change its teaching. Was the teaching in the past wrong? No. Historical circumstances change, so the older teaching was true in those circumstances and the newer teaching accepting religious freedom is true in the new historical circumstances.[13] In addition, it is even harder to change on these issues now, because the hierarchical magisterium has so constantly and publicly

---

[12] John L. Allen, "However Dramatic, the Synod of Bishops Was Just the Beginning," at www.cruxnow.com.

[13] Emile-Joseph de Smedt, "Religious Freedom," in *Council Speeches of Vatican II*, ed. Yves Congar, Hans Küng, and Daniel O'Hanlon (New York: Sheed & Ward, 1964), 157–68.

insisted on these teachings and often engaged in getting aspects of these teachings written into public law.

All recognize that Catholic spouses use artificial contraception in the same proportion as non-Catholics. Artificial contraception is not a real issue for almost all married Catholics today who have decided the issue in their own conscience. A primary reason for continuing the present teaching is that if the hierarchical magisterium should change its teaching on artificial contraception, it would logically open the door to change on other issues such as gay marriage.

What about the argument that many people have left and are continuing to leave the Catholic Church because of its teaching on these moral issues? One must put this in the proper context. The reality is that a greater percentage of people have left the mainstream Protestant churches in the United States than have left the Catholic Church. The Protestant churches, however, basically accept these moral sexual teachings that the Catholic Church does not accept. These issues, thus, are not the primary reason why people leave the Christian churches today. The real problem is secularism.

This is not the place to respond to these arguments in depth. It is enough to point out that the problem comes from the claim of the hierarchical magisterium to have certitude on particular moral issues in the area of sexuality. The hierarchical magisterium should have recognized publicly that its teachings here are noninfallible, that is, in reality fallible. They can be wrong. Some noninfallible teachings in the past were wrong. As pointed out, the problem does not exist in the area of hierarchical teaching on social issues precisely because the teaching did not claim to have certitude on very specific issues. In the long run, to admit change or error in claiming certitude in these areas should help the credibility of the church. But in the short run, what about those who, with great personal sacrifice, tried to live in accord with these teachings? No doubt this situation would be an important pastoral issue. The church would have to ask forgiveness from these people and honor them for their commitments. I remember in the days after *Humanae Vitae* a married faculty colleague at the Catholic University was talking with me about this issue. He pointed out that he and his wife lived in accord with the teaching against artificial contraception, but prayed that his children would not have to do so. The largeness of heart exemplified in such a response indicates the best of what it means to be a Christian.

In summary, Pope Francis has already contributed much to the ongoing reform of the church and the Catholic moral tradition. With Vatican II he insists that all Christians are called to holiness in their daily lives in the world. The primary emphasis and priority frequently given in the past to the observance of some absolute moral norms is misplaced. God's mercy is ever present for all who are striving to live the Christian moral life. The distinction between moral teaching and a pastoral approach has concrete consequences, but the exact meaning of the law of gradualness needs much more development. As a loyal son of the church, Francis accepts and is committed to what his predecessors have authoritatively taught is of divine or natural law. With regard to the social tradition, he gives priority to the needs of the poor and the importance of peace. Francis also emphasizes care for immigrants, climate control, and ecology. He is strongly committed to seeing the social mission of the church as a constitutive dimension of the preaching of the gospel and the church's own mission.

With regard to methodology, many of his comments such as the recognition that God is present and working in the world today indicate an acceptance of the role of historical consciousness. Recall that chapter 8 criticized the lack of historical consciousness in the teaching of Pope John Paul II on marriage and sexuality. In his understanding of the church, Francis does not limit the teaching role only to the hierarchical magisterium. There is a very important prophetic role in the church, the *sensus fidei* of all the baptized, and popular piety as a *locus theologicus*. These two methodological developments leave the door slightly ajar for some changes in the future regarding the disputed issues.

All in the church are called to continual reform and growth in our own individual lives and in the life of the church. Those of us who are convinced that the good of the church requires a change in some of its specific moral teachings need to continue to work to bring that about.

INDEX

Abel, Francisco, 141
abortion, 143, 157, 178
absolution, 230
activism, 86
ACTU. *See* Association of Catholic Trade
    Unionists
adultery, 162
Aeterni Patris (Leo XIII), 10–11
AFL-CIO, 82
Africa, religious tradition of, 120
African Americans, situation for, in the US,
    119, 120–21
African American theology, world religions
    and, 120
Africentric Christianity (Roberts), 120
Africentrism, 120
agape, 169
Alexander of Hales, 10
Alfrink, Bernard, 199
Alinksy, Saul, 44
Allen, Joseph L., 93
Alphonsian Academy, 241
*American Catholic Social Ethics: Twentieth-
    Century Approaches* (Curran), 129
American Catholic Sociological Review, 41–42
American Catholic Sociological Society, 41–42
analogical thinking, 116–17, 251
angels, orders of, 16–17
anthropology, 94, 150–52
    Catholic, 15–16, 17, 121–22, 224–25
    marriage and, 166
Antoninus, 143
apocalyptic eschatology, 151
Aquinas, Thomas, 5, 10–11, 16, 18, 26–27, 152
    anthropology of, 94
    on forgiveness, 236
    insisting on faith and reason, 119
    ius in writings of, 94–95
    on justice, 27
    primacy of, 98
    on religious freedom, 100
    on religious vows, 203
Aristotle, 5, 10, 16, 122
art, prayer and, 214–15
artificial insemination, 182

Association of Catholic Trade Unionists, 41
Augustine of Hippo, 9, 100, 254
auricular confession, 229, 236–37
authoritarianism
    in the Catholic Church, 247
    Catholicism's tolerance of, 96

Bainton, Roland, 103
baptism, interchurch celebration of, 217
baptismal commitment, primacy of, 204
Baptists, 103
Barth, Karl, 116, 117–19
Baum, Gregory, 54
Bea, Augustin, 198–99
Bellarmine, Robert, 23
Benedict XV, 193
Bergoglio, Jorge Mario. *See* Francis
Bernard of Clairvaux, 234
Bernardin, Joseph, 48, 81
Between Chaos and New Creation (McDonagh),
    213–14, 220–21
Bible and Labor, The (Husslein), 38
biblical renewal, 212
bioethics, 62. *See also* medical ethics
    breadth of, 153
    Catholic approaches to, 154
    growth of, 146, 153
    prehistory of, 141–42
    religious ethics and, 155–56
    specialization in, 154
bishops
    international synods of, 270–71
    national conferences of, 45–46, 61
"Bishops' Program of Social Reconstruction"
    (National Catholic Welfare Conference),
    32–33
black Catholic theology, 115–16
black culture, Jesus and, 125
black Messiah, 125
Black Political Theology, A (Roberts), 118,
    120, 126
Black Power, 86, 120, 126
black theology, 5, 114, 115, 119–20, 131
    Catholic dialogue with, 113
    holistic understanding of, 119, 120

281